THE

POETICAL WORKS

OF

EDMUND SPENSER.

THE

TEXT CAREFULLY REVISED, AND ILLUSTRATED WITH
NOTES, ORIGINAL AND SELECTED,

BY

FRANCIS J. CHILD.

VOLUME II.

BOSTON:
LITTLE, BROWN, AND COMPANY.
NEW YORK:
PHINNEY, BLAKEMAN, AND MASON.
M.DCCC.LX.

CONTENTS

OF THE SECOND VOLUME.

THE FAERIE QUEENE.

APPENDIX.

THE

FAERIE QUEENE.

DISPOSED INTO TWELVE BOOKS,

FASHIONING

XII. MORALL VERTUES.

LONDON:
PRINTED FOR WILLIAM PONSONBIE.
1590.

THE SECOND BOOKE

OF

THE FAERIE QUEENE,

CONTAYNING

THE LEGEND OF SIR GUYON, OR OF TEMPERAUNCE.

CANTO VII.

Guyon findes Mamon in a delve,[1]
Sunning his threasure hore[2];
Is by him tempted, and led downe
To see his secrete store.

1 As pilot well expert in perilous wave,
That to a stedfast starre his course hath bent,
When foggy mistes or cloudy tempests have
The faithfull light of that faire lampe yblent,[3]
And cover'd heaven with hideous dreriment,[4]
Upon his card and compas firmes[5] his eye,
The maysters of his long experiment,

[1] *Delve*, dell.
[2] *Hore*, mouldy.
[3] *Yblent*, blinded, put out.
[4] *Dreriment*, gloom.
[5] *Firmes*, firmly fixes.

I. 7. — *The maysters of his long experiment.*] His guides in the long voyage he is trying. H.

And to them does the steddy helme apply,
Bidding his winged vessell fairely forward fly:

2 So Guyon, having lost his trustie guyde,
Late left beyond that Ydle Lake, proceedes
Yet on his way, of none accompanyde;
And evermore himselfe with comfort feedes
Of his own vertues and praise-worthie deedes.
So, long he yode,[1] yet no adventure found,
Which Fame of her shrill trompet worthy reedes[2]:
For still he traveild through wide wastfull[3] ground,
That nought but desert wildernesse shewed all around.

3 At last he came unto a gloomy glade,
Cover'd with boughes and shrubs from heavens light,
Whereas he sitting found in secret shade
An uncouth, salvage, and uncivile wight,
Of griesly hew and fowle ill-favour'd sight;
His face with smoke was tand, and eies were bleard,
His head and beard with sout[4] were ill bedight,[5]
His cole-blacke hands did seeme to have ben seard
In smythes fire-spitting forge, and nayles like clawes appeard.

4 His yron cote, all overgrowne with rust,
Was underneath enveloped with gold;
Whose glistring glosse, darkned with filthy dust,
Well yet appeared to have beene of old

1 *Yode*, went.
2 *Reedes*, deems.
3 *Wastfull*, uninhabited.
4 *Sout*, soot.
5 *Bedight*, covered.

A worke of rich entayle[1] and curious mould
Woven with antickes[2] and wyld ymagery:
And in his lap a masse of coyne he told,
And turned upside downe, to feede his eye
And covetous desire with his huge threasury.

5 And round about him lay on every side
Great heapes of gold that never could be spent;
Of which some were rude owre, not purifide,
Of Mulcibers devouring element;
Some others were new driven, and distent[3]
Into great ingowes[4] and to wedges square;
Some in round plates withouten moniment[5]:
But most were stampt, and in their metal bare
The ántique shapes of kings and kesars[6] straung and rare.

6 Soone as he Guyon saw, in great affright
And haste he rose for to remove aside
Those pretious hils from straungers envious sight,
And downe them poured through an hole full wide
Into the hollow earth, them there to hide:
But Guyon, lightly to him leaping, stayd
His hand that trembled as one terrifyde;
And though himselfe were at the sight dismayd,
Yet him perforce restraynd, and to him doubtfull[7] sayd:

1 *Entayle*, carving.
2 *Antickes*, fantastic figures.
3 *Distent*, beaten out.
4 *Ingowes*, ingots.
5 *Moniment*, stamp.
6 *Kesars*, emperors.
7 *Doubtfull*, fearful.

7 "What art thou, Man, (if man at all thou art,)
That here in desert hast thine habitaunce,
And these rich hils of welth doest hide apart
From the worldes eye, and from her right usaunce?"
Thereat, with staring eyes fixed askaunce,
In great disdaine he answerd: "Hardy Elfe,
That darest vew my direfull countenaunce!
I read[1] thee rash and heedlesse of thyselfe,
To trouble my still seate and heapes of pretious pelfe.

8 "God of the world and worldlings I me call,
Great Mammon, greatest god below the skye,
That of my plenty poure out unto all,
And unto none my graces do envýe:
Riches, renowme, and principality,
Honour, estate, and all this worldës good,
For which men swinck[2] and sweat incessantly,
Fro me do flow into an ample flood,
And in the hollow earth have their eternall brood.

9 "Wherefore, if me thou deigne to serve and sew,[3]
At thy commaund, lo! all these mountaines bee;
Or if to thy great mind, or greedy vew,
All these may not suffise, there shall to thee
Ten times so much be nombred[4] francke and free."
"Mammon," said he, "thy godheads vaunt is vaine,
And idle offers of thy golden fee;
To them that covet such eye-glutting gaine
Proffer thy giftes, and fitter servaunts entertaine.

1 *Read*, deem.
2 *Swinck*, toil.
3 *Sew*, follow.
4 *Nombred*, counted out.

10 "Me ill besits,[1] that in derdoing[2] armes
And honours suit my vowed daies do spend,
Unto thy bounteous baytes and pleasing charmes,
With which weake men thou witchest, to attend;
Regard of worldly mucke[3] doth fowly blend[4]
And low abase the high heroicke spright,
That ioyes for crownes and kingdomes to contend;
Faire shields, gay steedes, bright armes, be my delight;
Those be the riches fit for an advent'rous knight."

11 "Vaine glorious Elfe," saide he, "doest not thou weet,[5]
That money can thy wantes at will supply?
Sheilds, steeds, and armes, and all things for thee meet,
It can purvay in twinckling of an eye;
And crownes and kingdomes to thee multiply.
Doe not I kings create, and throw the crowne
Sometimes to him that low in dust doth ly,
And him that raignd into his rowme thrust downe,
And whom I lust[6] do heape with glory and renowne?"

12 "All otherwise," saide he, "I riches read,[7]
And deeme them roote of all disquietnesse;
First got with guile, and then preserv'd with dread,

1 *Besits*, becomes.
2 *Derdoing*, (literally) doing daring deeds.
3 *Mucke*, dirt.
4 *Blend*, pollute.
5 *Weet*, know.
6 *Lust*, please.
7 *Read*, conceive of.

And after spent with pride and lavishnesse,
Leaving behind them griefe and heavinesse:
Infinite mischiefes of them doe arize;
Strife and debate, bloodshed and bitternesse,
Outrageous wrong and hellish covetize;
That noble heart, as great dishonour, doth despize.

13 "Ne thine be kingdomes, ne the scepters thine;
But realmes and rulers thou doest both confound,
And loyall truth to treason doest incline:
Witnesse the guiltlesse blood pourd oft on ground;
The crowned often slaine; the slayer cround;
The sacred diademe in peeces rent;
And purple robe gored with many a wound;
Castles surprizd; great citties sackt and brent[1]:
So mak'st thou kings, and gaynest wrongfull government!

14 "Long were to tell the troublous stormes that tosse
The private state, and make the life unsweet:
Who swelling sayles in Caspian sea doth crosse,
And in frayle wood on Adrian gulf doth fleet,[2]
Doth not, I weene, so many evils meet."
Then Mammon wexing wroth, "And why then," sayd,
"Are mortall men so fond and undiscreet
So evill thing to seeke unto their ayd;
And having not, complaine; and having it, upbrayd?"

[1] *Brent*, burned. [2] *Fleet*, float.

15 "Indeede," quoth he, "through fowle intemperaunce,
Frayle men are oft captív'd to covetise:
But would they thinke with how small allowaunce
Untroubled nature doth herselfe suffise,
Such superfluities they would despise,
Which with sad cares empeach [1] our native ioyes.
At the well-head the purest streames arise;
But mucky filth his braunching armes annoyes,
And with uncomely weedes the gentle wave accloyes.[2]

16 "The antique world, in his first flowring youth,
Fownd no defect in his Creators grace;
But with glad thankes, and unreproved [3] truth,
The guifts of soveraine bounty did embrace:
Like angels life was then mens happy cace:
But later ages pride, like corn-fed steed,
Abusd her plenty and fat-swolne encreace
To all licentious lust, and gan exceed
The measure of her meane [4] and naturall first need.

17 "Then gan a cursed hand the quiet wombe
Of his great grandmother with steele to wound,
And the hid treasures in her sacred tombe
With sacriledge to dig. Therein he fownd
Fountaines of gold and silver to abownd,
Of which the matter of his huge desire
And pompous pride eftsoones [5] he did compownd;
Then Avarice gan through his veines inspire
His greedy flames, and kindled life-devouring fire."

1 *Empeach*, hinder.
2 *Accloyes*, chokes.
3 *Unreproved*, blameless.
4 *Meane*, moderate portion.
5 *Eftsoones*, immediately.

18 "Sonne," said he then, "lett be thy bitter scorne,
And leave the rudenesse of that ántique age
To them, that liv'd therin in state forlorne.
Thou, that doest live in later times, must wage[1]
Thy workes for wealth, and life for gold engage.
If then thee list my offred grace to use,
Take what thou please of all this surplusage;
If thee list not, leave have thou to refuse:
But thing refused doe not afterward accuse."

19 "Me list not," said the Elfin Knight, "receave
Thing offred, till I know it well be gott;
Ne wote[2] I but thou didst these goods bereave
From rightfull owner by unrighteous lott,
Or that blood-guiltinesse or guile them blott."
"Perdy," quoth he, "yet never eie did vew,
Ne tong did tell,[3] ne hand these handled not;
But safe I have them kept in secret mew[4]
From hevens sight and powre of al which them poursew."

20 "What secret place," quoth he, "can safely hold
So huge a masse, and hide from heavens eie?
Or where hast thou thy wonne,[5] that so much gold
Thou canst preserve from wrong and robbery?"
"Come thou," quoth he, "and see." So by and by
Through that thick covert he him led, and fownd
A darkesome way, which no man could descry,

1 *Wage*, let out on hire.
2 *Wote*, know.
3 *Tell*, count.
4 *Mew*, hiding-place.
5 *Wonne*, dwelling.

That deep descended through the hollow grownd,
And was with dread and horror compassed arownd.

21 At length they came into a larger space,
That stretcht itselfe into an ample playne;
Through which a beaten broad high way did trace
That streight did lead to Plutoes griesly rayne[1]:
By that wayes side there sate infernall Payne,
And fast beside him sat tumultuous Strife;
The one in hand an yron whip did strayne,
The other brandished a bloody knife;
And both did gnash their teeth, and both did threten Life.

22 On th' other side in one consórt[2] there sate
Cruell Revenge, and rancorous Despight,
Disloyall Treason, and hart-burning Hate;
But gnawing Gealosy, out of their sight
Sitting alone, his bitter lips did bight;
And trembling Feare still to and fro did fly,
And found no place wher safe he shroud him might.
Lamenting Sorrow did in darknes lye;
And Shame his ugly face did hide from living eye.

23 And over them sad Horror with grim hew
Did alwaies sore, beating his yron wings;
And after him owles and night-ravens flew,
The hatefull messengers of heavy things,
Of death and dolor[3] telling sad tidíngs;

1 *Rayne*, reign, kingdom.
2 *Consórt*, company.
3 *Dolor*, grief.

Whiles sad Celeno, sitting on a clifte,
A song of bale[1] and bitter sorrow sings,
That hart of flint asonder could have rifte[2];
Which having ended, after him she flyeth swifte.

24 All these before the gates of Pluto lay;
By whom they passing spake unto them nought.
But th' Elfin Knight with wonder all the way
Did feed his eyes, and fild his inner thought.
At last him to a litle dore he brought,
That to the gate of hell, which gaped wide,
Was next adioyning, ne them parted ought:
Betwixt them both was but a litle stride,
That did the house of Richesse from hell-mouth divide.

25 Before the dore sat selfe-consuming Care,
Day and night keeping wary watch and ward,
For feare least Force or Fraud should unaware
Breake in, and spoile the treasure there in gard:
Ne would he suffer Sleepe once thether-ward
Approch, albe[3] his drowsy den were next;
For next to Death is Sleepe to be compard;
Therefore his house is unto his annext:
Here Sleep, ther Richesse, and hel-gate them both betwext.

26 So soone as Mammon there arrivd, the dore
To him did open and affoorded way:

[1] *Bale*, woe. [2] *Rifte*, riven. [3] *Albe*, although.

XXIII. 6.—*Sad Celeno.*] *Celeno* was the name of one of the Harpies. H.

Him followed eke Sir Guyon evermore,
Ne darkenesse him ne daunger might dismay.
Soone as he entred was, the dore streightway
Did shutt, and from behind it forth there lept
An ugly feend, more fowle then dismall day[1];
The which with monstrous stalke behind him stept,
And ever as he went dew watch upon him kept.

27 Well hoped hee, ere long that hardy guest,
If ever covetous hand, or lustfull eye,
Or lips he layd on thing that likte him best,
Or ever sleepe his eie-strings did untye,
Should be his pray: and therefore still on hye
He over him did hold his cruell clawes,
Threatning with greedy gripe to doe him dye,
And rend in peeces with his ravenous pawes,
If ever he transgrest the fatall Stygian lawes.

28 That houses forme within was rude and strong,
Lyke an huge cave hewne out of rocky clifte,
From whose rough vaut the ragged breaches hong
Embost with massy gold of glorious guifte,[2]
And with rich metall loaded every rifte,
That heavy ruine they did seeme to threatt;
And over them Arachne high did lifte
Her cunning web, and spred her subtile nett,
Enwrapped in fowle smoke and clouds more black then iett.

[1] I. e. day of doom, or death, as in Can. viii. v. 51.
[2] *Guifte*, gift; i. e. gifted with glorious richness.

29 Both roofe, and floore, and walls, were all of gold,
But overgrowne with dust and old decay,
And hid in darkenes, that none could behold
The hew thereof: for vew of cherefull day
Did never in that house itselfe display,
But a faint shadow of uncertein light;
Such as a lamp, whose life does fade away;
Or as the moone, cloathed with clowdy night,
Does shew to him that walkes in feare and sad affright.

30 In all that rowme was nothing to be seene
But huge great yron chests, and coffers strong,
All bard with double bends,[1] that none could weene
Them to efforce by violence or wrong;
On every side they placed were along.
But all the grownd with sculs was scattered
And dead mens bones, which round about were flong;
Whose lives, it seemed, whilome there were shed,
And their vile carcases now left unburied.

31 They forward passe; ne Guyon yet spoke word,
Till that they came unto an yron dore,
Which to them opened of his owne accord,
And shewd of richesse such exceeding store,
As eie of man did never see before,
Ne ever could within one place be fownd,
Though all the wealth which is, or was of yore,
Could gathered be through all the world arownd,
And that above were added to that under grownd.

[1] *Bends*, bands.

32 The charge thereof unto a covetous spright
Commaunded was, who thereby did attend,
And warily awaited day and night,
From other covetous feends it to defend,
Who it to rob and ransacke did intend.
Then Mammon, turning to that warriour, said:
"Loe, here the worldës blis! loe, here the end,
To which al men doe ayme, rich to be made!
Such grace now to be happy is before thee laid."

33 "Certes," sayd he, "I n'ill[1] thine offred grace,
Ne to be made so[2] happy doe intend!
Another blis before mine eyes I place,
Another happines, another end.
To them that list, these base regardes[3] I lend:
But I in armes, and in atchievements brave,
Do rather choose my flitting houres to spend,
And to be lord of those that riches have,
Then them to have my selfe, and be their servile sclave."

34 Thereat the Feend his gnashing teeth did grate,
And griev'd, so long to lacke his greedie pray;
For well he weened that so glorious bayte
Would tempt his guest to take thereof assay[4]:
Had he so doen, he had him snatcht away
More light then culver[5] in the faulcons fist:
Eternall God thee save from such decay!

1 *N'ill*, will not have.
2 *So*, in this way.
3 *Regardes*, considerations.
4 *Assay*, trial.
5 *Culver*, pigeon.

But, whenas Mammon saw his purpose mist,
Him to entrap unwares another way he wist.

35 Thence, forward he him ledd and shortly brought
Unto another rowme, whose dore forthright
To him did open as it had beene taught:
Therein an hundred raunges weren pight,[1]
And hundred fournaces all burning bright;
By every fournace many feendes did byde,
Deformed creatures, horrible in sight;
And every feend his busie paines applyde
To melt the golden metall, ready to be tryde.

36 One with great bellowes gathered filling ayre,
And with forst wind the fewell did inflame;
Another did the dying bronds repayre
With yron tongs, and sprinckled ofte the same
With liquid waves, fiers Vulcans rage to tame,
Who, maystring[2] them, renewd his former heat:
Some scumd the drosse that from the metall came;
Some stird the molten owre with ladles great:
And every one did swincke,[3] and every one did sweat.

37 But, when an earthly wight they present saw
Glistring in armes and battailous aray,
From their whot work they did themselves withdraw
To wonder at the sight; for, till that day,
They never creature saw that cam that way:
Their staring eyes sparckling with fervent fyre

1 *Pight*, placed.
2 *Maystring*, mastering, or subduing.
3 *Swincke*, toil.

And ugly shapes did nigh the man dismay,
That, were it not for shame, he would retyre;
Till that him thus bespake their soveraine lord and syre:

38 "Behold, thou Faeries sonne, with mortall eye,
That living eye before did never see!
The thing that thou didst crave so earnestly,
To weet whence all the wealth late shewd by mee
Proceeded, lo! now is reveald to thee.
Here is the fountaine of the worldës good!
Now therefore, if thou wilt enriched bee,
Avise[1] thee well, and chaunge thy wilfull mood;
Least thou perhaps hereafter wish, and be withstood."

39 "Suffise it then, thou Money-god," quoth hee,
"That all thine ydle offers I refuse.
All that I need I have; what needeth mee
To covet more then I have cause to use?
With such vaine shewes thy worldlinges vyle abuse;
But give me leave to follow mine emprise."
Mammon was much displeasd, yet no'te[2] he chuse
But beare the rigour of his bold mesprise[3];
And thence him forward ledd, him further to entise.

40 He brought him, through a darksom narrow strayt,
To a broad gate all built of beaten gold:
The gate was open; but therein did wayt
A sturdie villein, stryding stiffe and bold,
As if the highest God defy he would:

1 *Avise*, bethink.
2 *No'te*, could not.
3 *Mesprise*, contempt.

In his right hand an yron club he held,
But he himselfe was all of golden mould,
Yet had both life and sence, and well could weld
That cursed weapon, when his cruell foes he queld.

41 Disdayne he called was, and did disdayne
To be so cald, and who so did him call:
Sterne was his looke, and full of stomacke[1] vayne;
His portaunce[2] terrible, and stature tall,
Far passing th' hight of men terrestriall;
Like an huge gyant of the Titans race;
That made him scorne all creatures great and small,
And with his pride all others powre deface:
More fitt emongst black fiendes then men to have his place.

42 Soone as those glitterand armes he did espye,
That with their brightnesse made that darknes light,
His harmefull club he gan to hurtle[3] hye,
And threaten batteill to the Faery Knight;
Who likewise gan himselfe to batteill dight,[4]
Till Mammon did his hasty hand withhold,
And counseld him abstaine from perilous fight;
For nothing might abash that villein bold,
Ne mortall steele emperce his miscreated mould.

43 So having him with reason pacifyde,
And the fiers carle commaunding to forbeare,

1 *Stomacke*, haughtiness.
2 *Portaunce*, bearing.
3 *Hurtle*, brandish.
4 *Dight*, prepare.

He brought him in. The rowme was large and wyde,
As it some gyeld[1] or solemne temple weare;
Many great golden pillours did upbeare
The massy roofe, and riches huge sustayne;
And every pillour decked was full deare[2]
With crownes, and diademes, and titles vaine,
Which mortall princes wore whiles they on earth did rayne.

44 A route of people there assembled were,
Of every sort and nation under skye,
Which with great uprore preaced[3] to draw nere
To th' upper part, where was advaunced hye
A stately siege[4] of soveraine maiestye;
And thereon satt a woman gorgeous gay,
And richly cladd in robes of royaltye,
That never earthly prince in such aray
His glory did enhaunce, and pompous pryde display.

45 Her face right wondrous faire did seeme to bee,
That her broad beauties beam great brightnes threw
Through the dim shade, that all men might it see;
Yet was not that same her owne native hew,
But wrought by art and counterfetted shew,
Thereby more lovers unto her to call;
Nath'lesse most hevenly faire in deed and vew
She by creation was, till she did fall;
Thenceforth she sought for helps to cloke her crime withall.

1 *Gyeld*, guild (-hall).
2 *Deare*, richly.
3 *Preaced*, pressed.
4 *Siege*, seat.

46 There, as in glistring glory she did sitt,
She held a great gold chaine ylincked well,
Whose upper end to highest heven was knitt,
And lower part did reach to lowest hell;
And all that preace[1] did rownd about her swell
To catchen hold of that long chaine, thereby
To climbe aloft, and others to excell:
That was Ambition, rash desire to sty,[2]
And every linck thereof a step of dignity.

47 Some thought to raise themselves to high degree
By riches and unrighteous reward;
Some by close shouldring; some by flatteree;
Others through friendes; others for base regard;
And all, by wrong waies, for themselves prepard:
Those that were up themselves, kept others low;
Those that were low themselves, held others hard,
Ne suffred them to ryse or greater grow;
But every one did strive his fellow downe to throw.

48 Which whenas Guyon saw, he gan inquire,
What meant that preace[1] about that ladies throne,
And what she was that did so high aspyre?
Him Mammon answered: "That goodly one,
Whom all that folke with such contention
Doe flock about, my deare, my daughter is:
Honour and dignitie from her alone
Derived are, and all this worldës blis,
For which ye men doe strive; few gett, but many mis.

1 *Preace*, press. 2 *Sty*, ascend.

49 "And fayre Philotimé[1] she rightly hight,
The fairest wight that wonneth[2] under skye;
But that this darksom neather world her light
Doth dim with horror and deformity,
Worthie of heven and hye felicitie,
From whence the gods have her for envy thurst:
But, sith thou hast found favour in mine eye,
Thy spouse I will her make, if that thou lust[3];
That she may thee advance for works and merits iust."

50 "Gramercy, Mammon," said the gentle Knight,
"For so great grace and offred high estate;
But I, that am fraile flesh and earthly wight,
Unworthy match for such immortall mate
Myselfe well wote,[4] and mine unequall fate:
And were I not, yet is my trouth yplight,[5]
And love avowd to other lady late,
That to remove the same I have no might:
To chaunge love causelesse is reproch to warlike knight."

51 Mammon emmoved was with inward wrath;
Yet, forcing it to fayne, him forth thence ledd,
Through griesly shadowes by a beaten path,
Into a gardin goodly garnished
With hearbs and fruits, whose kinds mote not be redd[6]:
Not such as earth out of her fruitfull woomb

[1] *Philotimé* (Greek), Ambition.
[2] *Wonneth*, dwelleth.
[3] *Lust*, list, desire.
[4] *Wote*, know.
[5] *Yplight*, plighted.
[6] *Redd*, conceived of.

Throwes forth to men, sweet and well savored,
But direfull deadly black, both leafe and bloom,
Fitt to adorne the dead and deck the drery toombe.

52 There mournfull cypresse grew in greatest store;
And trees of bitter gall; and heben[1] sad;
Dead sleeping poppy; and black hellebore;
Cold coloquintida; and tetra mad;
Mortall samnitis; and cicuta[2] bad,
With which th' uniust Atheniens made to dy
Wise Socrates, who, thereof quaffing glad,
Pourd out his life and last philosophy
To the fayre Critias, his dearest belamy[3]!

53 The Gardin of Prosérpina this hight:
And in the midst thereof a silver seat,
With a thick arber goodly overdight,[4]
In which she often usd from open heat
Herselfe to shroud, and pleasures to entreat.[5]
Next thereunto did grow a goodly tree,

1 *Heben*, ebony.
2 *Cicuta*, hemlock.
3 *Belamy* (*bel ami*, Fr.), fair friend.
4 *Overdight*, overspread.
5 *Entreat*, woo, or enjoy.

LII. 4, 5. — There are no such plants as *tetra* and *samnitis* Upton conjectures that Spenser meant by the former the deadly nightshade, and that *samnitis* is the *arbor sabina*, or savin-tree, which was thought to produce abortion. C.

LII. 6-9. It is Theramenes, and not Socrates, of whom this incident is related. Spenser was perhaps led into the mistake by the resemblance of the name of *Critias* to that of *Crito*, who was an intimate friend of Socrates, and with him at the time of his death. H.

With braunches broad dispredd and body great,
Clothed with leaves, that none the wood mote see,
And loaden all with fruit as thick as it might bee.

54 Their fruit were golden apples glistring bright,
That goodly was their glory to behold;
On earth like never grew, ne living wight
Like ever saw, but they from hence were sold;
For those, which Hercules with conquest bold
Got from great Atlas daughters, hence began,
And planted there did bring forth fruit of gold;
And those, with which th' Eubæan young man wan
Swift Atalanta, when through craft he her out ran.

55 Here also sprong that goodly golden fruit,
With which Acontius got his lover trew,
Whom he had long time sought with fruitlesse suit;
Here eke that famous golden apple grew,
The which emongest the gods false Ate threw;
For which th' Idæan Ladies disagreed,

LIV. 6.—*Got from great Atlas daughters.*] The Hesperides, who were, according to one account, the daughters of Atlas and Hesperis, daughter of Hesperus. C.

LIV. 9.—*Swift Atalanta.*] Hippomenes vanquished Atalanta in a foot-race, by dropping before her, whenever she was likely to get the start of him, an apple of gold, which she stopped to gather. H.

LV. 2.—*Acontius.*] Acontius was a youth of humble origin, who fell in love with Cydippe, of Delos, and, being unsuccessful in his suit, wrote on an apple, which he gave to her, the words, "By Diana, I will wed Acontius." Cydippe read the words, and felt constrained to marry her lover, by the involuntary oath she had uttered. H.

Till partiall Paris dempt[1] it Venus dew,
And had of her fayre Helen for his meed,
That many noble Greekes and Troians made to bleed.

56 The warlike Elfe much wondred at this tree,
So fayre and great, that shadowed all the ground;
And his broad braunches, laden with rich fee,[2]
Did stretch themselves without the utmost bound
Of this great gardin, compast with a mound:
Which overhanging, they themselves did steepe
In a blacke flood, which flow'd about it round;
That is the river of Cocytus deepe,
In which full many soules do endlesse wayle and weepe.

57 Which to behold he clomb up to the bancke,
And, looking downe, saw many damned wightes
In those sad waves, which direfull deadly stancke,
Plonged continually of[3] cruell sprightes,
That with their piteous cryes, and yelling shrightes[4]
They made the further shore resounden wide:
Emongst the rest of those same ruefull sightes,
One cursed creature he by chaunce espide,
That drenched lay full deepe under the garden side.

58 Deepe was he drenched to the upmost chin,
Yet gaped still, as coveting to drinke
Of the cold liquour which he waded in;
And, stretching forth his hand, did often thinke
To reach the fruit which grew upon the brincke;

1 *Dempt*, deemed, adjudged.
2 *Fee*, property.
3 *Of*, by.
4 *Shrightes*, shrieks.

But both the fruit from hand, and flood from mouth,
Did fly abacke, and made him vainely swincke[1];
The whiles he sterv'd with hunger, and with drouth
He daily dyde, yet never throughly[2] dyen couth.[3]

59 The Knight, him seeing labour so in vaine,
Askt who he was, and what he ment thereby?
Who, groning deepe, thus answerd him againe:
"Most cursed of all creatures under skye,
Lo Tantalus, I here tormented lye!
Of whom high Iove wont whylome[4] feasted bee;
Lo, here I now for want of food doe dye!
But, if that thou be such as I thee see,
Of grace I pray thee give to eat and drinke to mee!"

60 "Nay, nay, thou greedy Tantalus," quoth he,
"Abide the fortune of thy present fate;
And, unto all that live in high degree,
Ensample be of mind intemperate,
To teach them how to use their present state."
Then gan the cursed wretch alowd to cry,
Accusing highest Iove and gods ingrate;
And eke blaspheming heaven bitterly,
As authour of uniustice, there to let him dye.

1 *Swincke*, labor.
2 *Throughly*, thoroughly.
3 *Couth*, could.
4 *Whylome*, formerly.

LIX. 6. — Tantalus was admitted to the table of Jupiter, and *once* entertained the gods with a banquet. He was punished for abusing the celestial hospitality, or, according to another legend, for his insatiable desires, his "mind intemperate." C.

61 He lookt a litle further, and espyde
Another wretch, whose carcas deepe was drent[1]
Within the river which the same did hyde:
But both his handes, most filthy feculent,
Above the water were on high extent,[2]
And faynd[3] to wash themselves incessantly,
Yet nothing cleaner were for such intent,
But rather fowler seemed to the eye;
So lost his labour vaine and ydle industry.

62 The Knight, him calling, asked who he was?
Who, lifting up his head, him answerd thus:
"I Pilate am, the falsest iudge, alas!
And most uniust; that, by unrighteous
And wicked doome, to Iewes despiteous[4]
Delivered up the Lord of Life to dye,
And did acquite a murdrer felonous;
The whiles my handes I washt in purity,[5]
The whiles my soule was soyld with fowle iniquity."

63 Infinite moe[6] tormented in like paine
He there beheld, too long here to be told:
Ne Mammon would there let him long remayne,
For terrour of the tortures manifold,
In which the damned soules he did behold,
But roughly him bespake: "Thou fearefull foole,
Why takest not of that same fruite of gold?

1 *Drent*, drenched.
2 *Extent*, raised.
3 *Faynd*, pretended, seemed.
4 *Despiteous*, malicious.
5 *Purity*, i. e. in pure water.
6 *Moe*, more.

Ne sittest downe on that same silver stoole,
To rest thy weary person in the shadow coole?"

64 All which he did to do him deadly fall
In frayle intemperaunce through sinfull bayt;
To which if he inclyned had at all,
That dreadfull feend, which did behinde him wayt,
Would him have rent in thousand peeces strayt:
But he was wary wise in all his way,
And well perceived his deceiptfull sleight,
Ne suffred lust[1] his safety to betray:
So goodly did beguile the guyler of his pray.

65 And now he has so long remained theare,
That vitall powres gan wexe both weake and wan
For want of food and sleepe, which two upbeare,
Like mightie pillours, this frayle life of man,
That none without the same enduren can:
For now three dayes of men were full outwrought,
Since he this hardy enterprize began:
Forthy[2] great Mammon fayrely he besought
Into the world to guyde him backe, as he him brought.

66 The God, though loth, yet was constraynd t' obay;
For lenger time then that, no living wight
Below the earth might suffred be to stay:
So backe againe him brought to living light.
But all so soone as his enfeebled spright
Gan sucke this vitall ayre into his brest,

[1] *Lust*, desire (of gold). [2] *Forthy*, therefore.

As overcome with too exceeding might,
The life did flit away out of her nest,
And all his sences were with deadly fit opprest.*

* In the swoon of Sir Guyon, it has been conjectured that Spenser means to express that state of torpid inaction into which the best faculties of the mind and heart fall, from the too eager and exclusive pursuit of wealth. H.

CANTO VIII.

Sir Guyon, layd in swowne, is by
  Acrates sonnes despoyld;
Whom Arthure soone hath reskewed
  And Paynim brethren foyld.

1 AND is there care in heaven? And is there love
  In heavenly spirits to these creatures bace,
  That may compassion of their evilles move?
  There is: — else much more wretched were the cace
  Of men then beasts. But O th' exceeding grace
  Of Highest God, that loves his creatures so,
  And all his workes with mercy doth embrace,
  That blessed Angels he sends to and fro,
To serve to wicked man, to serve his wicked foe!

2 How oft do they their silver bowers leave
  To come to succour us that succour want!
  How oft do they with golden pineons cleave
  The flitting[1] skyes, like flying pursuivant,
  Against fowle feendes to ayd us militant!
  They for us fight, they watch and dewly ward,
  And their bright squadrons round about us plant;
  And all for love and nothing for reward:
O, why should hevenly God to men have such regard!

[1] *Flitting*, yielding.

3 During the while that Guyon did abide
In Mamons house, the Palmer, whom whyleare[1]
That wanton Mayd of passage had denide,
By further search had passage found elsewhere;
And, being on his way, approched neare
Where Guyon lay in traunce; when suddeinly
He heard a voyce that called lowd and cleare,
"Come hether, hether, O come hastily!"
That all the fields resounded with the ruefull cry.

4 The Palmer lent his eare unto the noyce,
To weet who called so impórtunely:
Againe he heard a more efforced voyce,
That bad him come in haste. He by and by[2]
His feeble feet directed to the cry;
Which to that shady delve[3] him brought at last,
Where Mammon earst did sunne his threasury:
There the good Guyon he found slumbring fast
In senceles dreame; which sight at first him sore aghast.[4]

5 Beside his head there satt a faire young man,
Of wondrous beauty and of freshest yeares,
Whose tender bud to blossome new began,
And florish faire above his equall peares:
His snowy front, curled with golden heares,

1 *Whyleare*, a little while before.
2 *By and by*, immediately.
3 *Delve*, dell.
4 *Aghast*, terrified.

III. 3.— *That wanton Mayd*, &c.] Phædria. See Canto VI. Stanza 19. H.

Like Phœbus face adornd with sunny rayes,
Divinely shone; and two sharpe winged sheares,
Decked with diverse plumes, like painted iayes,
Were fixed at his backe to cut his ayery wayes.

6 Like as Cupido on Idæan hill,
When having laid his cruell bow away
And mortall arrowes, wherewith he doth fill
The world with murdrous spoiles and bloody pray,
With his faire mother he him dights[1] to play,
And with his goodly sisters, Graces three;
The goddesse, pleased with his wanton play,
Suffers herselfe through sleepe beguild to bee,
The whiles the other ladies mind theyr mery glee.

7 Whom when the Palmer saw, abasht he was
Through fear and wonder, that he nought could say,
Till him the childe bespoke: "Long lackt, alas!
Hath bene thy faithfull aide in hard assay,[2]
Whiles deadly fitt thy pupill doth dismay.
Behold this heavy sight, thou reverend Sire!
But dread of death and dolor[3] doe away;
For life ere long shall to her home retire,
And he, that breathlesse seems, shal corage bold respire.

8 "The charge, which God doth unto me arrett,[4]
Of his deare safety, I to thee commend;
Yet will I not forgoe, ne yet forgett
The care thereof myselfe unto the end,

[1] *Dights*, prepares.
[2] *Assay*, trial.
[3] *Dolor*, grief.
[4] *Arrett*, appoint.

But evermore him succour, and defend
Against his foe and mine. Watch thou, I pray;
For evill is at hand him to offend."
So having said, eftsoones he gan display
His painted nimble wings, and vanisht quite away.

9 The Palmer seeing his lefte empty place,
And his slow eies beguiled of their sight,
Woxe sore affraid, and standing still a space
Gaz'd after him, as fowle[1] escapt by flight:
At last, him, turning to his charge behight,[2]
With trembling hand his troubled pulse gan try;
Where finding life not yet dislodged quight,
He much reioyst, and courd[3] it tenderly,
As chicken newly hatcht, from dreaded destiny.

10 At last he spide where towards him did pace
Two Paynim knights al armd as bright as skie,
And them beside an aged sire did trace,[4]
And far before a light-foote page did flie
That breathed strife and troublous enmitie.
Those were the two sonnes of Acrates old,
Who, meeting earst with Archimago slie
Foreby that Idle Strond, of him were told
That he, which earst them combatted, was Guyon bold.

1 *Fowle*, bird.
2 *Behight*, intrusted.
3 *Courd*, covered.
4 *Trace*, walk.

X. 3.— *An aged Sire.*] Archimago.
X. 4.— *A light-foot Page.*] Atin.
X. 7.— *Who, meeting earst.*] See Canto VI. Stanza 47.

11 Which to avenge on him they dearly vowd,
Where ever that on ground they mote him find:
False Archimage provokte their corage prowd,
And stryful Atin in their stubborne mind
Coles of contention and whot[1] vengeaunce tind.[2]
Now bene they come whereas the Palmer sate,
Keeping that slombred corse to him assind:
Well knew they both his person, sith of late
With him in bloody armes they rashly did debate.

12 Whom when Pyrochles saw, inflam'd with rage
That Sire he fowl bespake: "Thou dotard vile,
That with thy brutenesse shendst[3] thy comely age,
Abandon soone, I read,[4] the caytive spoile
Of that same outcast carcas, that erewhile
Made itselfe famous through false trechery,
And crownd his coward crest with knightly stile;
Loe where he now inglorious doth lye,
To proove he lived il, that did thus fowly dye."

13 To whom the Palmer fearlesse answered
"Certes, Sir Knight, ye bene too much to blame,
Thus for to blott the honor of the dead,
And with fowle cowardize his carcas shame
Whose living handes immortalizd his name.
Vile is the vengeaunce on the ashes cold;
And envy base to barke at sleeping fame:
Was never wight that treason of him told:
Yourself his prowesse prov'd, and found him fiers and bold."

1 *Whot*, hot.
2 *Tind*, kindled.
3 *Shendst*, disgracest.
4 *Read*, advise.

14 Then sayd Cymochles : "Palmer, thou doest dote,
Ne canst of prowesse ne of knighthood deeme,
Save as thou seest or hearst: but well I wote,
That of his puissaunce tryall made extreeme:
Yet gold al is not that doth golden seeme;
Ne all good knights that shake well speare and shield:
The worth of all men by their end esteeme;
And then dew praise or dew reproch them yield:
Bad therefore I him deeme that thus lies dead on field."

15 "Good or bad," gan his brother fiers reply,
"What doe I recke, sith that he dide entire[1]?
Or what doth his bad death now satisfy
The greedy hunger of revenging yre,
Sith wrathfull hand wrought not her owne desire?
Yet, since no way is lefte to wreake my spight,
I will him reave[2] of armes, the victors hire,
And of that shield, more worthy of good knight;
For why should a dead dog be deckt in armour bright?"

16 "Fayr Sir," said then the Palmer suppliaunt,
"For knighthoods love doe not so fowle a deed,
Ne blame[3] your honor with so shamefull vaunt
Of vile revenge. To spoile the dead of weed[4]
Is sacrilege, and doth all sinnes exceed:
But leave these relicks of his living might
To decke his herce, and trap his tomblacke steed."

1 *Entire*, i. e. unwounded.
2 *Reave*, strip.
3 *Blame*, bring reproach upon.
4 *Weed*, clothing.

"What herce or steed," said he, "should he have
dight,
But be entombed in the raven or the kight?"

17 With that, rude hand upon his shield he laid,
And th' other brother gan his helme unlace;
Both fiercely bent to have him disaraid;
Till that they spyde where towards them did pace
An armed knight, of bold and bounteous grace,
Whose squire bore after him an heben[1] launce
And coverd shield. Well kend him so far space
Th' Enchaunter by his armes and amenaunce,[2]
When under him he saw his Lybian steed to praunce,

18 And to those brethren sayd: "Rise, rise bylive,[3]
And unto batteil doe yourselves addresse;
For yonder comes the prowest[4] knight alive,
Prince Arthur, flowre of grace and nobilesse,
That hath to Paynim knights wrought gret distresse,
And thousand Sar'zins fowly donne to dye."
That word so deepe did in their harts impresse,
That both eftsoones upstarted furiously,
And gan themselves prepare to batteill greedily.

19 But fiers Pyrochles, lacking his owne sword,
The want thereof now greatly gan to plaine,

1 *Heben*, ebony.
2 *Amenaunce*, carriage.
3 *Bylive*, quickly.
4 *Prowest*, bravest.

XVII. 7.—*And coverd shield.*] See Book I. Canto VII. Stanza 33.

And Archimage besought, him that afford
Which he had brought for Braggadochio vaine.
"So would I," said th' Enchaunter, "glad and faine
Beteeme[1] to you this sword, you to defend,
Or ought that els your honor might maintaine;
But that this weapons powre I well have kend[2]
To be contrâry to the worke which ye intend:

20 "For that same knights owne sword this is, of yore
Which Merlin made by his almightie art
For that his noursling, when he knighthood swore,
Therewith to doen his foes eternall smart.
The metall first he mixt with medæwart,
That no enchauntment from his dint might save,
Then it in flames of Aetna wrought apart,
And seven times dipped in the bitter wave
Of hellish Styx, which hidden vertue to it gave.

21 "The vertue is, that nether steele nor stone
The stroke thereof from entraunce may defend,
Ne ever may be used by his fone[3];
Ne forst his rightful owner to offend;
Ne ever will it breake, ne ever bend;
Wherefore *Morddure*[4] it rightfully is hight.
In vaine therefore, Pyrochles, should I lend
The same to thee, against his lord to fight;
For sure yt would deceive thy labor and thy might."

1 *Beteeme*, grant.
2 *Kend*, learned.
3 *Fone*, foes.
4 *Morddure*, Hard-biter.

XX. 5.—*Medœwart.*] Meadow-wort, or meadow-sweet. C.

22 "Foolish old man," said then the Pagan wroth,
"That weenest words or charms may force withstond:
Soone shalt thou see, and then beleeve for troth,[1]
That I can carve with this inchaunted brond
His lords owne flesh." Therewith out of his hond
That vertuous steele he rudely snatcht away;
And Guyons shield about his wrest he bond:
So ready dight, fierce battaile to assay,
And match his brother proud in battailous aray.

23 By this, that straunger knight in presence came,
And goodly salued[2] them; who nought againe
Him answered, at courtesie became;
But with sterne lookes, and stomachous[3] disdaine,
Gave signes of grudge and discontentment vaine:
Then, turning to the Palmer, he gan spy
Where at his feet, with sorrowfull demayne[4]
And deadly hew, an armed corse did lye,
In whose dead face he redd great magnanimity.

24 Sayd he then to the Palmer: "Reverend Syre,
What great misfortune hath betidd this knight?
Or did his life her fatall date expyre,
Or did he fall by treason, or by fight?
However, sure I rew his pitteous plight."
"Not one, nor other," sayd the Palmer grave,
"Hath him befalne; but cloudes of deadly night

1 *Troth*, truth.
2 *Salued*, saluted.
3 *Stomachous*, haughty.
4 *Demayne*, demeanor, appearance.

Awhile his heavy eylids cover'd have,
And all his sences drowned in deep sencelesse wave:

25 "Which those his cruell foes, that stand hereby,
Making advauntage, to revenge their spight,
Would him disarme and treaten shamefully;
Unworthie usage of redoubted knight!
But you, faire Sir, whose honourable sight
Doth promise hope of helpe and timely grace,
Mote I beseech to succour his sad plight,
And by your powre protect his feeble cace?
First prayse of knighthood is, fowle outrage to de-
face.[1]"

26 "Palmer," said he, "no knight so rude, I weene,
As to doen outrage to a sleeping ghost[2]:
Ne was there ever noble corage[3] seene,
That in advauntage would his puissaunce bost.
Honour is least, where oddes appeareth most.
May bee, that better reason will aswage
The rash revengers heat. Words, well despost,
Have secrete powre t' appease inflamed rage:
If not, leave unto me thy knights last patronage.[4]"

27 Tho, turning to those brethren, thus bespoke:
"Ye warlike payre, whose valorous great might,
It seemes, iust wronges to vengeaunce doe provoke,
To wreake your wrath on this dead-seeming knight,
Mote ought allay the storme of your despight,

1 *Deface*, defeat, prevent.
2 *Ghost*, spirit.
3 *Corage*, heart.
4 *Patronage*, defence.

And settle patience in so furious heat?
Not to debate the chalenge[1] of your right,
But for his carkas pardon I entreat,
Whom fortune hath already laid in lowest seat."

28 To whom Cymochles said: "For what art thou,
That mak'st thyselfe his dayes-man,[2] to prolong
The vengeaunce prest[3]? Or who shall let[4] me now
On this vile body from to wreak my wrong,
And make his carkas as the outcast dong?
Why should not that dead carrion satisfye
The guilt, which, if he lived had thus long,
His life for dew revenge should deare abye[5]?
The trespas still doth live, albee[6] the person dye."

29 "Indeed," then said the Prince, "the evill donne
Dyes not, when breath the body first doth leave;
But from the grandsyre to the nephewes[7] sonne
And all his seede the curse doth often cleave,
Till vengeaunce utterly the guilt bereave:
So streightly[8] God doth iudge. But gentle knight,
That doth against the dead his hand upreare,*
His honour staines with rancour and despight,
And great disparagment makes to his former might."

1 *Chalenge*, claim, title.
2 *Dayes-man*, umpire.
3 *Prest*, ready at hand.
4 *Let*, hinder.
5 *Abye*, abide.
6 *Albee*, although.
7 *Nephewes*, grandson's.
8 *Streightly*, strictly.

* Qu. *upheave?*

30 Pyrochles gan reply the second tyme,
And to him said: "Now, felon, sure I read,[1]
How that thou art partaker of his cryme:
Therefore by Termagaunt thou shalt be dead."
With that, his hand, more sad[2] then lomp of lead,
Uplifting high, he weened with Morddure,
His owne good sword Morddure, to cleave his head.
The faithfull steele such treason no'uld[3] endure,
But, swarving from the marke, his lordes life did assure.

31 Yet was the force so furious and so fell,
That horse and man it made to reele asyde:
Nath'lesse the Prince would not forsake his sell,[4]
(For well of yore he learned had to ryde,)
But full of anger fiersly to him cryde:
"False traitour miscreaunt, thou broken hast
The law of armes, to strike foe undefide:
But thou thy treasons fruit, I hope, shalt taste
Right sowre, and feele the law, the which thou hast defast.[5]"

32 With that his balefull speare he fiercely bent
Against the Pagans brest, and therewith thought
His cursed life out of her lodg have rent:

1 *Read*, perceive.
2 *Sad*, heavy.
3 *No'uld*, would not.
4 *Sell*, saddle.
5 *Defast*, i. e. broken.

XXX. 4. — *By Termagaunt*, &c.] *Termagaunt* is the name given in old romances to a supposed god of the Saracens. H.

But, ere the point arrived where it ought,
That seven-fold shield, which he from Guyon brought,
He cast between to ward the bitter stownd[1]:
Through all those foldes the steelehead passage wrought,
And through his shoulder perst; wherwith to ground
He groveling fell, all gored in his gushing wound.

33 Which when his brother saw, fraught with great griefe
And wrath, he to him leaped furiously,
And fowly saide: "By Mahoune, cursed thiefe,
That direfull stroke thou dearely shalt aby."
Then, hurling up his harmefull blade on hy,
Smote him so hugely on his haughtie crest,
That from his saddle forced him to fly:
Els mote it needes downe to his manly brest
Have cleft his head in twaine, and life thence dispossest.

34 Now was the Prince in daungerous distresse,
Wanting his sword when he on foot should fight:
His single[2] speare could doe him small redresse
Against two foes of so exceeding might,
The least of which was match for any knight.
And now the other, whom he earst did daunt,
Had reard himselfe againe to cruel fight
Three times more furious and more puissaunt,
Unmindfull of his wound, of his fate ignoraunt.

1 *Stownd*, time (of peril). 2 *Single*, alone.

35 So both attonce him charge on either syde
With hideous strokes and ímportable[1] powre,
That forced him his ground to traverse wyde,
And wisely watch to ward that deadly stowre[2].
For in his shield, as thicke as stormie showre,
Their strokes did raine; yet did he never quaile,
Ne backward shrinke; but as a stedfast towre,
Whom foe with double battry doth assaile,
Them on her bulwarke beares, and bids them nought
availe,—

36 So stoutly he withstood their strong assay;
Till that at last, when he advantage spyde,
His poynant[3] speare he thrust with puissant sway
At proud Cymochles, whiles his shield was wyde,[4]
That through his thigh the mortall steele did
gryde[5]:
He, swarving with the force, within his flesh
Did breake the launce, and let the head abyde:
Out of the wound the red blood flowed fresh,
That underneath his feet soone made a purple plesh.[6]

37 Horribly then he gan to rage and rayle,
Cursing his gods, and himselfe damning deepe:
Als[7] when his brother saw the red blood rayle[8]
Adowne so fast, and all his armour steepe,
For very felnesse[9] lowd he gan to weepe,

1 *Importable*, not to be borne.
2 *Stowre*, danger.
3 *Poynant*, piercing.
4 *Wyde*, turned away.
5 *Gryde*, pierce.
6 *Plesh*, plash, pool.
7 *Als*, also.
8 *Rayle*, flow.
9 *Felnesse*, fury.

And said: "Caytive, cursse on thy cruell hond,
That twise hath spedd[1]; yet shall it not thee keepe
From the third brunt of this my fatall brond:
Lo, where the dreadfull Death behynd thy backe doth stond!"

38 With that he strooke, and th' other strooke withall,
That nothing seemd mote beare so monstrous might:
The one upon his covered shield did fall,
And glauncing downe would not his owner byte:
But th' other did upon his troncheon[2] smyte;
Which hewing quite asunder, further way
It made, and on his hacqueton did lyte,
The which dividing with impórtune sway,
It seizd[3] in his right side, and there the dint did stay.

39 Wyde was the wound, and a large lukewarme flood,
Red as the rose, thence gushed grievously;
That when the Paynym spyde the streaming blood,
Gave him great hart and hope of victory.
On th' other side, in huge perplexity
The Prince now stood, having his weapon broke;
Nought could he hurt, but still at warde did ly:
Yet with his troncheon he so rudely stroke
Cymochles twise, that twise him forst his foot revoke.

1 *Spedd*, succeeded.
2 *Troncheon*, the staff of the spear.
3 *Seizd*, fixed.

XXXVIII. 7.—*His hacqueton.*] The *hacqueton* was a military garment, worn sometimes alone, sometimes under the hauberk. It was generally made of buckram and stuffed with cotton. C.

40 Whom when the Palmer saw in such distresse,
Sir Guyons sword he lightly to him raught,[1]
And said: "Fayre sonne, great God thy right hand blesse,
To use that sword so well as he it ought[2]!"
Glad was the Knight, and with fresh courage fraught,
Whenas againe he armed felt his hond:
Then like a lyon, which had long time saught
His robbed whelpes, and at the last them fond
Emongst the shepeheard swaynes, then wexeth wood and yond[3]:

41 So fierce he laid about him, and dealt blowes
On either side, that neither mayle could hold,
Ne shield defend the thunder of his throwes:
Now to Pyrochles many strokes he told;
Eft[4] to Cymochles twise so many fold;
Then, backe againe turning his busie hond,
Them both atonce compeld with courage bold
To yield wide way to his hart-thrilling[5] brond;
And though they both stood stiffe, yet could not both withstond.

42 As salvage bull, whom two fierce mastives bayt,
When rancour doth with rage him once engore,[6]
Forgets with wary warde them to awayt,
But with his dreadfull hornes them drives afore,

1 *Raught*, reached.
2 *He it ought*, he that owned it.
3 *Wood and yond*, mad and furious.
4 *Eft*, afterwards.
5 *Hart-thrilling*, heart-piercing.
6 *Engore*, pierce, prick.

Or flings aloft, or treades downe in the flore,
Breathing out wrath, and bellowing disdaine,
That all the forest quakes to heare him rore:
So rag'd Prince Arthur twixt his foemen twaine,
That neither could his mightie puissaunce sustaine.

43 But ever at Pyrochles when he smitt,
(Who Guyons shield cast ever him before,
Whereon the Faery Queenes pourtract was writt,)
His hand relented and the stroke forbore,
And his deare hart the picture gan adore;
Which oft the Paynim sav'd from deadly stowre[1]:
But him henceforth the same can save no more;
For now arrived is his fatall howre,
That no'te[2] avoyded be by earthly skill or powre.

44 For when Cymochles saw the fowle reproch,
Which them appeached[3]; prickt with guiltie shame
And inward griefe, he fiercely gan approch,
Resolv'd to put away that loathly blame,
Or dye with honour and desert of fame;
And on the haubergh[4] stroke the Prince so sore,
That quite disparted all the linked frame,
And pierced to the skin, but bit no more;
Yet made him twise to reele, that never moov'd afore.

45 Whereat renfierst[5] with wrath and sharp regret,
He stroke so hugely with his borrowd blade,

1 *Stowre*, peril.
2 *No'te*, might not.
3 *Appeached*, impeached.
4 *Haubergh*, coat of mail.
5 *Renfierst*, reënforced.

That it empierst the Pagans burganet[1];
And, cleaving the hard steele, did deepe invade
Into his head, and cruell passage made
Quite through his brayne: He, tombling downe on ground,
Breathd out his ghost, which, to th' infernall shade
Fast flying, there eternall torment found
For all the sinnes wherewith his lewd life did abound.

46 Which when his german[2] saw, the stony feare
Ran to his hart, and all his sence dismayd;
Ne thenceforth life ne corage did appeare:
But, as a man whom hellish feendes have frayd,[3]
Long trembling still he stoode; at last thus sayd:
"Traytour, what hast thou doen! How ever may
Thy cursed hand so cruelly have swayd
Against that knight! Harrow[4] and well away!
After so wicked deede why liv'st thou lenger[5] day!"

47 With that all desperate, as loathing light,
And with revenge desyring soone to dye,
Assembling all his force and utmost might,
With his owne[6] swerd he fierce at him did flye,
And strooke, and foynd,[7] and lasht outrageously,
Withouten reason or regard. Well knew
The Prince, with pacience and sufferaunce sly,

1 *Burganet*, helmet.
2 *German*, brother.
3 *Frayd*, terrified.
4 *Harrow*, alas.
5 *Lenger*, longer.
6 *Owne*, i. e. Arthur's.
7 *Foynd*, pushed.

So hasty heat soone cooled to subdew:
Tho, when this breathlesse woxe, that batteil gan renew.

48 As when a windy tempest bloweth hye,
That nothing may withstand his stormy stowre,[1]
The clowdes, as thinges affrayd, before him flye;
But, all so soone as his outrageous powre
Is layd, they fiercely then begin to showre;
And, as in scorne of his spent stormy spight,
Now all attonce their malice forth do poure:
So did Prince Arthur beare himselfe in fight,
And suffred rash Pyrochles waste his ydle might.

49 At last whenas the Sarazin perceiv'd
How that straunge[2] sword refusd to serve his neede,
But, when he stroke most strong, the dint deceiv'd,
He flong it from him; and, devoyd of dreed,
Upon him lightly leaping without heed,
Twixt his two mighty armes engrasped fast,
Thinking to overthrowe and downe him tred:
But him in strength and skill the Prince surpast,
And through his nimble sleight did under him down cast.

50 Nought booted it the Paynim then to strive;
For as a bittur[3] in the eagles clawe,

1 *Stowre*, violence.
2 *Straunge*, not belonging to him.
3 *Bittur*, bittern.

XLVII. 9.— *Tho, when*, &c.] Then when *this* Paynim grew breathless, *that* Prince renewed the battle. H.

That may not hope by flight to scape alive,
Still waytes for death with dread and trembling aw;
So he, now subiect to the victours law,
Did not once move, nor upward cast his eye,
For vile disdaine and rancour, which did gnaw
His hart in twaine with sad melâncholy;
As one that loathed life, and yet despysd to dye.

51 But, full of princely bounty and great mind,
The conquerour nought cared him to slay;
But, casting wronges and all revenge behind,
More glory thought to give life then decay,[1]
And sayd: "Paynim, this is thy dismall day[2];
Yet if thou wilt renounce thy miscreaunce,[3]
And my trew liegeman yield thyselfe for ay,
Life will I graunt thee for thy valiaunce,
And all thy wronges will wipe out of my sovenaunce.[4]"

52 "Foole," sayd the Pagan, "I thy gift defye;
But use thy fortune, as it doth befall;
And say, that I not overcome doe dye,
But in despight of life for death doe call."
Wroth was the Prince, and sory yet withall,
That he so wilfully refused grace;
Yet, sith his fate so cruelly did fall,
His shining helmet he gan soone unlace,
And left his headlesse body bleeding all the place.

1 *Then decay*, than death.
2 *Dismall day*, doomsday. (And so, Canto VII. 26.)
3 *Miscreaunce*, false faith.
4 *Sovenaunce*, memory.

53 By this, Sir Guyon from his traunce awakt,
Life having maystered her sencelesse foe;
And looking up, whenas his shield he lakt
And sword saw not, he wexed wondrous woe.[1]
But when the Palmer, whom he long ygoe
Had lost, he by him spyde, right glad he grew,
And saide: "Deare Sir, whom wandring to and fro
I long have lackt, I ioy thy face to vew!
Firme is thy faith, whom daunger never fro me drew.

54 "But read[2] what wicked hand hath robbed mee
Of my good sword and shield?" The Palmer, glad
With so fresh hew uprysing him to see,
Him answered: "Fayre sonne, be no whit sad
For want of weapons; they shall soone be had."
So gan he to discourse the whole debate,[3]
Which that straunge Knight for him sustained had,
And those two Sarazins confounded late,
Whose carcases on ground were horribly prostrâte.

55 Which when he heard, and saw the tokens trew,
His hart with great affection was embayd,[4]
And to the Prince, bowing with reverence dew,
As to the patrone[5] of his life, thus sayd:
"My Lord, my Liege, by whose most gratious ayd
I live this day, and see my foes subdewd,
What may suffise to be for meede repayd

1 *Woe*, sad.
2 *Read*, tell me.
3 *Debate*, contest.
4 *Embayd*, bathed.
5 *Patrone*, protector.

Of so great graces as ye have me shewd,
But to be ever bound — "

56 To whom the Infant[1] thus : " Fayre Sir, what need
Good turnes be counted, as a servile bond,
To bind their dooers to receive their meed ?
Are not all knightes by oath bound to withstond
Oppressours powre by armes and puissant hond ?
Suffise, that I have done my dew[2] in place."
So goodly purpose[3] they together fond[4]
Of kindnesse and of courteous aggrace[5] ;
The whiles false Archimage and Atin fled apace.

1 *Infant*, youth, or knight. (Compare F. Q. VI., VIII. 15.)
2 *Dew*, duty.
3 *Purpose*, discourse.
4 *Fond*, found.
5 *Aggrace*, favor.

LVI. 1.—*Fayre Sir, what need*, &c.] This remark of Prince Arthur expresses the sentiment of a beautiful maxim of De la Rochefoucauld, that the too eager desire to return a favor is, in itself, a species of ingratitude. H.

CANTO IX.

The House of Temperance, in which
  Doth sober Alma dwell,
Besiegd of many foes, whom straung
  er Knightes to flight compell.

1 Of all Gods workes, which doe this worlde adorne,
  There is no one more faire and excellent
  Then is mans body, both for powre and forme,
  Whiles it is kept in sober government;
  But none then it more fowle and indecent,
  Distempred through misrule and passions bace;
  It growes a monster, and incontinent[1]
  Doth loose his dignity and native grace:
Behold, who list, both one and other in this place.

2 After the Paynim brethren conquer'd were,
  The Briton Prince recov'ring his stolne sword,
  And Guyon his lost shield, they both yfere[2]
  Forth passed on their way in fayre accord,

[1] *Incontinent*, immediately. [2] *Yfere*, together.

I. 9. — *In this place.*] In the persons of Prince Arthur and of the two brothers, Cymochles and Pyrochles. H.

Till him the Prince with gentle court did bord[1].
"Sir Knight, mote I of you this court'sy read,[2]
To weet why on your shield, so goodly scord,
Beare ye the picture of that ladies head?
Full lively[3] is the semblaunt, though the substance dead."

3 "Fayre Sir," sayd he, "if in that picture dead
Such life ye read, and vertue in vaine shew;
What mote ye weene, if the trew lively-head[4]
Of that most glorious visage ye did vew!
But ẏf the beauty of her mind ye knew,
That is, her bounty, and imperiall powre,
Thousand times fairer then her mortal hew,
O how great wonder would your thoughts devoure,
And infinite desire into your spirite poure!

4 "Shee is the mighty Queene of Faëry,
Whose faire retraitt[5] I in my shield doe beare;
Shee is the flowre of grace and chastity,
Throughout the world renowmed far and neare,
My Liefe,[6] my Liege, my Soveraine, my Deare,
Whose glory shineth as the morning starre,
And with her light the earth enlumines cleare;
Far reach her mercies, and her praises farre,
As well in state of peace, as puissaunce in warre."

1 *Bord*, address.
2 *Read*, understand, i. e. will your courtesy explain this.
3 *Lively*, lifelike.
4 *Lively-head*, lifelikeness, or living original.
5 *Retraitt*, portrait.
6 *Liefe*, dear, or love.

5 "Thrise happy man," said then the Briton Knight,
"Whom gracious lott and thy great valiaunce
Have made thee soldier of that princesse bright,
Which with her bounty and glad countenaunce
Doth blesse her servaunts, and them high advaunce;
How may straunge knight hope ever to aspire,
By faithfull service and meete amenaunce,[1]
Unto such blisse? Sufficient were that hire
For losse of thousand lives, to die at her desire."

6 Said Guyon, "Noble Lord, what meed so great,
Or grace of earthly prince so soveraine,
But by your wondrous worth and warlike feat
Ye well may hope, and easely attaine?
But were your will her sold to entertaine,[2]
And numbred be mongst Knights of Maydenhed,
Great guerdon, well I wote, should you remaine,
And in her favor high bee reckoned,
As Arthegall and Sophy now beene honored."

7 "Certes," then said the Prince, "I God avow,[3]
That sith I armes and knighthood first did plight,
My whole desire hath beene, and yet is now,
To serve that Queene with al my powre and might.
Seven times the sunne with his lamp-burning light

[1] *Amenaunce*, deportment.
[2] *Sold to entertaine*, receive her pay.
[3] *Avow*, vow to.

VI. 9.—*As Arthegall and Sophy.*] Of Arthegall we hear hereafter, but not of Sophy. H.

VII. 5.—*Seven times*, &c.] In Book I. Canto IX. Stanza 5. Arthur says he has already been nine months in quest of the Faerie

Hath walkte about the world, and I no lesse,
Sith of that goddesse I have sought the sight,
Yet no where can her find; such happinesse
Heven doth to me envý and fortune favourlesse."

8 "Fortune, the foe of famous chevisaunce,[1]
Seldome," said Guyon, "yields to vertue aide,
But in her way throwes mischiefe and mischaunce,
Whereby her course is stopt and passage staid.
But you, faire Sir, be not herewith dismaid,
But constant keepe the way in which ye stand;
Which were it not that I am els delaid
With hard adventure, which I have in hand,
I labour would to guide you through al Fary land."

9 "Gramercy,[2] Sir," said he; "but mote I weete
What straunge adventure doe ye now pursew?
Perhaps my succour or advizement meete
Mote stead[3] you much your purpose to subdew."
Then gan Sir Guyon all the story shew
Of false Acrasia, and her wicked wiles;
Which to avenge, the Palmer him forth drew

1 *Chevisaunce*, enterprise.
2 *Gramercy*, many thanks.
3 *Stead*, help.

Queene. He now says that he has sought for her seven years. In the thirty-eighth stanza of this canto he is said to have rambled *three* years. These inconsistencies are removed in the second edition, which reads "twelve months" in Stanza 38, and in this place, —

"Now hath the sunne with his lamp-burning light
Walkt round about the world, and I no lesse." C.

From Faery court. So talked they, the whiles
They wasted had much way, and measurd many miles.

10 And now faire Phoebus gan decline in haste
His weary wagon to the westerne vale,
Whenas they spide a goodly castle, plaste
Foreby[1] a river in a pleasaunt dale;
Which choosing for that evenings hospitale,[2]
They thether marcht: but when they came in sight,
And from their sweaty coursers did avale,[3]
They found the gates fast barred long ere night,
And every loup[4] fast lockt, as fearing foes despight.

11 Which when they saw, they weened fowle reproch
Was to them doen, their entraunce to forstall;
Till that the Squire gan nigher to approch,
And wind his horne under the castle wall,
That with the noise it shooke as it would fall.
Eftsoones forth looked from the highest spire
The watch, and lowd unto the knights did call,
To weete what they so rudely did require:
Who gently answered, They entraunce did desire.

12 "Fly, fly, good Knights," said he, "fly fast away,
If that your lives ye love, as meete ye should;
Fly fast, and save yourselves from neare decay[5];
Here may ye not have entraunce, though we would
We would and would againe, if that we could;

[1] *Foreby*, near to.
[2] *Hospitale*, inn.
[3] *Avale*, alight.
[4] *Loup*, loophole.
[5] *Decay*, destruction.

But thousand enemies about us rave,
And with long siege us in this castle hould:
Seven yeares this wize they us besieged have,
And many good knights slaine that have us sought to save."

13 Thus as he spoke, loe! with outragious cry
A thousand villeins rownd about them swarmd
Out of the rockes and caves adioyning nye;
Vile caitive wretches, ragged, rude, deformd,
All threatning death, all in straunge manner armd;
Some with unweldy clubs, some with long speares,
Some rusty knifes, some staves in fier warmd:
Sterne was their looke; like wild amazed steares,
Staring with hollow eies, and stiffe upstanding heares.

14 Fiersly at first those knights they did assayle,
And drove them to recoile: but, when againe
They gave fresh charge, their forces gan to fayle
Unhable their encounter to sustaine;
For with such puissaunce and impetuous maine
Those champions broke on them, that forst them fly,
Like scattered sheepe, whenas the shepherds swaine
A lyon and a tigre doth espye
With greedy pace forth rushing from the forest nye.

XII. 8. — *They us besieged have.*] It will hardly be necessary to remind the reader that *this castle* is the human body; that *Alma* is the mind; and that the *besiegers* are the unruly passions, &c. Spenser says *seven years*, perhaps in allusion to the seven ages of the world, or else to the various stages of man's life. UPTON.

15 A while they fled, but soone retournd againe
With greater fury then before was fownd;
And evermore their cruell capitaine
Sought with his raskall routs t' enclose them rownd,
And overronne to tread them to the grownd:
But soone the knights with their bright-burning blades
Broke their rude troupes, and orders did confownd,
Hewing and slashing at their idle shades;
For though they bodies seem, yet substaunce from them fades.

16 As when a swarme of gnats at eventide
Out of the fennes of Allan doe arise,
Their murmuring small trompetts sownden[1] wide,
Whiles in the aire their clustring army flies,
That as a cloud doth seeme to dim the skies;
Ne man nor beast may rest or take repast
For their sharpe wounds and noyous iniuries,
Till the fierce northerne wind with blustring blast
Doth blow them quite away, and in the ocean cast.

17 Thus when they had that troublous rout disperst,
Unto the castle gate they come againe,
And entraunce crav'd, which was denied erst.
Now when report of that their perlous[2] paine,

1 *Sownden*, sound. 2 *Perlous*, perilous.

XVI. 2. — *Fennes of Allan.*] Probably the great bog of Allen in the eastern part of Ireland.

And combrous conflict which they did sustaine,
Came to the Ladies eare which there did dwell,
Shee forth issèwed with a goodly traine
Of squires and ladies equipaged well,
And entertained them right fairely, as befell.

18 Alma she called was; a virgin bright,
That had not yet felt Cupides wanton rage;
Yet was shee wooed of many a gentle knight,
And many a lord of noble parentage,
That sought with her to lincke in marriage:
For shee was faire, as faire mote ever bee,
And in the flowre now of her freshest age;
Yet full of grace and goodly modestee,
That even heven reioyced her sweete face to see.

19 In robe of lilly white she was arayd,
That from her shoulder to her heele downe raught[1];
The traine whereof loose far behind her strayd,
Braunched[2] with gold and perle most richly wrought,
And borne of two faire damsels which were taught
That service well: her yellow golden heare
Was trimly woven and in tresses wrought,
Ne other tire[3] she on her head did weare,
But crowned with a garland of sweete rosiere.[4]

20 Goodly shee entertaind those noble knights,
And brought them up into her castle hall;

1 *Raught*, reached.
2 *Braunched*, sprigged, embroidered.
3 *Tire*, head-dress.
4 *Rosiere*, rose-tree.

Where gentle court and gracious delight
Shee to them made, with mildnesse virginall,
Shewing herselfe both wise and liberall.
Then when they rested had a season dew,
They her besought of favour speciall
Of that faire castle to affoord them vew:
Shee graunted; and, them leading forth, the same did
shew.

21 First she them led up to the castle wall,
That was so high as foe might not it clime,
And all so faire and fensible[1] withall;
Not built of bricke, ne yet of stone and lime,
But of thing like to that Ægyptian slime,
Whereof King Nine whilome built Babell towre:
But O great pitty that no lenger time
So goodly workemanship should not endure!
Soone it must turne to earth: no earthly thing is sure.

22 The frame thereof seemd partly circulare,
And part triangulare; O worke divine!
Those two the first and last proportions are;
The one imperfect, mortall, fœminine;

[1] *Fensible*, capable of being defended.

XXI. 5.— Possibly Spenser had in his mind the account of Diodorus, according to which the slime left by the overflow of the Nile generated animals of itself. See Book I. Canto I. 21. C.

XXII. — This verse describes the plan and proportions of Alma's castle, the human body. The circular part is the head, the triangular, the legs, the base of the triangle being wanting. The quadrate or parallelogram which forms the base of both is the trunk. The triangle and the circle are called "the first and last pro-

Th' other immortall, perfect, masculine;
And twixt them both a quadrate was the base,
Proportioned equally by seven and nine;
Nine was the circle sett in heavens place:
All which compacted made a goodly diapase.

23 Therein two gates were placed seemly well:
The one before, by which all in did pas,
Did th' other far in workmanship excell;
For not of wood, nor of enduring bras,
But of more worthy substance fram'd it was:
Doubly disparted, it did locke and close,
That, when it locked, none might thorough pas,
And, when it opened, no man might it close;
Still open to their friendes, and closed to their foes.

---

portions," because they include respectively the least and the greatest space in the same perimeter, or perhaps simply because they are the extremities. The triangle is imperfect, as wanting a base and denoting the animal nature; mortal, because it is altogether fleshly and contains no spiritual part; feminine, because it includes the generative power, of which the female is the type. The circle is immortal, for it contains the imperishable mind; perfect, not only as complete in itself, but because the soul is made in the image of God; and masculine, because it is the seat of the spiritual principle which exercises sway over the body. The breadth of the trunk (including the arms) is to the length from the shoulders to the thigh nearly as seven to nine, and the longer side of the parallelogram is affirmed to be equal to the circumference of the head,— "Nine was the circle sett in heavens place" (or topping this noble structure). All parts of the edifice fitly joined together made "a goodly diapase," or concord. The mystical interpretation of this verse by Sir Kenelm Digby and Upton is, to say the least, quite unnecessary. I am indebted for some parts of this explanation to a writer in the London Athenæum, No. 1085. C.

24 Of hewen stone the porch was fayrely wrought,
Stone more of valew, and more smooth and fine,
Then iett or marble far from Ireland brought;
Over the which was cast a wandring vine,
Enchaced with a wanton yvie twine:
And over it a fayre portcullis hong,
Which to the gate directly did incline,
With comely compasse and compacture strong,
Nether unseemly short, nor yet exceeding long.

25 Within the barbican[1] a Porter sate,
Day and night duely keeping watch and ward;
Nor wight nor word mote passe out of the gate,
But in good order, and with dew regard;
Utterers of secrets he from thence debard,
Bablers of folly, and blazers of cryme:
His larum-bell might lowd and wyde be hard
When cause requyrd, but never out of time;
Early and late it rong, at evening and at prime.

26 And rownd about the porch on every syde
Twise sixteene Warders satt, all armed bright
In glistring steele, and strongly fortifyde:
Tall yeomen seemed they, and of great might,
And were enraunged ready still for fight.
By them as Alma passed with her guestes,

[1] *Barbican*, outwork.

XXIV.—The porch is the upper lip; the wandering vine, the moustache; the portcullis, the nose; the barbican, the cavity of the mouth, the porter of which is the tongue, while the twice sixteen warders are the teeth. C.

They did obeysaunce, as beseemed right,
And then againe retourned to their restes:
The Porter eke to her did lout[1] with humble gestes.[2]

27 Thence she them brought into a stately hall,
Wherein were many tables fayre dispred.
And ready dight with drapets[3] festivall,
Against the viaundes should be ministred.
At th' upper end there sate, yclad in red
Downe to the ground, a comely personage,
That in his hand a white rod menaged;
He steward was, hight Diet; rype of age,
And in demeanure sober, and in counsell sage.

28 And through the hall there walked to and fro
A iolly yeoman, marshall of the same,
Whose name was Appetite; he did bestow
Both guestes and meate, whenever in they came,
And knew them how to order without blame,
As him the steward badd. They both attone[4]
Did dewty to their Lady, as became;
Who, passing by, forth ledd her guestes anone
Into the kitchin rowme, ne spard for nicenesse none.

29 It was a vaut[5] ybuilt for great dispence,[6]
With many raunges reard along the wall,
And one great chimney, whose long tonnell thence
The smoke forth threw: and in the midst of all

1 *Lout*, bow.
2 *Gestes*, gestures.
3 *Drapets*, linen cloths.
4 *Attone*, together
5 *Vaut*, vault.
6 *Dispence*, expense

There placed was a caudron wide and tall
Upon a mightie fornace, burning whott,
More whott then Aetn', or flaming Mongiball:
For day and night it brent, ne ceased not,
So long as any thing it in the caudron gott.

30 But to delay[1] the heat, least by mischaunce
It might breake out and set the whole on fyre,
There added was by goodly ordinaunce
An huge great payre of bellowes, which did styre[2]
Continually, and cooling breath inspyre.
About the caudron many cookes accoyld[3]
With hookes and ladles, as need did requyre;
The whyles the viaundes in the vessell boyld,
They did about their businesse sweat, and sorely toyld.

31 The maister cooke was cald Concoction;
A carefull man, and full of comely guyse:
The kitchin clerke, that hight Digestion,
Did order all th' achates[4] in seemely wise,
And set them forth, as well he could devise.
The rest had severall offices assynd;
Some to remove the scum as it did rise;
Others to beare the same away did mynd;
And others it to use according to his kynd.

1 *Delay*, temper.
2 *Styre*, stir, move.
3 *Accoyld*, bustled.
4 *Achates*, provisions.

XXIX. 5.—*A caudron.*] This *caudron* is the stomach. H.
XXIX. 7.—*Mongiball.*] *Mongiball* is another name for Mount Ætna. H.
XXX. 4.—*Payre of bellowes.*] These are the lungs. H.

32 But all the liquour, which was fowle and waste,
Not good nor serviceable elles for ought,
They in another great rownd vessel plaste,
Till by a conduit pipe it thence were brought;
And all the rest, that noyous was and nought,
By secret wayes, that none might it espy,
Was close convaid, and to the backgate brought,
That cleped was Port Esquiline, whereby
It was avoided quite, and throwne out privily.

33 Which goodly order and great workmans skill
Whenas those knightes beheld, with rare delight
And gazing wonder they their mindes did fill;
For never had they seene so straunge a sight.
Thence backe againe faire Alma led them right,
And soone into a goodly parlour brought,
That was with royall arras richly dight,[1]
In which was nothing poúrtrahed nor wrought;
Not wrought nor poúrtrahed, but easie to be thought.

34 And in the midst thereof upon the floure
A lovely bevy of faire ladies sate,
Courted of many a iolly[2] paramoure,

1 *Dight*, covered. 2 *Iolly*, handsome.

XXXII. 8.—*Port Esquiline.*] The Campus Esquilinus, outside of the Esquiline gate of Rome, was used as a burial-place for the poor. The mean purposes to which it was devoted account for the word being employed here. H.

XXXIV. 2.—*Of faire ladies.*] These *faire ladies* represent the various affections; the parlor being the heart. H.

The which them did in modest wise amate,[1]
And each one sought his lady to aggrate[2];
And eke emongst them litle Cupid playd
His wanton sportes, being retourned late
From his fierce warres, and having from him layd
His cruel bow, wherewith he thousands hath dismayd.

35 Diverse delights they fownd themselves to please;
Some song in sweet consórt[3]; some laught for ioy;
Some plaid with strawes; some ydly satt at ease;
But other some could not abide to toy,
All pleasaunce was to them griefe and annoy:
This fround; that faund; the third for shame did blush;
Another seemed envious, or coy;
Another in her teeth did gnaw a rush:
But at these straungers presence every one did hush.

36 Soone as the gracious Alma came in place,
They all attonce out of their seates arose,
And to her homage made with humble grace:
Whom when the knights beheld, they gan dispose
Themselves to court, and each a damzell chose:
The Prince by chaunce did on a lady light,
That was right faire and fresh as morning rose,
But somwhat sad and solemne eke in sight,[4]
As if some pensive thought constraind her gentle spright.

1 *Amate*, accompany.
2 *Aggrate*, please.
3 *Consórt*, concert.
4 *In sight*, in appearance, or expression.

37 In a long purple pall, whose skirt with gold
Was fretted all about, she was arayd;
And in her hand a poplar braunch did hold;
To whom the Prince in courteous maner sayd:
"Gentle Madáme, why beene ye thus dismayd,
And your faire beautie doe with sadnes spill[1]?
Lives any that you hath thus ill apayd[2]?
Or doen you love, or doen you lack your will?
Whatever bee the cause, it sure beseemes you ill."

38 "Fayre Sir," said she, halfe in disdainefull wise,
"How is it that this word in me ye blame,
And in yourselfe doe not the same advise[3]?
Him ill beseemes anothers fault to name,
That may unwares bee blotted with the same:
Pensive I yeeld I am, and sad in mind,
Through great desire of glory and of fame;
Ne ought I weene are ye therein behynd,
That have three years * sought One, yet no where can Her find."

39 The Prince was inly moved at her speach,
Well weeting trew what she had rashly[4] told;
Yet with faire semblaunt[5] sought to hyde the breach,

1 *Spill*, spoil, obscure.
2 *Apayd*, satisfied.
3 *Advise*, perceive.
4 *Rashly*, at a venture.
5 *Semblaunt*, appearance.

XXXVII. 3. — *A poplar braunch.*] The poplar was sacred to Hercules, which is the reason why this lady, who represents the love of distinction, has a branch of it in her hands, that hero being so distinguished for that quality. H.

* Three years. 2d Edition, *twelve months*. See Stanza 7.

Which chaunge of colour did perforce unfold,
Now seeming flaming whott, now stony cold:
Tho, turning soft aside, he did inquyre
What wight she was that poplar braunch did hold:
It answered was, her name was Prays-desire,
That by well doing sought to honour to aspyre.

40 The whyles, the Faery Knight did entertayne
Another damsell of that gentle crew,
That was right fayre and modest of demayne,[1]
But that too oft she chaung'd her native hew:
Straunge was her tyre, and all her garment blew,
Close rownd about her tuckt with many a plight[2]:
Upon her fist the bird which shonneth vew
And keepes in coverts close from living wight,
Did sitt, as yet ashamd how rude Pan did her dight.[3]

41 So long as Guyon with her commoned,
Unto the grownd she cast her modest eye,
And ever and anone with rosy red
The bashfull blood her snowy cheekes did dye,
That her became, as polisht yvory
Which cunning craftesman hand hath overlayd
With fayre vermilion or pure castory.

1 *Demayne*, demeanor.
2 *Plight*, fold.
3 *Dight*, treat.

XL. 7.—*The bird*, &c.] The nymph Echo bore to Pan a daughter named Jynx, who was changed by Juno into a bird of the same name, the wryneck, or cuckoo's mate.

XLI. 7.—*Castory.*] This appears from the context to be a red coloring matter. I can give no account of the word. It can hardly be *castoreum*, the secretion of the beaver. C.

Great wonder had the Knight to see the mayd
So straungely passioned,[1] and to her gently said:

42 "Fayre Damzell, seemeth by your troubled cheare,
That either me too bold ye weene, this wise
You to molest, or other ill to feare
That in the secret of your hart close lyes,
From whence it doth, as cloud from sea, aryse:
If it be I, of pardon I you pray;
But, if ought else that I mote not devyse,
I will, if please you it discure,[2] assay
To ease you of that ill, so wisely as I may."

43 She answerd nought, but more abasht for shame
Held downe her head, the whiles her lovely face
The flashing blood with blushing did inflame,
And the strong passion[3] mard her modest grace,
That Guyon mervayld at her uncouth[4] cace;
Till Alma him bespake: "Why wonder yee,
Faire Sir, at that which ye so much embrace[5]?
She is the fountaine of your modestee;
You shamefast are, but Shamefastnes itselfe is shee."

44 Thereat the Elfe did blush in privitee,
And turnd his face away; but she the same
Dissembled faire, and faynd to oversee.
Thus they awhile with court and goodly game
Themselves did solace each one with his dame,
Till that great Lady thence away them sought

1 *Passioned*, moved.
2 *Discure*, discover.
3 *Passion*, emotion.
4 *Uncouth*, singular.
5 *So much embrace*, of which you have so much.

To vew her castles other wondrous frame:
Up to a stately turret she them brought,
Ascending by ten steps of alablaster wrought.

45 That turrets frame most admirable was,
Like highest heaven compassed around,
And lifted high above this earthly masse,
Which it survewd,[1] as hils doen lower ground:
But not on ground mote like to this be found;
Not that, which antique Cadmus whylome built
In Thebes, which Alexander did confound;
Nor that proud towre of Troy, though richly guilt,[2]
From which young Hectors blood by cruell Greekes was spilt.

46 The roofe hereof was arched over head,
And deckt with flowers and herbars[3] daintily;
Two goodly beacons, set in watches stead,
Therein gave light, and flamd continually:
For they of living fire most subtilly
Were made, and set in silver sockets bright,
Cover'd with lids deviz'd of substance sly,[4]
That readily they shut and open might.
O, who can tell the prayses of that makers might!

1 *Survewd*, overlooked.
2 *Guilt*, gilded.
3 *Herbars*, plants.
4 *Sly*, subtile, finely wrought.

XLV. 9. — *From which young Hectors blood*, &c.] Astyanax, the son of Hector, was thrown from the walls of Troy by the Greeks. H.

XLVI. 1. — *The roofe*, &c.] The arched roof is the skull; the flowers and herbars, the hair; the two goodly beacons, the eyes. H.

47 Ne can I tell, ne can I stay to tell,
This parts great workemanship and wondrous powre,
That all this other worldes worke doth excell,
And likest is unto that heavenly towre
That God hath built for his owne blessed bowre.
Therein were divers rowmes, and divers stages;
But three the chiefest and of greatest powre,
In which there dwelt three honorable Sages,
The wisest men, I weene, that lived in their ages.

48 Not he whom Greece, the nourse of all good arts,
By Phœbus doome the wisest thought alive,
Might be compar'd to these by many parts:
Nor that sage Pylian syre, which did survive
Three ages, such as mortall men contrive,[1]
By whose advise old Priams cittie fell,
With these in praise of pollicies mote strive.
These three in these three rowmes did sondry dwell,
And counselled faire Alma how to governe well.

49 The first of them could things to come foresee;
The next could of thinges present best advize;
The third things past could keepe in memoree:
So that no time nor reason could arize,
But that the same could one of these comprize.
Forthy[2] the first did in the forepart sit,

[1] *Contrive*, wear out, spend. [2] *Forthy*, therefore.

XLVIII. 1.—*Not he*, &c.] Socrates, whom the oracle at Delphi pronounced the wisest of men. The Pylian syre is Nestor.

XLIX. 1.—*The first of them.*] The first of these personages is Imagination, the second, Judgment, and the third, Memory. H.

That nought mote hinder his quicke preiudize[1],
He had a sharpe foresight and working wit
That never idle was, ne once would rest a whit.

50 His chamber was dispainted all within
With sondry colours, in the which were writ
Infinite shapes of thinges dispersed thin;
Some such as in the world were never yit,
Ne can devized be of mortall wit;
Some daily seene and knowen by their names,
Such as in idle fantasies doe flit;
Infernall hags, centaurs, feendes, hippodames,[2]
Apes, lyons, aegles, owles, fooles, lovers, children, dames.

51 And all the chamber filled was with flyes,
Which buzzed all about, and made such sound
That they encombred all mens eares and eyes;
Like many swarmes of bees assembled round,
After their hives with honny do abound.
All those were idle thoughtes and fantasies,
Devices, dreames, opinions unsound,
Shewes, visions, sooth-sayes, and prophesies;
And all that fained is, as leasings, tales, and lies.

52 Emongst them all sate he which wonned[3] there,
That hight Phantastes by his nature trew;
A man of yeares yet fresh, as mote appere,
Of swarth complexion, and of crabbed hew,

1 *Preiudize*, foresight.
2 *Hippodames*, river-horses (hippopotamuses.)
3 *Wonned*, dwelt.

That him full of melāncholy did shew;
Bent hollow beetle browes, sharpe staring eyes,
That mad or foolish seemd: one by his vew
Mote deeme him borne with ill-disposed skyes,
When oblique[1] Saturne sate in the house of agonyes.

53 Whom Alma having shewed to her guestes,
Thence brought them to the second rowme, whose
wals
Were painted faire with memorable gestes[2]
Of famous wisards; and with picturals
Of magistrates, of courts, of trībunals,
Of commen-wealthes, of states, of pollicy,
Of lawes, of iudgementes, and of dēcretals,
All artes, all science, all philosophy,
And all that in the world was ay thought wittily.[3]

54 Of those that rowme was full; and them among
There sate a man of ripe and perfect age,
Who did them meditate all his life long,
That through continuall practise and usāge
He now was growne right wise and wondrous sage:
Great plesure had those straunger knightes to see
His goodly reason and grave personage,

1 *Oblique*, unpropitious.
2 *Gestes*, deeds.
3 *Wittily*, wisely.

LII. 9.— *The house of agonyes.*] The twelfth house of the celestial sphere according to astrologers, in which, they say, "Saturn greatly joyeth." "The twelfth house, being the house of tribulation, resolves all questions of sorrow, affliction, anxiety of mind, trouble, distress, imprisonment, persecution, malice, secret enemies, suicide, treason," &c. Sibly's Astrology. C.

That his disciples both desyrd to bee:
But Alma thence them led to th' hindmost rowme of three.

55 That chamber seemed ruinous and old,
And therefore was removed far behind,
Yet were the wals, that did the same uphold,
Right firme and strong, though somwhat they declind[1];
And therein sat an old, old man, halfe blind,
And all decrepit in his feeble corse,
Yet lively vigour rested in his mind,
And recompenst him with a better scorse[2]:
Weake body well is chang'd for minds redoubled forse.

56 This man of infinite remembraunce was,
And things foregone through many ages held,
Which he recorded still as they did pas,
Ne suffred them to perish through long eld,[3]
As all things els the which this world doth weld[4];
But laid them up in his immortall scrine,[5]
Where they for ever incorrupted dweld:
The warres he well remembred of King Nine,
Of old Assaracus, and Inachus divine.

57 The yeares of Nestor nothing were to his,
Ne yet Mathusalem, though longest liv'd;
For he remembred both their infancis:

1 *Declind*, i. e. from the perpendicular.
2 *Scorse*, exchange.
3 *Eld*, age.
4 *Weld*, control.
5 *Scrine*, desk.

Ne wonder then if that he were depriv'd
Of native strength now that he them surviv'd.
His chamber all was hangd about with rolls
And old records from auncient times derivd,
Some made in books, some in long parchment scrolls,
That were all worm-eaten and full of canker holes.

58 Amidst them all he in a chaire was sett,
Tossing and turning them withouten end;
But for he was unhable them to fett,[1]
A litle boy did on him still attend
To reach, whenever he for ought did send:
And oft when thinges were lost, or laid amis,
That boy them sought and unto him did lend[2]:
Therefore he Anamnestes cleped is;
And that old man Eumnestes, by their propertis.

59 The Knightes there entring did him reverence dew,
And wondred at his endlesse exercise.
Then as they gan his library to vew,
And antique regesters for to avise,[3]
There chaunced to the Princes hand to rize
An auncient booke, hight *Briton Moniments*,
That of this lands first conquest did devize,

1 *Fett*, fetch.
2 *Lend*, hand, reach.
3 *Avise*, examine.

LVIII. 4.—*A litle boy*, &c.] The *boy* sustains to the *old man* the relation of Recollection to Memory.—*Eumnestes* means a person of good memory; *Anamnestes*, one who puts in mind of something which has been forgotten. It is not improbable that Spenser intended by Anamnestes, *Anagnostes*, a reader.

And old division into regiments[1]
Till it reduced was to one mans governements.

60 Sir Guyon chaunst eke on another booke,
That hight *Antiquitee of Faery Lond:*
In which whenas he greedily did looke,
Th' ofspring of Elves and Faryes there he fond,
As it delivered was from hond to hond:
Whereat they, burning both with fervent fire
Their countreys auncestry to understond,
Crav'd leave of Alma and that aged sire
To read those bookes; who gladly graunted their desire.

1 *Regiments*, governments.

CANTO X.

A Chronicle of Briton Kings,*
From Brute to Uthers rayne;
And rolls of Elfin Emperours,
Till time of Gloriane.

1 Who now shall give unto me words and sound
Equall unto this haughty[1] enterprise?
Or who shall lend me wings, with which from ground
My lowly verse may loftily arise,
And lift itselfe unto the highest skyes?
More ample spirit then hetherto was wount[2]
Here needes me, whiles the famous auncestryes
Of my most dreaded Soveraigne I recount,
By which all earthly princes she doth far surmount.

2 Ne under sunne that shines so wide and faire,
Whence all that lives does borrow life and light,
Lives ought that to her linage may compaire;

1 *Haughty*, high, bold. 2 *Wount*, wont.

* Some parts of this Chronicle appear to be taken from Holinshed, others from Geoffrey of Monmouth, the oldest authority for these fabulous stories. There are two or three unimportant particulars, not found in either, which I have not succeeded in tracing to their original. C.

Which though from earth it be derived right,
Yet doth itselfe stretch forth to hevens hight,
And all the world with wonder overspred;
A labor huge, exceeding far my might!
How shall fraile pen, with feare disparaged,[1]
Conceive such soveraine glory and great bountyhed[2]

3 Argument worthy of Mœonian quill;
Or rather worthy of great Phoebus rote,[3]
Whereon the ruines of great Ossa hill,
And triumphes of Phlegræan Iove, he wrote,
That all the gods admird his lofty note.
But, if some relish of that hevenly lay
His learned daughters would to me report
To decke my song withall, I would assay
Thy name, O soveraine Queene, to blazon far away.

4 Thy name, O soveraine Queene, thy realme, and race,
From this renowmed Prince derived arre,
Who mightily upheld that royall mace
Which now thou bear'st, to thee descended farre
From mighty kings and conquerours in warre,
Thy fathers and great grandfathers of old,
Whose noble deeds above the northern starre
Immortall Fame for ever hath enrold;
As in that Old Mans booke they were in order told.

1 *Disparaged*, i. e. deprived of its ordinary power.
2 *Bountyhed*, goodness.
3 *Rote*, lyre. (Celtic, *chrotta;* English, *crowd.*)

5 The land which warlike Britons now possesse,
And therein have their mighty empire raysd,
In antique times was salvage wildernesse,
Unpeopled, unmannurd, unprovd,[1] unpraysd;
Ne was it island then, ne was it paysd[2]
Amid the ocean waves, ne was it sought
Of merchaunts farre for profits therein praysd;
But was all desolate, and of some thought
By sea to have bene from the Celticke mayn-land brought.

6 Ne did it then deserve a name to have,
Till that the venturous mariner that way,
Learning his ship from those white rocks to save,
Which all along the southerne sea-coast lay,
Threatning unheedy wrecke and rash decay,
For safëty that same his sea-marke made,
And namd it ALBION: but later day,
Finding in it fit ports for fishers trade,
Gan more the same frequent, and further to invade.

7 But far in land a salvage nation dwelt
Of hideous giaunts, and halfe-beastly men,
That never tasted grace, nor goodnes felt;
But wild like beastes lurking in loathsome den,
And flying fast as roebucke through the fen,
All naked without shame or care of cold,
By hunting and by spoiling liveden[3];
Of stature huge, and eke of corage bold,
That sonnes of men amazd their sternesse to behold.

[1] *Unprovd*, not worked or cultivated.
[2] *Paysd*, poised.
[3] *Liveden*, lived.

8 But whence they sprong, or how they were begott,
Uneath[1] is to assure[2]; uneath to wene[3]
That monstrous error which doth some assott,[4]
That Dioclesians fifty daughters shene[5]
Into this land by chaunce have driven bene;
Where, companing with feends and filthy sprights
Through vaine illusion of their lust unclene,
They brought forth geaunts, and such dreadful wights
As far exceeded men in their immeasurd mights.

9 They held this land, and with their filthinesse
Polluted this same gentle soyle long time;
That their owne mother loathd their beastlinesse,
And gan abhorre her broods unkindly[6] crime,
All were they borne of her owne native slime:
Until that Brutus, anciently deriv'd
From roiall stocke of old Assaracs line,
Driven by fatall error[7] here arriv'd,
And them of their uniust possession depriv'd.

10 But ere he had established his throne,
And spred his empire to the utmost shore,
He fought great batteils with his salvage fone[8]:

1 *Uneath*, hard.
2 *Assure*, to assert confidently.
3 *Wene*, believe.
4 *Assott*, infatuate.
5 *Shene*, bright.
6 *Unkindly*, unnatural.
7 *Fatall error*, foreordained wandering.
8 *Fone*, foes.

VIII. 4. — This Dioclesian is a fabled king of Assyria. Holinshed, without vouching for the story, says that the name is a mistake for Danaus. C.

In which he them defeated evermore,
And many giaunts left on groning flore[1]:
That well can witnes yet unto this day
The westerne Hogh, besprincled with the gore
Of mighty Goëmot, whome in stout fray
Corineus conquered, and cruelly did slay.

11 And eke that ample pitt, yet far renownd
For the large leape which Debon did compell
Coulin to make, being eight lugs[2] of grownd,
Into the which retourning backe he fell:
But those three monstrous stones doe most excell,
Which that huge sonne of hideous Albion,
Whose father Hercules in Fraunce did quell,
Great Godmer threw, in fierce contention,
At bold Canutus; but of him was slaine anon.

12 In meed of these great conquests by them gott,
Corineus had that province utmost west
To him assigned for his worthy lott,
Which of his name and memorable gest[3]
He called Cornwaile, yet so called best:
And Debons shayre was that is Devon shyre:
But Canute had his portion from the rest,
The which he cald Canutium, for his hyre;
Now Cantium, which Kent we comenly inquyre.[4]

1 *Flore*, ground.
2 *Lugs*, rods.
3 *Gest*, exploit.
4 *Inquyre* (i. e. inquire for by the name of), call (?).

X. 7.—The Hogh is the Haw near Plymouth. 8. Goëmot is Gogmagog. 9. Corineus was said to be the leader of a party of Trojans that had emigrated with Antenor. C.

13 Thus Brute this realme unto his rule subdewd,
And raigned long in great felicity,
Lov'd of his freends, and of his foes eschewd:
He left three sonnes, his famous progeny,
Borne of fayre Inogene of Italy;
Mongst whom he parted his imperiall state,
And Locrine left chiefe lord of Britany.
At last ripe age bad him surrender late
His life, and long good fortune, unto finall fate.

14 Locrine was left the soveraine lord of all;
But Albanact had all the northerne part,
Which of himselfe Albania he did call;
And Camber did possesse the westerne quart,[1]
Which Severne now from Logris[2] doth depart:
And each his portion peaceably enioyd,
Ne was there outward breach, nor grudge in hart,
That once their quiet government annoyd;
But each his paynes to others profit still employd.

15 Untill a nation straung,[3] with visage swart
And corage fierce that all men did affray,
Which through the world then swarmd in every part,
And overflow'd all countries far away,
Like Noyes great flood, with their importune[4] sway,
This land invaded with like violence,
And did themselves through all the north display;

[1] *Quart*, quarter.
[2] *Logris*, England.
[3] I. e. the Huns.
[4] *Importune*, unrelenting, irresistible.

Untill that Locrine, for his realmes defence,
Did head against them make and strong munificence.[1]

16 He them encountred, a confused rout,
Foreby[2] the river that whylóme was hight
The ancient Abus, where with courage stout
He them defeated in victorious fight,
And chaste so fiercely after fearefull flight,
That forst their chiefetain, for his safeties sake,
(Their cheifetain Humber named was aright,)
Unto the mighty streame him to betake,
Where he an end of batteill and of life did make.

17 The king retourned proud of victory,
And insolent wax through unwonted ease,
That shortly he forgot the ieopardy,
Which in his land he lately did appease,
And fell to vaine voluptuous disease:
He lov'd faire Ladie Estrild, leudly lov'd,
Whose wanton pleasures him too much did please,
That quite his hart from Guendolene remov'd,
From Guendolene his wife, though alwaies faithful prov'd.

18 The noble daughter of Corinëus
Would not endure to bee so vile disdaind,
But, gathering force and corage valorous,

1 *Munificence* (i. e. munition), defence. 2 *Foreby*, near to.

XVII. 6.—The Lady Estrild was said to be the daughter of a German king. C.

Encountred him in batteill well ordaind,
In which him vanquisht she to fly constraind:
But she so fast pursewd, that him she tooke
And threw in bands, where he till death remaind:
Als[1] his faire leman flying through a brooke
She overhent,[2] nought moved with her piteous looke:

19 But both herselfe, and eke her daughter deare
Begotten by her kingly paramoure,
The faire Sabrina, almost dead with feare,
She there attached,[3] far from all succoúre:
The one she slew upon the present floure[4];
But the sad virgin innocent of all
Adowne the rolling river she did poure,
Which of her name now Severne men do call:
Such was the end that to disloyall love did fall.

20 Then for her sonne, which she to Locrin bore,
(Madan was young, unmeet the rule to sway,)
In her owne hand the crowne she kept in store,
Till ryper yeares he raught[5] and stronger stay:
During which time her powre she did display
Through all this realme, the glory of her sex,
And first taught men a woman to obay:

1 *Als*, also.
2 *Overhent*, overtook.
3 *Attached*, seized.
4 *The present floure*, i. e. the spot where she was.
5 *Raught*, reached.

XIX. 3.— *The faire Sabrina.*] This is the "Sabrina fair" of Milton's Comus, in which her sad fate is commemorated in a passage of great beauty. H.

But when her sonne to mans estate did wex,[1]
She it surrendred, ne her selfe would lenger vex.

21 Tho Madan raignd, unworthie of his race;
For with all shame that sacred throne he fild.
Next Memprise, as unworthy of that place,
In which being consorted with Manild,
For thirst of single kingdom him he kild.
But Ebranck salved[2] both their infamies
With noble deedes, and warreyd on Brunchild
In Henault, where yet of his victories
Brave moniments remaine, which yet that land envies.

22 An happy man in his first dayes he was,
And happy father of faire progeny:
For all so many weekes, as the yeare has,
So many children he did multiply;
Of which were twentie sonnes, which did apply
Their mindes to prayse and chevalrous desyre:
Those germans[3] did subdew all Germany,
Of whom it hight; but in the end their syre
With foule repulse from Fraunce was forced to retyre.

23 Which blott his sonne succeeding in his seat,
The second Brute, the second both in name
And eke in semblaunce of his puissaunce great,
Right well recur'd, and did away that blame
With recompence of everlasting fame:
He with his victour sword first opened
The bowels of wide Fraunce, a forlorne dame,

1 *Wex*, grow.
2 *Salved*, healed.
3 *Germans*, brothers.

And taught her first how to be conquered;
Since which, with sondrie spoiles she hath bene ransacked.

24 Let Scaldis tell, and let tell Hania,
And let the marsh of Esthambruges tell,
What colour were their waters that same day,
And all the moore twixt Elversham and Dell,
With blood of Henalois which therein fell.
How oft that day did sad Brunchildis see
The *greene shield* dyde in dolorous vermell?
That not *scuith guiridh* it mote seeme to bee,
But rather *y scuith gogh*, signe of sad crueltee.

25 His sonne, King Leill, by fathers labour long,
Enioyd an heritage of lasting peace,
And built Cairleill, and built Cairleon strong.
Next Huddibras his realme did not encrease,
But taught the land from wearie wars to cease.
Whose footsteps Bladud following, in artes
Exceld at Athens all the learned preace,[1]
From whence he brought them to these salvage parts,
And with sweet science mollifide their stubborne harts.

[1] *Preace*, throng.

XXIV. 8. — *Scuith guiridh.*] These are Welsh words, meaning "green shield." *Yscuith gogh* means "the red shield." These words, and all of the ninth line except "but," are not printed in some copies of the first edition. C.

XXV. 3. — *Cair* is city; *Cairleill*, Carlisle; *Cairleon* (City of the Legion), Chester; *Cairbadon* (XXVI. 2), Bath. C.

26 Ensample of his wondrous faculty,
Behold the boyling bathes at Cairbadon,
Which seeth with secret fire eternally,
And in their entrailles, full of quick brimstón,
Nourish the flames which they are warmd upon,
That to their people wealth they forth do well,
And health to every forreyne nation:
Yet he at last, contending to excell
The reach of men, through flight into fond mischief fell.

27 Next him King Leyr in happie peace long raynd,
But had no issue male him to succeed;
But three faire daughters, which were well uptraind
In all that seemed fitt for kingly seed;
Mongst whom his realme he equally decreed
To have divided. Tho, when feeble age
Nigh to his utmost date he saw proceed,
He cald his daughters, and with speeches sage
Inquyrd, which of them most did love her parentage.

28 The eldest Gonorill gan to protest,
That she much more then her owne life him lov'd;
And Regan greater love to him profest
Then all the world, when ever it were proov'd;
But Cordeill said she lov'd him as behoov'd:

XXVI. 9.—*Fond mischief.*] Foolish death or ruin. The story is, that, in attempting to fly, he fell and was dashed in pieces. H.

XXVII. 1.—*King Leyr.*] At the time this stanza was written, Spenser little dreamed of the immortality which this name was destined to enjoy. "King Lear" was published about sixteen years after the Faerie Queene. The magic of Shakespeare's genius has made these the only interesting stanzas in the whole canto. H.

Whose simple answere, wanting colours fayre
To paint it forth, him to displeasaunce moov'd,
That in his crown he counted her no hayre,
But twixt the other twain his kingdom whole did shayre.

29 So wedded th' one to Maglan, king of Scottes,
And th' other to the king of Cambria,
And twixt them shayrd his realme by equall lottes;
But, without dowre, the wise Cordelia
Was sent to Aggannip of Celtica[1]:
Their aged syre, thus eased of his crowne,
A private life ledd in Albania
With Gonorill, long had in great renowne,
That nought him griev'd to beene from rule deposed downe.

30 But true it is that, when the oyle is spent,
The light goes out, and weeke is throwne away;
So, when he had resignd his regiment,[2]
His daughter gan despise his drouping day,[3]
And wearie wax of his continuall stay:
Tho to his daughter Regan he repayrd,
Who him at first well used every way;
But when of his departure she despayrd,
Her bountie she abated, and his cheare empayrd.

31 The wretched man gan then avise[4] to late,
That love is not where most it is profest;
Too truely tryde in his extremest state!

[1] I. e. France.
[2] *Regiment*, government.
[3] *Drouping day*, declining years.
[4] *Avise*, perceive.

At last, resolv'd likewise to prove the rest,
He to Cordelia himselfe addrest,
Who with entyre affection him receav'd,
As for her syre and king her seemed best;
And after all an army strong she leav'd,[1]
To war on those which him had of his realme bereav'd.

32 So to his crowne she him restord againe;
In which he dyde, made ripe for death by eld,[2]
And after wild it should to her remaine:
Who peaceably the same long time did weld,[3]
And all mens harts in dew obedience held;
Till that her sisters children, woxen strong,
Through proud ambition against her rebeld,
And overcommen kept in prison long,
Till weary of that wretched life herselfe she hong.

33 Then gan the bloody brethren both to raine:
But fierce Cundah gan shortly to envý
His brother Morgan, prickt with proud disdaine
To have a pere in part of soverainty;
And, kindling coles of cruell enmity,
Raisd warre, and him in batteill overthrew:
Whence as he to those woody hilles did fly,
Which hight of him Glamorgan, there him slew:
Then did he raigne alone, when he none equall knew.

34 His sonne Rivall' his dead rowme did supply;
In whose sad time blood did from heaven rayne.
Next great Gurgustus, then faire Cæcily,

1 *Leav'd*, levied. 2 *Eld*, age. 3 *Weld*, wield.

In constant peace their kingdomes did contayne.
After whom Lago and Kinmarke did rayne,
And Gorbogud, till far in yeares he grew:
Then his ambitious sonnes unto them twayne
Arraught[1] the rule, and from their father drew;
Stout Ferrex and sterne Porrex him in prison threw.

35 But O! the greedy thirst of royall crowne,
That knowes no kinred, nor regardes no right,
Stird Porrex up to put his brother downe;
Who, unto him assembling forreigne might,
Made warre on him, and fell himselfe in fight:
Whose death t' avenge, his mother mercilesse,
Most mercilesse of women, Wyden hight,
Her other sonne fast sleeping did oppresse,
And with most cruell hand him murdred pittilesse.

36 Here ended Brutus sacred progeny,
Which had seven hundred yeares this scepter borne
With high renowme and great felicity:
The noble braunch from th' antique stocke was torne
Through discord, and the roiall throne forlorne.[2]
Thenceforth this realme was into factions rent,
Whilest each of Brutus boasted to be borne,
That in the end was left no moniment
Of Brutus, nor of Britons glorie auncient.

1 *Arraught*, seized. 2 *Forlorne*, left vacant.

XXXIV. 9. — *Stout Ferrex and sterne Porrex.*] *Ferrex* and *Porrex* have afforded the subject of the earliest tragedy in the English language, written by Lord Buckhurst and Thomas Nor ton, called "Gorboduc," or sometimes "Ferrex and Porrex." H.

37 Then up arose a man of matchlesse might,
And wondrous wit to menage high affayres,
Who, stird with pitty of the stressed[1] plight
Of this sad realme, cut into sondry shayres
By such as claymd themselves Brutes rightfull hayres,
Gathered the princes of the people loose[2]
To taken counsell of their common cares;
Who, with his wisedom won, him streight did choose
Their king, and swore him fëalty, to win or loose.

38 Then made he head against his enimies,
And Ymner slew of Logris miscreate;
Then Ruddoc and proud Stater, both allyes,
This of Albány newly nominate,
And that of Cambry king confirmed late,
He overthrew through his owne valiaunce;
Whose countries he redus'd to quiet state,
And shortly brought to civile governaunce,
Now one, which earst were many made through variaunce.

39 Then made he sacred lawes, which some men say
Were unto him reveald in vision;
By which he freed the traveilers high-way,
The churches part, and ploughmans portion,
Restraining stealth and strong extortion;
The gratious Numa of great Britany:
For, till his dayes, the chiefe dominion
By strength was wielded without pollicy:
Therefore he first wore crowne of gold for dignity.

1 *Stressed*, distressed. 2 *Loose*, scattered.

40 Donwallo dyde, (for what may live for ay?)
And left two sonnes, of pearelesse prowesse both,
That sacked Rome too dearely did assay,
The recompence of their periúred oth;
And ransackt Greece wel tryde, when they were wroth;
Besides subiected France and Germany,
Which yet their praises speake, all be they loth,
And inly tremble at the memory
Of Brennus and Belinus, kinges of Britany.

41 Next them did Gurgiunt, great Belinus sonne,
In rule succeede, and eke in fathers praise;
He Easterland subdewd, and Denmarke wonne,
And of them both did foy[1] and tribute raise,
The which was dew in his dead fathers daies:
He also gave to fugitives of Spayne,
Whom he at sea found wandring from their waies,
A seate in Ireland safely to remayne,
Which they should hold of him as subiect to Britáyne.

42 After him raigned Guitheline his hayre,
The iustest and trewest in his daies,
Who had to wife Dame Mertia the fayre,
A woman worthy of immortall praise,
Which for this realme found[2] many goodly layes,[3]

[1] *Foy*, i. e. money paid as sign of fidelity.
[2] *Found*, devised. [3] *Layes*, laws.

XL. 3.—I. e. Rome made proof of their prowess to her cost. The Romans swore fealty to the British kings, and then treacherously attempted to destroy them; for which the brothers sacked the city. This Brennus is meant to be the same person as the antagonist of Camillus. C.

And wholesome statutes to her husband brought:
Her many deemd to have beene of the Fayes,
As was Aegerié that Numa tought:
Those yet of her be Mertian lawes both nam'd and thought.

43 Her sonne Sisillus after her did rayne;
And then Kimarus; and then Danius:
Next whom Morindus did the crowne sustayne;
Who, had he not with wrath outrageous
And cruell rancour dim'd his valorous
And mightie deedes, should matched have the best:
As well in that same field victorious
Against the forreine Morands [1] he exprest;
Yet lives his memorie, though carcas sleepe in rest.

44 Five sonnes he left begotten of one wife,
All which successively by turnes did rayne:
First Gorboman, a man of vertuous life;
Next Archigald, who for his proud disdayne
Deposed was from princedome soverayne,
And pitteous Elidure put in his sted;
Who shortly it to him restord agayne,
Till by his death he it recovered;
But Peridure and Vigent him disthronized.

45 In wretched prison long he did remaine,
Till they out-raigned had their utmost date,
And then therein reseized [2] was againe,
And ruled long with honorable state,

1 *Morands*, people of the northwest coast of France.
2 *Reseized*, reseated.

Till he surrendred realme and life to fate.
Then all the sonnes of these five brethren raynd
By dew successe,[1] and all their nephewes[2] late;
Even thrise eleven descents the crowne retaynd,
Till aged Hely by dew heritage it gaynd.

46 He had two sonnes, whose eldest, called Lud,
Left of his life most famous memory,
And endlesse moniments of his great good:
The ruin'd wals he did reædifye[3]
Of Troynovant,[4] gainst force of enimy,
And built that gate which of his name is hight,
By which he lyes entombed solemnly:
He left two sonnes, too young to rule aright,
Androgeus and Tenantius, pictures of his might.

47 Whilst they were young, Cassibalane their eme[5]
Was by the people chosen in their sted,
Who on him tooke the roiall diademe,
And goodly well long time it governed;
Till the prowde Romanes him disquieted,
And warlike Cæsar, tempted with the name
Of this sweet island never conquered,
And envying the Britons blazed fame,
(O hideous hunger of dominion!) hether came.

1 *Successe*, succession.
2 *Nephewes*, descendants.
3 *Reædifye*, rebuild.
4 *Troynovant*, London.
5 *Eme*, uncle.

XLVII. 1.— *Cassibalane.*] Caswallon, who made a brave resistance to Cæsar, but was obliged at last to purchase the evacuation of Britain by the Romans at the price of a nominal submission. C.

48 Yet twise they were repulsed backe againe,
And twise renforst backe to their ships to fly;
The whiles with blood they all the shore did staine,
And the gray ocean into purple dy:
Ne had they footing found at last perdie,
Had not Androgeus, false to native soyle,
And envious of uncles soveraintie,
Betrayd his countrey unto forreine spoyle.
Nought els but treason from the first this land did foyle!

49 So by him Cæsar got the victory,
Through great bloodshed and many a sad assay,
In which himselfe was charged heavily
Of hardy Nennius, whom he yet did slay,
But lost his sword, yet to be seene this day.
Thenceforth this land was tributarie made
T' ambitious Rome, and did their rule obay,
Till Arthur all that reckoning defrayd:
Yet oft the Briton kings against them strongly swayd.

50 Next him Tenantius raignd; then Kimbeline,
What time th' Eternall Lord in fleshly slime
Enwombed was, from wretched Adams line
To purge away the guilt of sinfull crime.
O ioyous memorie of happy time,
That heavenly grace so plenteously displayd!
O too high ditty for my simple rime! —
Soone after this the Romanes him warrayd;
For that their tribute he refusd to let be payd.

L. 1. — *Kimbeline.*] This is Shakespeare's Cymbeline. H.

51 Good Claudius, that next was emperour,
An army brought, and with him batteile fought,
In which the king was by a treachetour[1]
Disguised slaine, ere any thereof thought:
Yet ceased not the bloody fight for ought:
For Arvirage his brothers place supplyde
Both in his armes and crowne, and by that draught[2]
Did drive the Romanes to the weaker syde,
That they to peace agreed. So all was pacifyde.

52 Was never king more highly magnifide,
Nor dredd of Romanes, then was Arvirage;
For which the emperour to him allide
His daughter Genuiss' in marriage:
Yet shortly he renounst the vassallage
Of Rome againe, who hether hastly sent
Vespasian, that with great spoile and rage
Forwasted[3] all, till Genuissa gent[4]
Persuaded him to ceasse, and her lord to relent

53 He dide; and him succeeded Marius,
Who ioyd his dayes in great tranquillity.
Then Coyll; and after him good Lucius,
That first received Christianity,
The sacred pledge of Christes Evangely.
Yet true it is, that long before that day

1 *Treachetour*, traitor.
2 *Draught*, device.
3 *Forwasted*, laid waste.
4 *Gent*, noble.

LI. 3.—The king here should be Guiderius, not Kimbeline. C.

LII. 7.—Vespasian fought thirty battles in Britain, subdued the Isle of Wight, overcame two nations, and took twenty places. C.

Hither came Ioseph of Arimathy,
Who brought with him the Holy Grayle, (they say,)
And preacht the truth; but since it greatly did decay.

54 This good king shortly without issew dide,
Whereof great trouble in the kingdome grew,
That did herselfe in sondry parts divide,
And with her powre her owne selfe overthrew,
Whilest Romanes daily did the weake subdew:
Which seeing, stout Bunduca up arose,
And, taking armes, the Britons to her drew;
With whom she marched streight against her foes,
And them unwares besides the Severne did enclose.

55 There she with them a cruell batteill tryde,
Not with so good successe as shee deserv'd,
By reason that the captaines on her syde,
Corrupted by Paulinus, from her swerv'd:
Yet, such as were through former flight preserv'd
Gathering againe, her host she did renew,
And with fresh corage on the victor serv'd:
But being all defeated, save a few,
Rather then fly, or be captív'd, herselfe she slew.

56 O famous moniment of womens prayse!
Matchable either to Semiramis,

LIII. 8.—*The Holy Grayle.*] The dish in which the paschal lamb was placed at the Last Supper (Saint Graal). It was carried to England by Joseph of Arimathea, and its subsequent loss occasioned the famous quest for its recovery. At the beginning of the twelfth century it appeared in Genoa, and there it was preserved until Napoleon transported it to Paris. For an account of the word *graal*, see Diez, Etym. Wörterb., p. 647. The mistaken derivation from *sang réel* is still given in books. C.

Whom antique history so high doth rayse,
Or to Hypsiphil', or to Thomiris:
Her host two hundred thousand numbred is;
Who, whiles good fortune favoured her might,
Triumphed oft against her enemis;
And yet, though overcome in haplesse fight,
Shee triumphed on death, in enemies despight.

57 Her reliques Fulgent having gathered,
Fought with Severus, and him overthrew;
Yet in the chace was slaine of them that fled;
So made them victors whome he did subdew.
Then gan Carausius tirannize anew,
And gainst the Romanes bent their proper[1] powre;
But him Allectus treacherously slew,
And tooke on him the robe of emperoure:
Nath'lesse the same enioyed but short happy howre:

[1] *Their proper*, their own.

LVI. 4.— *Or to Hypsiphil', or to Thomiris.*] *Hypsiphile* was a queen of Lemnos, who headed an attack made by her female subjects upon their male relations. — *Thomiris* or *Tomyris* was a queen of the Massagetæ, who, according to Herodotus, defeated and slew Cyrus the Great. H.

LVII. 1.— *Fulgent.*] *Fulgentius* is said to be the name of a Caledonian chief, who headed the armies which the Emperor Severus met in his march into Caledonia. But this was a hundred and fifty years after the time of Boadicea. H.

LVII. 5.— *Carausius.*] Carausius, a Menapian, was intrusted with extensive powers, by the Emperors Diocletian and Maximian, for the defence of the northern coasts of the Empire. He entered into an alliance with the Saxon pirates, renounced his allegiance to Rome, and assumed the imperial title in Britain. He was mur-

58 For Asclepiodate him overcame,
And left inglorious on the vanquisht playne,
Without or robe or rag to hide his shame :
Then afterwards he in his stead did raigne ;
But shortly was by Coyll in batteill slaine :
Who after long debate, since Lucies tyme,
Was of the Britons first crownd soveraine.
Then gan this realme renew her passed prime :
He of his name Coylchester built of stone and lime.

59 Which when the Romanes heard, they hether sent
Constantius, a man of mickle might,
With whome King Coyll made an agreëment,
And to him gave for wife his daughter bright,
Fayre Helena, the fairest living wight,
Who in all godly thewes[1] and goodly praise
Did far excell, but was most famous hight[2]
For skil in musicke of all in her daies,
As well in curious instruments as cunning laies:

60 Of whom he did great Constantine begett,
Who afterward was emperour of Rome ;
To which whiles absent he his mind did sett,

1 *Thewes*, qualities. 2 *Hight*, called.

dered in 293, by Allectus, who usurped his empire, but was defeated by the Romans after a reign of three years. C.

LIX. 2.— *Constantius.*] Constantius Chlorus, the father of Constantine, died at York (then Eboracum), A. D. 306. His wife (the mother of Constantine) was named Helena, and was, according to Geoffrey, the daughter of "King Cole."

LX., LXI.— Octavius, according to the legend, was a Welsh prince. Traherne was one of the Empress Helena's three uncles,

Octavius here lept into his roome,
And it usurped by unrighteous doome:
But he his title iustifide by might,
Slaying Traherne, and having overcome
The Romane legion in dreadfull fight:
So settled he his kingdome, and confirmd his right:

61 But, wanting yssew male, his daughter deare
He gave in wedlocke to Maximian,
And him with her made of his kingdome heyre,
Who soone by meanes thereof the empire wan,
Till murdred by the freends of Gratian.
Then gan the Hunnes and Picts invade this land,
During the raigne of Maximinian;
Who dying left none heire them to withstand;
But that they overran all parts with easy hand.

62 The weary Britons, whose war-hable[1] youth
Was by Maximian lately ledd away,
With wretched miseryes and woefull ruth
Were to those Pagans made an open pray,
And daily spectacle of sad decay:
Whome Romane warres, which now fowr hundred yeares
And more had wasted, could no whit dismay;

[1] *War-hable*, able to serve in war.

---

and Maximian, or Maximus, was her cousin, and the son of Traherne's brother. Maximinian (LXI. 7) seems to be put by oversight for Valentinian. C.

LXII. 2.—*Ledd away.*] For the conquest of Armorica. C.

Til, by consent of Commons and of Peares,
They crownd the second Constantine with ioyous teares:

63 Who having oft in batteill vanquished
Those spoylefull Picts, and swarming Easterlings,
Long time in peace his realme established,
Yet oft annoyd with sondry bordragings[1]
Of neighbour Scots, and forrein scatterlings[2]
With which the world did in those dayes abound:
Which to outbarre, with painefull pyonings[3]
From sea to sea he heapt a mighty mound,
Which from Alcluid to Panwelt did that border bownd.

64 Three sonnes he dying left, all under age;
By meanes whereof their uncle Vortigere
Usurpt the crowne during their pupillage;
Which th' infants tutors gathering to feare,[4]
Them closely into Armorick did beare:
For dread of whom, and for those Picts annoyes,
He sent to Germany straunge aid to reare[5];
From whence eftsoones arrived here three hoyes[6]
Of Saxons, whom he for his safëty imployes.

1 *Bordragings*, border forays.
2 *Scatterlings*, vagrants.
3 *Pyonings*, works of pioneers.
4 *Gathering to feare*, considering a cause of alarm.
5 *Reare*, raise.
6 *Hoyes*, boats.

LXII. 9.—*The second Constantine.*] A common soldier of the name of Constantine was made Emperor at the beginning of the fifth century. H.

LXIII. 2.—*Easterlings.*] The Northern pirates.

65 Two brethren were their capitayns, which hight
Hengist and Horsus, well approv'd in warre,
And both of them men of renowmed might;
Who making vantage of their civile iarre,
And of those forreyners which came from farre,
Grew great, and got large portions of land,
That in the realme ere long they stronger arre
Then they which sought at first their helping hand,
And Vortiger have forst the kingdome to aband.[1]

66 But, by the helpe of Vortimere his sonne,
He is againe unto his rule restord;
And Hengist, seeming sad for that was donne,
Received is to grace and new accord,
Through his faire daughters face and flattring word.
Soone after which, three hundred lords he slew
Of British blood, all sitting at his bord;
Whose dolefull moniments who list to rew,[2]
Th' eternall marks of treason may at Stonheng vew.

67 By this the sonnes of Constantine, which fled,
Ambrose and Uther, did ripe yeares attayne,
And, here arriving, strongly challenged
The crowne which Vortiger did long detayne;
Who, flying from his guilt, by them was slayne:
And Hengist eke soone brought to shamefull death.
Thenceforth Aurelius peaceably did rayne,
Till that through poyson stopped was his breath;
So now entombed lies at Stoneheng by the heath.

[1] *Aband*, abandon.

[2] *List to rew*, wishes to pity.

68 After him Uther, which Pendragon hight,
Succeeding —— There abruptly it did end,
Without full point, or other cesure[1] right;
As if the rest some wicked hand did rend,
Or th' author selfe could not at least attend
To finish it: that so untimely breach
The Prince himselfe halfe seemed to offend;
Yet secret pleasure did offence empeach,[2]
And wonder of antiquity long stopt his speach.

69 At last, quite ravisht with delight to heare
The royall ofspring[3] of his native land,
Cryde out: "Deare Countrey! O how dearely deare
Ought thy remembraunce and perpetual band
Be to thy foster childe, that from thy hand
Did commun breath and nouriture receave!
How brutish is it not to understand
How much to her we owe, that all us gave;
That gave unto us all whatever good we have!"

70 But Guyon all this while his booke did read,
Ne yet has ended: for it was a great
And ample volume, that doth far excead
My leasure so long leaves here to repeat:
It told how first Prometheus did create

1 *Cesure*, stop.
2 *Empeach*, prevent.
3 *Ofspring*, origin, ancestors.

LXVIII. 2.— *There abruptly it did end.*] The history is brought down to Uther Pendragon, the father of Arthur, and there ends. Prince Arthur was at that time ignorant of his parentage. H.

A man, of many parts from beasts deryv'd,
And then stole fire from heven to animate
His worke, for which he was by Iove depryv'd
Of life himself, and hart-strings of an aegle ryv'd.

71 That man so made he called Elfe, to weet
Quick, the first author of all Elfin kynd;
Who, wandring through the world with wearie feet,
Did in the gardins of Adonis fynd
A goodly creature, whom he deemd in mynd
To be no earthly wight, but either spright,
Or angell, th' authour of all woman kynd;
Therefore a Fay he her according hight,
Of whom all Faryes spring, and fetch their lignage right.

72 Of these a mighty people shortly grew,
And puissant kinges which all the world warrayd,[1]
And to themselves all nations did subdew:
The first and eldest, which that scepter swayd,
Was Elfin: him all India obayd,
And all that now America men call:
Next him was noble Elfinan, who laid
Cleopolis foundation first of all:
But Elfiline enclosd it with a golden wall.

73 His sonne was Elfinell, who overcame
The wicked Gobbelines[2] in bloody field:
But Elfant was of most renowmed fame,
Who all of christall did Panthea build:

1 *Warrayd*, warred upon. 2 *Gobbelines*, goblins.

Then Elfar, who two brethren gyauntes kild,
The one of which had two heades, th' other three:
Then Elfinor, who was in magick skild;
He built by art upon the glassy see
A bridge of bras, whose sound hevens thunder seem'd
to bee.

74 He left three sonnes, the which in order raynd,
And all their ofspring, in their dew descents;
Even seven hundred princes, which maintaynd
With mightie deedes their sondry governments:
That were too long their infinite contents
Here to record, ne much materiall:
Yet should they be most famous moniments,
And brave ensample, both of martiall
And civil rule, to kinges and states imperiall.

75 After all these Elficleos did rayne,
The wise Elficleos in great maiestie,
Who mightily that scepter did sustayne,
And with rich spoyles and famous victorie
Did high advaunce the crowne of Faëry:
He left two sonnes, of which faire Elferon,
The eldest brother, did untimely dy;
Whose emptie place the mightie Oberon
Doubly supplide, in spousall and dominion.

LXXV. 1. —*Elficleos.*] In this and the succeeding stanza there are obvious allusions to history. Elficleos is Henry VII.; Elferon is Prince Arthur, his son, who died young; Oberon is Henry VIII., who married his brother's betrothed bride; and Tanaquill, or Gloriana, his daughter, is Queen Elizabeth. It will be observed that no mention is made of Edward VI. or of Mary. H.

76 Great was his power and glorie over all
Which, him before, that sacred seate did fill,
That yet remaines his wide memoriall:
He dying left the fairest Tanaquill,
Him to succeede therein, by his last will:
Fairer and nobler liveth none this howre,
Ne like in grace, ne like in learned skill;
Therefore they Glorian call that glorious flowre:
Long mayst thou, Glorian, live in glory and great powre!

77 Beguyld thus with delight of novelties,
And naturall desire of countryes state,
So long they redd in those antiquities,
That how the time was fled they quite forgate;
Till gentle Alma, seeing it so late,
Perforce their studies broke, and them besought
To thinke how supper did them long awaite:
So halfe unwilling from their bookes them brought,
And fayrely feasted as so noble knightes she ought.

CANTO XI.

The Enimies of Temperaunce
  Besiege her dwelling place;
Prince Arthure them repelles, and fowle
  Maleger doth deface.

1 WHAT warre so cruel, or what siege so sore,
As that, which strong affections[1] doe apply
Against the forte of Reason evermore,
To bring the sowle into captivity!
Their force is fiercer through infirmity
Of the fraile flesh, relenting to their rage;
And exercise most bitter tyranny
Upon the partes, brought into their bondáge:
No wretchednesse is like to sinfull vellenage.[2]

2 But in a body which doth freely yeeld
His partes to Reasons rule obedient,
And letteth her, that ought, the scepter weeld,
All happy peace and goodly government
Is setled there in sure establishment.
There Alma, like a Virgin Queene most bright,
Doth florish in all beautie excellent;
And to her guestes doth bounteous banket dight,[3]
Attempred goodly well for health and for delight.

1 *Affections*, passions.
2 *Vellenage*, servitude.
3 *Dight*, prepare.

3 Early, before the Morne with cremosin[1] ray
The windowes of bright heaven opened had,
Through which into the world the dawning day
Might looke, that maketh every creature glad,
Uprose Sir Guyon in bright armour clad,
And to his purposd iourney him prepar'd:
With him the Palmer eke in habit sad[2]
Himselfe addrest to that adventure hard:
So to the rivers syde they both together far'd:

4 Where them awaited ready at the ford
The Ferriman, as Alma had behight,[3]
With his well-rigged bote. They goe abord,
And he eftsoones[4] gan launch his barke forthright.
Ere long they rowed were quite out of sight,
And fast the land behynd them fled away.
But let them pas, whiles winde and wether right
Doe serve their turnes: here I a while must stay,
To see a cruell fight doen by the Prince this day.

5 For, all so soone as Guyon thence was gon
Upon his voyage with his trustie guyde,
That wicked band of Villeins fresh begon
That castle to assaile on every side,
And lay strong siege about it far and wyde.
So huge and infinite their numbers were,
That all the land they under them did hyde;
So fowle and ugly, that exceeding feare
Their visages imprest, when they approched neare.

1 *Cremosin*, crimson.
2 *Sad*, grave.
3 *Behight*, commanded.
4 *Eftsoones*, immediately.

6 Them in twelve troupes their captein did dispart,
And round about in fittest steades[1] did place,
Where each might best offend his proper part,
And his contráry obiect most deface,
As every one seem'd meetest in that cace.
Seven of the same against the castle gate
In strong entrenchments he did closely place,
Which with incessaunt force and endlesse hate
They battred day and night, and entraunce did awate.

7 The other five, five sondry wayes he sett
Against the five great bulwarkes of that pyle,
And unto each a bulwarke did arrett,[2]
T' assayle with open force or hidden guyle,
In hope thereof to win victorious spoile.
They all that charge did fervently apply[3]
With greedie malice and importune toyle,
And planted there their huge artillery,
With which they dayly made most dreadfull battery.

8 The first troupe was a monstrous rablement
Of fowle misshapen wightes, of which some were
Headed like owles, with beckes[4] uncomely bent;
Others like dogs; others like gryphons dreare;
And some had wings, and some had clawes to teare:
And every one of them had lynces eyes;

1 *Steades*, places.
2 *Arrett*, appoint.
3 *Apply*, employ themselves with.
4 *Beckes*, beaks.

VI. 6. — *Seven*, &c.] These represent the seven deadly sins, and the *five* mentioned in the next stanza, the vices that attack the senses. UPTON.

And every one did bow and arrówes beare:
All those were lawlesse Lustes, corrupt Envýes,
And covetous Aspécts,[1] all cruel enimyes.

9 Those same against the Bulwarke of the Sight
Did lay strong siege and battailous assault,
Ne once did yield it respitt day nor night;
But soone as Titan gan his head exault,
And soone againe as he his light withhault,[2]
Their wicked engins they against it bent;
That is, each thing by which the eyes may fault:
But two then all more huge and violent,
Beautie and Money, they that Bulwarke sorely rent.

10 The second Bulwarke was the Hearing Sence,
Gainst which the second troupe assignment[3] makes;
Deformed creatures, in straunge difference:
Some having heads like harts, some like to snakes,
Some like wilde bores late rouzd out of the brakes;
Slaunderous Reproches, and fowle Infamies,
Leasinges, Backbytinges, and vaine-glorious Crakes,[4]
Bad Counsels, Prayses, and false Flatteries:
All those against that fort did bend their batteries.

11 Likewise that same third Fort, that is the Smell,
Of that third troupe was cruelly assayd;
Whose hideous shapes were like to feendes of hell,

1 *Aspects*, looks.
2 *Withhault*, withheld.
3 *Assignment*, disposition.
4 *Crakes*, boastings.

Some like to houndes, some like to apes, dismayd[1];
Some, like to puttockes,[2] all in plumes arayd;
All shap't according[3] their conditions[4]:
For, by those ugly formes weren pourtrayd
Foolish Delights, and fond Abusions,[5]
Which doe that sence besiege with light illusions.

12 And that fourth band which cruell battry bent
Against the fourth Bulwarke, that is the Taste,
Was, as the rest, a grysie rablement;
Some mouth'd like greedy oystriges[6]; some faste[7]
Like loathly toades; some fashioned in the waste
Like swine: for so deformd is Luxury,
Surfeat, Misdiet, and unthriftie Waste,
Vaine Feastes, and ydle Superfluity:
All those this sences fort assayle incessantly.

13 But the fift troupe, most horrible of hew
And ferce of force, is dreadfull to report;
For some like snailes, some did like spyders shew,
And some like ugly urchins[8] thick and short:
Cruelly they assayed that fift Fort,
Armed with dartes of sensuall Delight,

1 *Dismayd*, mismade (?).
2 *Puttockes*, kites.
3 *According*, according to.
4 *Conditions*, qualities.
5 *Abusions*, abuses.
6 *Oystriges*, ostriches.
7 *Faste*, faced.
8 *Urchins*, hedgehogs.

XII. 3.—*A grysie rablement.*] If we retain this reading, *grysie* must be explained *filthy*. But the word should probably be *gryslie* (grisly), for the fourth band was *hideous*, "as the rest." C.

With stinges of carnall Lust, and strong effórt
Of feeling Pleasures, with which day and night
Against that same fift Bulwarke they continued fight.

14 Thus these twelve troupes with dreadfull puissaunce
Against that castle restlesse siege did lay,
And evermore their hideous ordinaunce
Upon the bulwarkes cruelly did play,
That now it gan to threaten neare decay[1]:
And evermore their wicked Capitayn
Provoked them the breaches to assay,
Somtimes with threats, somtimes with hope of gayn,
Which by the ransack of that peece[2] they should attayn.

15 On th' other syde, th' asseiged castles ward[3]
Their stedfast stonds[4] did mightily maintaine,
And many bold repulse and many hard
Atchievement wrought, with perill and with payne,
That goodly frame from ruine to sustaine:
And those two brethren gyauntes did defend
The walles so stoutly with their sturdie mayne,[5]
That never entraunce any durst pretend,
But they to direfull death their groning ghosts did send.

1 *Decay*, ruin.
2 *Peece*, structure, castle.
3 *Ward*, guard.
4 *Stonds*, stations.
5 *Mayne*, force.

XV. 6. — *Brethren gyauntes.*] Arthur and Guyon (not the Squire) are intended. But Guyon had left the castle in the morning. C.

16 The noble virgin, Ladie of the place,
Was much dismayed with that dreadful sight,
For never was she in so evill cace:
Till that the Prince, seeing her wofull plight,
Gan her recomfort from so sad affright,
Offring his service and his dearest life
For her defence against that carle to fight,
Which was their chiefe and th' authour of that strife:
She him remercied[1] as the patrone[2] of her life.

17 Eftsoones himselfe in glitterand armes he dight,
And his well proved weapons to him hent[3];
So taking courteous congé,[4] he behight[5]
Those gates to be unbar'd, and forth he went.
Fayre mote he thee,[6] the prowest[7] and most gent[8]
That ever brandished bright steele on hye!
Whom soone as that unruly rablement
With his gay Squyre issewing did espye,
They reard a most outrageous dreadfull yelling cry:

18 And therewithall attonce at him let fly
Their fluttring arrowes, thicke as flakes of snow,
And round about him flocke impetuously,
Like a great water-flood, that, tombling low
From the high mountaines, threates to overflow
With suddein fury all the fertile playne,
And the sad husbandmans long hope doth throw

1 *Remercied*, thanked.
2 *Patrone*, defender.
3 *Hent*, took.
4 *Congé*, leave.
5 *Behight*, ordered.
6 *Mote he thee*, may he prosper.
7 *Prowest*, bravest.
8 *Gent*, noble.

Adowne the streame, and all his vowes make vayne;
Nor bounds nor banks his headlong ruine may sustayne.

19 Upon his shield their heaped hayle he bore,
And with his sword disperst the raskall[1] flockes,
Which fled asonder, and him fell before,
As withered leaves drop from their dryed stockes,
When the wroth western wind does reave[2] their locks:
And underneath him his courageous steed,
The fierce Spumador,[3] trode them downe like docks[4];
The fierce Spumador borne of heavenly seed,
Such as Laomedon of Phæbus race did breed.

20 Which suddeine horrour and confused cry
When as their Capteine heard, in haste he yode[5]
The cause to weet, and fault to remedy:
Upon a tygre swift and fierce he rode,
That as the winde ran underneath his lode,
Whiles his long legs nigh raught[6] unto the ground:
Full large he was of limbe, and shoulders brode;
But of such subtile substance and unsound,
That like a ghost he seem'd whose grave-clothes were unbound:

21 And in his hand a bended bow was seene,
And many arrowes under his right side,

1 *Raskall*, base, or low.
2 *Reave*, strip off.
3 *Spumador*, i. e. Foamer.
4 *Docks*, weeds
5 *Yode*, went.
6 *Raught*, reached.

All deadly daungerous, all cruell keene,
Headed with flint, and fethers bloody dide;
Such as the Indians in their quivers hide:
Those could he well direct and streight as line,
And bid them strike the marke which he had eyde;
Ne was there salve, ne was there medicine,
That mote recure their wounds; so inly they did tine.[1]

22 As pale and wan as ashes was his looke:
His body leane and meagre as a rake,
And skin all withered like a dryed rooke,
Thereto[2] as cold and drery as a snake,
That seemd to tremble evermore and quake:
All in a canvas thin he was bedight,[3]
And girded with a belt of twisted brake:
Upon his head he wore an helmet light,
Made of a dead mans skull, that seemd a ghastly sight:

23 Maleger was his name; and after him
There follow'd fast at hand two wicked hags,
With hoary lockes all loose and visage grim;
Their feet unshod, their bodies wrapt in rags,
And both as swift on foot as chased stags;
And yet the one her other legge[4] had lame,

1 *Tine*, burn.
2 *Thereto*, besides.
3 *Bedight*, dressed.
4 *Her other legge* (a classic idiom), *one* of her two legs.

XXIII. 1.— *Maleger was his name.*] Maleger signifies badly diseased; and from this and the description given of him, he seems to represent the various diseases which an indulgence in those "fleshly lusts which war against the soul" gives birth to. H.

Which with a staffe all full of litle snags
She did support, and Impotence her name:
But th' other was Impatience arm'd with raging flame.

24 Soone as the carle from far the Prince espyde
Glistring in armes and warlike ornament,
His beast he felly prickt on either syde,
And his mischiévous bow full readie bent,
With which at him a cruell shaft he sent:
But he was warie, and it warded well
Upon his shield, that it no further went,
But to the ground the idle quarrell[1] fell:
Then he another and another did expell.

25 Which to prevent, the Prince his mortall speare
Soone to him raught, and fierce at him did ride,
To be avenged of that shot whyleare[2]:
But he was not so hardy to abide
That bitter stownd,[3] but, turning quicke aside
His light-foot beast, fled fast away for feare:
Whom to poursue, the Infant[4] after hide
So fast as his good courser could him beare;
But labour lost it was to weene approch him neare.

26 For as the winged wind his tigre fled,
That vew of eye could scarse him overtake,
Ne scarse his feet on ground were seene to tred;
Through hils and dales he speedy way did make,
Ne hedge ne ditch his readie passage brake,

1 *Quarrell*, arrow.
2 *Whyleare*, just before.
3 *Stownd*, moment, exigency, peril.
4 *Infant*, youth.

And in his flight the Villein turn'd his face,
(As wonts the Tartar by the Caspian lake,
Whenas the Russian him in fight does chace,)
Unto his tygres taile, and shot at him apace.

27 Apace he shot, and yet he fled apace,
Still as the greedy Knight nigh to him drew;
And oftentimes he would relent[1] his pace,
That him his foe more fiercely should poursew:
But, when his uncouth[2] manner he did vew,
He gan avize[3] to follow him no more,
But keepe his standing, and his shaftes eschew,
Untill he quite had spent his perlous[4] store,
And then assayle him fresh, ere he could shift for more.

28 But that lame Hag, still as abroad he strew
His wicked arrowes, gathered them againe,
And to him brought, fresh batteill to renew;
Which he espying cast[5] her to restraine
From yielding succour to that cursed swaine,
And her attaching[6] thought her hands to tye;
But, soone as him dismounted on the plaine
That other Hag did far away espye
Binding her sister, she to him ran hastily;

29 And catching hold of him, as downe he lent,[7]
Him backeward overthrew, and downe him stayd[8]

1 *Relent*, slacken.
2 *Uncouth*, strange.
3 *Avize*, bethink.
4 *Perlous*, perilous.
5 *Cast*, considered how.
6 *Attaching*, attacking.
7 *Lent*, stooped.
8 *Stayd*, held.

With their rude handes and gryesly[1] graplement:
Till that the Villein, comming to their ayd,
Upon him fell, and lode upon him layd:
Full litle wanted, but he had him slaine,
And of the battell balefull end had made,
Had not his gentle Squire beheld his paine,
And commen to his reskew ere his bitter bane.

30 So greatest and most glorious thing on ground[2]
May often need the helpe of weaker hand;
So feeble is mans state, and life unsound,
That in assuraunce it may never stand,
Till it dissolved be from earthly band!
Proofe be thou, Prince, the prowest man alyve,
And noblest borne of all in Britayne land;
Yet thee fierce Fortune did so nearely[3] drive,
That, had not Grace thee blest, thou shouldest not survive.

31 The Squyre arriving, fiercely in his armes
Snatcht first the one, and then the other iade,
His chiefest letts[4] and authors of his harmes,
And them perforce withheld with threatned blade,
Least that his Lord they should behinde invade;
The whiles the Prince, prickt with reprochful shame,
As one awakte out of long slombring shade,
Revivyng thought of glory and of fame,
United all his powres to purge himselfe from blame.

1 *Gryesly*, frightful.
2 *On ground*, on earth.
3 *Nearely*, narrowly.
4 *Letts*, hinderances.

32 Like as a fire, the which in hollow cave
Hath long bene underkept and down supprest,
With murmurous disdayne doth inly rave,
And grudge, in so streight prison to be prest,
At last breakes forth with furious unrest,
And strives to mount unto his native seat;
All that did earst it hinder and molest,
Yt now devoures with flames and scorching heat,
And carries into smoake with rage and horror great.

33 So mightely the Briton Prince him rouzd
Out of his holde, and broke his caytive bands;
And as a beare, whom angry curres have touzd,[1]
Having off-shakt them and escapt their hands,
Becomes more fell, and all that him withstands
Treads down and overthrowes. Now had the Carle
Alighted from his tigre, and his hands
Discharged of his bow and deadly quar'le,[2]
To seize upon his foe flatt lying on the marle.

34 Which now him turnd to disavantage deare[3];
For neither can he fly, nor other[4] harme,
But trust unto his strength and manhood meare,
Sith now he is far from his monstrous swarme,
And of his weapons did himselfe disarme.
The Knight, yet wrothfull for his late disgrace,
Fiercely advaunst his valorous right arme,
And him so sore smott with his yron mace,
That groveling to the ground he fell, and fild his place.[5]

1 *Touzd*, worried.
2 *Quar'le*, arrows.
3 *Deare*, grievous.
4 *Other*, another person.
5 *Fild his place*, i. e. measured his length.

35 Wel weened hee that field was then his owne,
And all his labor brought to happy end;
When suddein up the Villeine overthrowne
Out of his swowne arose, fresh to contend,
And gan himselfe to second battaill bend,
As hurt he had not beene. Thereby there lay
An huge great stone, which stood upon one end,
And had not bene removed many a day;
Some land-marke seemd to bee, or signe of sundry way:

36 The same he snatcht, and with exceeding sway[1]
Threw at his foe, who was right well aware
To shonne the engin of his meant decay[2];
It booted not to thinke that throw to beare,
But grownd he gave, and lightly lept areare[3];
Efte[4] fierce retourning, as a faulcon fayre,
That once hath failed of her souse full neare,
Remounts againe into the open ayre,
And unto better fortune doth herselfe prepayre:

37 So brave retourning, with his brandisht blade,
He to the Carle himselfe agayn addrest,
And strooke at him so sternely, that he made
An open passage through his riven brest,
That halfe the steele behind his backe did rest;
Which drawing backe, he looked evermore
When the hart blood should gush out of his chest,
Or his dead corse should fall upon the flore;
But his dead corse upon the flore fell nathëmore[5]:

1 *Sway*, powerful swing.
2 *Meant decay*, intended destruction.
3 *Areare*, back.
4 *Efte*, again.
5 *Nathëmore*, none the more.

38 Ne drop of blood appeared shed to bee,
All[1] were the wownd so wide and wonderous
That through his carcas one might playnly see.
Halfe in amaze with horror hideous,
And halfe in rage to be deluded thus,
Again through both the sides he strooke him quight,
That made his spright to grone full piteous ;
Yet nathëmore forth fled his groning spright,
But freshly, as at first, prepard himselfe to fight.

39 Thereat he smitten was with great affright,
And trembling terror did his hart apall ;
Ne wist he what to thinke of that same sight,
Ne what to say, ne what to doe at all :
He doubted least it were some magicall
Illusion that did beguile his sense,
Or wandring ghost that wanted funerall,
Or aery spirite under false pretence,
Or hellish feend raysd up through divelish science.

40 His wonder far exceeded reasons reach,
That he began to doubt his dazeled sight,
And oft of error did himselfe appeach[2] :
Flesh without blood, a person without spright,
Wounds without hurt, a body without might,
That could doe harme, yet could not harmed bee,
That could not die, yet seemd a mortall wight,
That was most strong in most infirmitee ;
Like did he never heare, like did he never see.

1 *All*, although. 2 *Appeach*, impeach.

41 Awhile he stood in this astonishment,
Yet would he not for all his great dismay
Give over to effect his first intent,
And th' utmost meanes of victory assay,
Or th' utmost yssew of his owne decay.[1]
His owne good sword Mordure, that never fayld
At need till now, he lightly threw away,
And his bright shield that nought him now avayld;
And with his naked hands him forcibly assayld.

42 Twixt his two mighty armes him up he snatcht,
And crusht his carcas so against his brest,
That the disdainfull sowle he thence dispatcht,
And th' ydle breath all utterly exprest[2];
Tho, when he felt him dead, adowne he kest[3]
The lumpish corse unto the sencelesse grownd;
Adowne he kest it with so puissant wrest,
That backe againe it did alofte rebownd,
And gave against his mother Earth a gronefull sownd:

43 As when Ioves harnesse-bearing[4] bird from hye
Stoupes at a flying heron with proud disdayne,
The stone-dead quarrey falls so forciblye,
That yt rebownds against the lowly playne,
A second fall redoubling backe agayne.
Then thought the Prince all peril sure was past,
And that he victor onely did remayne;

1 *Decay*, destruction.
2 *Exprest*, pressed out.
3 *Kest*, cast.
4 *Harnesse-bearing*, armor-bearing.

No sooner thought, then that the Carle as fast
Gan heap huge strokes on him, as ere he down was cast.

44 Nigh his wits end then woxe th' amazed Knight,
And thought his labor lost, and travell[1] vayne,
Against this lifelesse shadow so to fight:
Yet life he saw, and felt his mighty mayne,
That, whiles he marveild still, did still him payne;
Forthy[2] he gan some other wayes advize,
How to take life from that dead-living swayne,
Whom still he marked freshly to arize
From th' earth, and from her womb new spirits to reprize.[3]

45 He then remembred well, that had bene sayd,
How th' Earth his mother was, and first him bore;
Shee eke, so often as his life decayd,
Did life with usury to him restore,
And reysd him up much stronger then before,
So soone as he unto her wombe did fall:
Therefore to grownd he would him cast no more,
Ne him committ to grave terrestriall,
But beare him farre from hope of succour usuall.

46 Tho up he caught him twixt his puissant hands,
And having scruzd[4] out of his carrion corse
The lothfull life, now loosd from sinfull bands,
Upon his shoulders carried him perforse
Above three furlongs, taking his full course,

1 *Travell*, travail, labor.
2 *Forthy*, therefore.
3 *Reprize*, take again.
4 *Scruzd*, squeezed.

Untill he came unto a standing lake;
Him thereinto he threw without remorse,
Ne stird, till hope of life did him forsake:
So end of that Carles days and his owne paynes did
make.

47 Which when those wicked Hags from far did spye,
Like two mad dogs they ran about the lands;
And th' one of them with dreadfull yelling crye,
Throwing away her broken chaines and bands,
And having quencht her burning fier-brands,
Hedlong herselfe did cast into that lake:
But Impotence with her owne wilfull hands
One of Malegers cursed darts did take,
So ryv'd her trembling hart, and wicked end did make.

48 Thus now alone he conquerour remaines:
Tho, cumming to his Squyre that kept his steed,
Thought to have mounted; but his feeble vaines
Him faild thereto, and served not his need,
Through losse of blood which from his wounds did
bleed,
That he began to faint, and life decay:
But his good Squyre, him helping up with speed,
With stedfast hand upon his horse did stay,
And led him to the Castle by the beaten way.

49 Where many groomes and squyres ready were
To take him from his steed full tenderly;
And eke the fayrest Alma mett him there
With balme, and wine, and costly spicery,
To comfort him in his infirmity:

Eftesoones shee causd him up to be convayd,
And of his armes despoyled easily,
In sumptuous bed shee made him to be layd;
And, al the while his wounds were dressing, by him stayd.

CANTO XII.

Guyon, by Palmers governaunce,
Passing through perilles great,
Doth overthrow the Bowre of Blis,
And Acrasy defeat.

1 Now ginnes[1] this goodly frame of Temperaunce
Fayrely to rise, and her adorned hed
To pricke[2] of highest prayse forth to advaunce,
Formerly grounded and fast setteled
On firme foundation of true bountyhed[3]:
And that brave Knight, that for this vertue fightes,
Now comes to point of that same perilous sted,[4]
Where Pleasure dwelles in sensuall delights,
Mongst thousand dangers and ten thousand magick mights.

2 Two dayes now in that sea he sayled has,
Ne ever land beheld, ne living wight,
Ne ought save perill, still as he did pas:

1 *Ginnes*, begins.
2 *Pricke*, the point.
3 *Bountyhed*, goodness.
4 *Sted*, place.

I. 4.—*Formerly grounded.*] Being first established on the foundation of true virtue, by the victory of Arthur over the foes of Alma. C.

Tho, when appeared the third morrow bright
Upon the waves to spred her trembling light,
An hideous roring far away they heard,
That all their sences filled with affright;
And streight they saw the raging surges reard
Up to the skyes, that them of drowning made affeard.

3 Said then the Boteman, "Palmer, stere aright,
And keepe an even course; for yonder way
We needes must pas; (God doe us well acquight[1]!)
That is the Gulfe of Greedinesse, they say,
That deepe engorgeth[2] all this worldës pray;
Which having swallowd up excessively,
He soone in vomit up againe doth lay,[3]
And belcheth forth his superfluity,
That all the seas for feare doe seeme away to fly.

4 "On th' other syde an hideous rock is pight[4]
Of mightie magnes stone,[5] whose craggie clift
Depending from on high, dreadfull to sight,
Over the waves his rugged armes doth lift,
And threatneth downe to throw his ragged rift[6]
On whoso cometh nigh; yet nigh it drawes
All passengers, that none from it can shift:
For, whiles they fly that gulfes devouring iawes,
They on this rock are rent, and sunck in helples wawes.[7]"

[1] *Acquight*, deliver.
[2] *Engorgeth*, swallows.
[3] *Lay*, throw.
[4] *Pight*, placed.
[5] *Magnes stone*, magnet.
[6] *Ragged rift*, rough fragments.
[7] *Wawes*, waves.

5 Forward they passe, and strongly he them rowes,
Untill they nigh unto that gulfe arryve,
Where streame more violent and greedy growes:
Then he with all his puisaunce doth stryve
To strike his oares, and mightily doth dryve
The hollow vessell through the threatfull wave;
Which, gaping wide to swallow them alyve
In th' huge abysse of his engulfing grave,
Doth rore at them in vaine, and with great terrour rave.

6 They, passing by, that grisely mouth did see
Sucking the seas into his entralles deepe,
That seemd more horrible then hell to bee,
Or that darke dreadfull hole of Tartare steepe
Through which the damned ghosts doen often creep
Backe to the world, bad livers to torment:
But nought that falles into this direfull deepe,
Ne that approcheth nigh the wyde descent,
May backe retourne, but is condemned to be drent.[1]

7 On th' other side they saw that perilous rocke,
Threatning itselfe on them to ruinate,[2]
On whose sharp cliftes the ribs of vessels broke
And shivered ships, which had beene wrecked late,
Yet stuck, with carcases exanimate[3]
Of such, as having all their substance spent
In wanton ioyes and lustes intemperate,
Did afterwardes make shipwrack violent
Both of their life and fame for ever fowly blent.[4]

1 *Drent*, drenched, drowned.
2 *Ruinate*, throw down.
3 *Exanimate*, lifeless.
4 *Blent*, polluted, disgraced.

8 Forthy this hight the Rock of vile Reproch,
A daungerous and détestable place,
To which nor fish nor fowle did once approch,
But yelling meawes, with seagulles hoars and bace,
And cormoyraunts, with birds of ravenous race,
Which still sat wayting on that wastfull clift
For spoile of wretches, whose unhappy cace,
After lost credit and consumed thrift,
At last them driven hath to this despairefull drift.

9 The Palmer, seeing them in safetie past,
Thus saide: "Behold th' ensamples in our sightes
Of lustfull luxurie and thriftlesse wast!
What now is left of miserable wightes
Which spent their looser daies in leud delightes,
But shame and sad reproch, here to be red
By these rent reliques speaking their ill plightes!
Let all that live hereby be counselled
To shunne Rock of Reproch, and it as death to dread!"

10 So forth they rowed; and that Ferryman
With his stiffe oares did brush the sea so strong,
That the hoare waters from his frigot ran,
And the light bubles daunced all along,
Whiles the salt brine out of the billowes sprong.
At last far off they many islandes spy
On every side floting the floodes emong:
Then said the Knight: "Lo! I the land descry;
Therefore, old Syre, thy course doe thereunto apply."

11 "That may not bee," said then the Ferryman,
"Least wee unweeting[1] hap to be fordonne[2]:
For those same islands, seeming[3] now and than,
Are not firme land, nor any certein wonne,[4]
But stragling plots, which to and fro doe ronne
In the wide waters: therefore are they hight
The Wandring Islands. Therefore doe them shonne;
For they have ofte drawne many a wandring wight
Into most deadly daunger and distressed plight.

12 "Yet well they seeme to him, that farre doth vew,
Both faire and fruitfull, and the grownd dispred
With grassy greene of délectable hew;
And the tall trees with leaves appareled
Are deckt with blossoms dyde in white and red,
That mote the passengers thereto allure;
But whosoever once hath fastened
His foot thereon, may never it recure,[5]
But wandreth evermore uncertein and unsure.

13 "As th' isle of Delos whylome, men report,
Amid th' Aegæan sea long time did stray,
Ne made for shipping any certeine port,

1 *Unweeting*, unknowing.
2 *Fordonne*, undone.
3 *Seeming*, i. e. which seem such.
4 *Wonne*, habitation.
5 *Recure*, recover.

XIII. 1. — *As th' isle of Delos*, &c.] This island is represented by the ancients as having been floating under water, until it was made to appear and remain fixed, in order that Latona might give birth there to Apollo and Diana; the Earth having been bound, by an oath imposed by Juno, not to give her a resting-place, by

Till that Latona, traveiling that way,
Flying from Iunoes wrath and hard assay,[1]
Of her fayre twins was there delivered,
Which afterwards did rule the night and day;
Thenceforth it firmely was established,
And for Apolloes temple highly herried.[2]"

14 They to him hearken, as beseemeth meete;
And passe on forward: so their way does ly,
That one of those same islands, which doe fleet[3]
In the wide sea, they needes must passen by,
Which seemd so sweet and pleasaunt to the eye,
That it would tempt a man to touchen there:
Upon the banck they sitting did espy
A daintie damsell dressing of her heare,
By whom a little skippet[4] floting did appeare.

15 She, them espying, loud to them can[5] call,
Bidding them nigher draw unto the shore,
For she had cause to busie them withall;
And therewith lowdly laught. But nathëmore
Would they once turne, but kept on as afore:
Which when she saw, she left her lockes undight,[6]
And running to her boat withouten ore,

1 *Assay*, persecution.
2 *Herried*, honored.
3 *Fleet*, float.
4 *Skippet*, skiff.
5 *Can*, i. e. gan.
6 *Undight*, undressed.

which oath this island was not deemed to be bound. Hence the name of *Delos*, which is a Greek word meaning *manifest*. H.

XV. 7. — *Withouten ore.*] This boat, it will be remembered, was moved by turning a pin. See Canto VI. Stanza 5. H.

From the departing land it launched light,
And after them did drive with all her power and might.

16 Whom overtaking, she in merry sort
Them gan to bord,[1] and purpose [2] diversly;
Now faining dalliaunce and wanton sport,
Now throwing forth lewd wordes immodestly;
Till that the Palmer gan full bitterly
Her to rebuke for being loose and light:
Which not abiding, but more scornfully
Scoffing at him that did her iustly wite,[3]
She turnd her bote about, and from them rowed quite.

17 That was the wanton Phœdria, which late
Did ferry him over the Idle Lake:
Whom nought regarding, they kept on their gate,[4]
And all her vaine allurements did forsake;
When them the wary Boteman thus bespake:
"Here now behoveth us well to avyse,[5]
And of our safëty good heede to take;
For here before a perlous [6] passage lyes,
Where many Mermayds haunt making false melodies:

18 "But by the way there is a great quicksand,
And a whirlepoole of hidden ieopardy;
Therefore, Sir Palmer, keepe an even hand;
For twixt them both the narrow way doth ly."
Scarse had he saide, when hard at hand they spy

1 *Bord*, accost.
2 *Purpose*, discourse.
3 *Wite*, blame.
4 *Gate*, way.
5 *Avyse*, consider.
6 *Perlous*, perilous.

That quicksand nigh with water covered;
But by the checked[1] wave they did descry
It plaine, and by the sea discoloured:
It called was the Quickesand of Unthriftyhed.

19 They, passing by, a goodly ship did see
Laden from far with precious merchandize,
And bravely furnished as a ship might bee,
Which through great disaventure, or mesprize,[2]
Herselfe had ronne into that hazardize[3];
Whose mariners and merchants with much toyle
Labour'd in vaine to have recur'd[4] their prize,
And the rich wares to save from pitteous spoyle,
But neither toyle nor traveill might her backe recoyle.[5]

20 On th' other side they see that perilous poole,
That called was the Whirlepoole of Decay;
In which full many had with haplesse doole[6]
Beene suncke, of whom no memorie did stay:
Whose circled waters rapt with whirling sway,
Like to a restlesse wheele, still ronning round,
Did covet, as they passed by that way,
To draw their bote within the utmost[7] bound
Of his wide labyrinth, and then to have them dround.

21 But th' heedfull Boteman strongly forth did stretch
His brawnie armes, and all his bodie straine,

1 *Checked*, interrupted.
2 *Mesprize*, mistake.
3 *Hazardize*, hazardous situation.
4 *Recur'd*, recovered.
5 *Recoyle*, push her back.
6 *Doole*, lot.
7 *Utmost*, outmost.

That th' utmost sandy breach they shortly fetch,
Whiles the dredd daunger does behind remaine.
Suddeine they see from midst of all the maine
The surging waters like a mountaine rise,
And the great sea, puft up with proud disdaine,
To swell above the measure of his guise,[1]
As threatning to devoure all that his powre despise.

22 The waves come rolling, and the billowes rore
Outragiously, as they enraged were,
Or wrathfull Neptune did them drive before
His whirling charet for exceeding feare;
For not one puffe of winde there did appeare;
That all the three thereat woxe much afrayd,
Unweeting what such horrour straunge did reare.[2]
Eftsoones they saw an hideous hoast arrayd
Of huge sea-monsters, such as living sence dismayd:

23 Most ugly shapes and horrible aspécts,
Such as Dame Nature selfe mote feare to see,
Or shame that ever should so fowle defects
From her most cunning hand escaped bee;
All dreadfull pourtraicts of deformitee:
Spring-headed hydres; and sea-shouldring whales,

[1] *Guise*, wont or custom. [2] *Reare*, raise.

XXI. 3.—*That th' utmost sandy breach*, &c.] They come to the extreme edge of that quicksand, on which the "checked" sea breaks (St. xviii. 7). C.

XXIII. 6.—*Spring-headed* (very bad English); having several heads springing or budding from their bodies. For a picture, see Gesner (Zurich, 1558), Vol. III. p. 543.—*Sea-shouldring;* so

Great whirlpooles, which all fishes make to flee;
Bright scolopendraes arm'd with silver scales;
Mighty monoceroses with immeasured[1] tayles;

24 The dreadfull fish that hath deserv'd the name
Of Death, and like him lookes in dreadfull hew;
The griesly wasserman, that makes his game
The flying ships with swiftnes to pursew;
The horrible sea-satyre, that doth shew
His fearefull face in time of greatest storme;
Huge ziffius, whom mariners eschew
No lesse then rockes, as travellers informe;
And greedy rosmarines with visages deforme:

25 All these, and thousand thousands many more,
And more deformed monsters thousand fold,
With dreadfull noise and hollow rombling rore
Came rushing, in the fomy waves enrold,[2]
Which seem'd to fly for feare them to behold:

1 *Immeasured*, immeasurable. 2 *Enrold*, enveloped.

called from the quantity of water they displace in moving. — 7. *Whirlpoole;* a fish of the whale kind, thus named from the vortexes it makes in the water. (G. p. 256.) — 8. *Scolopendra* is the name of the centipede, and is also applied to a huge cetaceous fish. (G. p. 1009.) — 9. *Monoceroses*, sea-unicorns. (G. p. 247.) C.

XXIV. 1. — The *dreadfull fish* is the Morse (*mors*), or Walrus. (G. p. 250.) — 3. Of the *wasserman*, merman, three varieties may be seen in Gesner; one in shape like a monk, another like a bishop. — 5. *Sea-satyre*, or Pan, a kind of ichthyocentaur. (G. p. 1197.) — 7. *Ziffius* (G. p. 249), a monster described in general terms as entirely unlike any other animal. — 9. *Rosmarine*, a kind of walrus, or sea-horse. (G. p. 249.) C.

Ne wonder, if these did the Knight appall;
For all that here on earth we dreadfull hold,
Be but as bugs to fearen[1] babes withall,
Compared·to the creatures in the seas entráll.[2]

26 "Feare nought," then saide the Palmer well aviz'd,
"For these same monsters are not these in deed,
But are into these fearefull shapes disguiz'd
By that same wicked witch, to worke us dreed,
And draw[3] from on this iourney to proceed."
Tho, lifting up his vertuous staffe on hye,
He smote the sea, which calmed was with speed,
And all that dreadfull armie fast gan flye
Into great Tethys bosome, where they hidden lye.

27 Quit from that danger forth their course they kept,
And as they went they heard a ruefull cry
Of one that wayld and pittifully wept,
That through the sea the resounding plaints did fly.
At last they in an island did espy
A seemely maiden, sitting by the shore,
That with great sorrow and sad agony
Seemed some great misfortune to deplore,
And lowd to them for succour called evermore.

28 Which Guyon hearing, streight his Palmer bad
To stere the bote towards that dolefull mayd,

[1] *Fearen*, frighten. [2] *Entráll*, entrails, depths.
[3] *Draw*, i. e. us from proceeding, &c.

XXVI. 4.— *Wicked witch.*] Acrasia.

That he might know and ease her sorrow sad;
Who, him avizing better, to him sayd:
"Faire Sir, be not displeasd if disobayd:
For ill it were to hearken to her cry;
For she is inly nothing ill apayd[1];
But onely womanish fine forgery,
Your stubborne hart t' affect with fraile infirmity:

29 "To which when she your courage[2] hath inclind
Through foolish pitty, then her guilefull bayt
She will embosome deeper in your mind,
And for your ruine at the last awayt."
The Knight was ruled, and the Boteman strayt
Held on his course with stayed[3] stedfastnesse,
Ne ever shroncke, ne ever sought to bayt[4]
His tryed armes for toylesome wearinesse:
But with his oares did sweepe the watry wildernesse.

30 And now they nigh approched to the sted[5]
Whereas those Mermayds dwelt. It was a still,
And calmy bay, on th' one side sheltered
With the brode shadow of an hoarie hill;
On th' other side an high rocke toured still,
That twixt them both a pleasaunt port they made,
And did like an halfe theatre fulfill.[6]
There those five sisters had continuall trade,[7]
And usd to bath themselves in that deceiptfull shade.

1 *Apayd*, contented.
2 *Courage*, heart.
3 *Stayed*, constant.
4 *Bayt*, rest.
5 *Sted*, place.
6 *Fulfill*, i. e. make up, as it were, an amphitheatre.
7 *Trade*, occupation, employment.

31 They were faire ladies, till they fondly striv'd
With th' Heliconian Maides for maystery;
Of whom they over-comen were depriv'd
Of their proud beautie, and th' one moyity
Transformd to fish for their bold surquedry[1];
But th' upper halfe their hew retayned still,
And their sweet skill in wonted melody;
Which ever after they abusd to ill,
T' allure weake traveillers, whom gotten they did kill.

32 So now to Guyon, as he passed by,
Their pleasaunt tunes they sweetly thus applyde:
"O thou fayre sonne of gentle Faëry,
That art in mightie armes most magnifyde
Above all knights that ever batteill tryde,
O turne thy rudder hetherward awhile:
Here may thy storme-bett vessell safely ryde;
This is the port of rest from troublous toyle,
The worldes sweet in[2] from paine and wearisome turmoyle."

33 With that the rolling sea, resounding soft,
In his big base them fitly answered;
And on the rocke the waves breaking aloft

1 *Surquedry*, presumption. 2 *In*, resting place.

XXXI. 1.—*Faire Ladies.*] The classic Sirens were two (some say three) in number, and were provided with wings, — of which they were deprived by the Muses for the reason above given. Spenser makes them five, to correspond with the five senses. It was very natural that they should be taken for mermaids by later poets. C.

A solemne meane[1] unto them measured;
The whiles sweet Zephyrus lowd whisteled
His treble, a straunge kinde of harmony;
Which Guyons senses softly tickeled,
That he the Boteman bad row easily,
And let him heare some part of their rare melody.

34 But him the Palmer from that vanity
With temperate advice discounselled,
That they it past, and shortly gan descry
The land to which their course they leveled[2],
When suddeinly a grosse fog over spred
With his dull vapour all that desert has,
And heavens chearefull face enveloped,
That all things one, and one as nothing was,
And this great universe seemd one confused mas.

35 Thereat they greatly were dismayd, ne wist
How to direct theyr way in darkenes wide,
But feard to wander in that wastefull mist,
For tombling[3] into mischiefe unespide:
Worse is the daunger hidden then descride.
Suddeinly an innumerable flight
Of harmefull fowles about them fluttering cride,
And with their wicked wings them ofte did smight
And sore annoyed, groping in that griesly night.

36 Even all the nation of unfortunate
And fatall birds about them flocked were,

1 *Meane*, (here) tenor.
2 *Leveled*, aimed.
3 *For tombling*, lest they should tumble.

Such as by nature men abhorre and hate;
The ill-faste owle, deaths dreadfull messengere;
The hoars night-raven, trump of dolefull drere[1];
The lether-winged batt, dayes enimy;
The ruefull strich,[2] still waiting on the bere;
The whistler shrill, that whoso heares doth dy;
The hellish harpyes, prophets of sad destiny:

37 All those, and all that els does horror breed,
About them flew, and fild their sayles with feare;
Yet stayd they not, but forward did proceed,
Whiles th' one did row, and th' other stifly steare,
Till that at last the weather gan to cleare,
And the faire land itselfe did playnly sheow.
Said then the Palmer: "Lo! where does appeare
The sacred[3] soile where all our perills grow!
Therfore, Sir Knight, your ready arms about you throw."

38 He hearkned, and his armes about him tooke,
The whiles the nimble bote so well her sped,
That with her crooked keele the land she strooke:
Then forth the noble Guyon sallied,
And his sage Palmer that him governed;
But th' other by his bote behind did stay.
They marched fayrly forth, of nought ydred,[4]
Both firmely armd for every hard assay,
With constancy and care, gainst daunger and dismay.

[1] *Drere*, sorrow.
[2] *Strich*, the screech-owl.
[3] *Sacred*, cursed.
[4] *Ydred*, afraid.

39 Ere long they heard an hideous bellowing
Of many beasts, that roard outrageously,
As if that hungers poynt or Venus sting
Had them enraged with fell surquedry[1];
Yet nought they feard, but past on hardily,
Untill they came in vew of those wilde beasts,
Who all attonce, gaping full greedily,
And rearing fercely their upstaring[2] crests,
Ran towards to devoure those unexpected guests.

40 But, soone as they approcht with deadly threat,
The Palmer over them his staffe upheld,
His mighty staffe, that could all charmes defeat:
Eftesoones their stubborne corages were queld,
And high advaunced crests downe meekely feld;
Instead of fraying,[3] they themselves did feare,
And trembled, as them passing they beheld:
Such wondrous powre did in that staffe appeare,
All monsters to subdew to him that did it beare.

41 Of that same wood it fram'd was cunningly,
Of which Caducëus whilome was made,
Caducëus, the rod of Mercury,
With which he wonts the Stygian realmes invade,
Through ghastly horror and eternall shade;
Th' infernall feends with it he can asswage,

1 *Surquedry*, presumption.
2 *Upstaring*, elevated.
3 *Fraying*, terrifying.

XL. 2.—*His staffe upheld.*] The virtues of this staff express that power over the inferior appetites which springs from habits of temperance and self-control. H.

And Orcus tame, whome nothing cah persuade,
And rule the Furyes when they most doe rage:
Such vertue in his staffe had eke this Palmer sage.

42 Thence passing forth, they shortly doe arryve
Whereas the Bowre of Blisse was situate;
A place pickt out by choyce of best alyve,
That natures worke by art can imitate:
In which whatever in this worldly state
Is sweete and pleasing unto living sense,
Or that may dayntest[1] fantasy aggrate,[2]
Was poured forth with plentifull dispence,[3]
And made there to abound with lavish affluence.

43 Goodly it was enclosed rownd about,
As well their entred guestes to keep within,
As those unruly beasts to hold without;
Yet was the fence thereof but weake and thin;
Nought feard theyr force that fortilage[4] to win,
But Wisedomes powre, and Temperaunces might,
By which the mightiest things efforced bin:
And eke the gate was wrought of substaunce light,
Rather for pleasure then for battery or fight.

44 Yt framed was of precious yvory,
That seemd a worke of admirable witt;

1 *Dayntest*, daintiest, most delicate.
2 *Aggrate*, gratify.
3 *Dispence*, expense.
4 *Fortilage*, fortress.

XLIII. 5.—*Nought feard*, &c.] Their force did not fear that anything could win that fortress, except the power of wisdom and the might of temperance. H.

And therein all the famous history
Of Iason and Medæa was ywritt;
Her mighty charmes, her furious loving fitt;
His goodly conquest of the golden fleece,
His falsed fayth, and love too lightly flitt[1];
The wondred[2] Argo, which in venturous peece[3]
First through the Euxine seas bore all the flowr of Greece.

45 Ye might have seene the frothy billowes fry[4]
Under the ship as thorough them she went,
That seemd the waves were into yvory,
Or yvory into the waves were sent;
And otherwhere the snowy substaunce sprent[5]
With vermell,[6] like the boyes blood therein shed,
A piteous spectacle did represent;
And otherwhiles with gold besprinkeled
Yt seemd th' enchaunted flame, which did Crëusa wed.

1 *Flitt*, departed.
2 *Wondred*, admired.
3 *Peece*, structure, ship.
4 *Fry*, foam.
5 *Sprent*, sprinkled.
6 *Vermell*, vermilion.

XLIV., XLV. — Many parts of this Canto are imitated or translated from Tasso. These verses were suggested by the description of the gates of Armida's palace, Jerus. Deliv. xvi. 1-7. Stanzas 50, 51 are in imitation of Canto xv. 53, 54; 58, 59, of xvi. 9, 10; 63-68, of xv. 58-62; 71, of xvi. 12; 74, 75, 78, of xvi. 14, 15, 18. C.

XLV. 6. — *The boyes blood.*] Medea put to death the children she had by Jason, and presented Creusa, the destined wife of Jason, with a robe and a diadem which consumed her to ashes. H.

46 All this and more might in that goodly gate
Be red, that ever open stood to all
Which thether came: but in the porch there sate
A comely personage of stature tall,
And semblaunce pleasing, more then naturall,
That traveilers to him seemd to entize;
His looser garment to the ground did fall,
And flew about his heeles in wanton wize,
Not fitt for speedy pace or manly exercize.

47 They in that place him Genius did call:
Not that celestiall powre, to whom the care
Of life, and generation of all
That lives, perteines in charge particulare,
Who wondrous things concerning our welfare,
And straunge phantomes, doth lett us ofte foresee,
And ofte of secret ill bids us beware:
That is our Selfe, whom though we doe not see,
Yet each doth in himselfe it well perceive to bee:

48 Therefore a god him sage Antiquity
Did wisely make, and good Agdistes call:
But this same was to that quite contrary,
The foe of life, that good envýes to all,
That secretly doth us procure to fall
Through guilefull semblants, which he makes us see:

XLVII. 1.—A Genius, so called from *gignendo*, either because he is born with us, or because he has particular charge of "the generation of all that lives," is believed to govern our whole life, by inciting us to such actions as conduce to our welfare, or restraining us when we are disposed to pursue the "guilefull semblants" with which malignant demons tempt us astray. In later times this Genius was called Agdistes.—This is the substance of a passage cited by Warton from Natalis Comes. C.

He of this Gardin had the governall,
And Pleasures Porter was devizd to bee,
Holding a staffe in hand for more formalitee.

49 With diverse flowres he daintily was deckt,
And strowed rownd about; and by his side
A mighty mazer[1] bowle of wine was sett,
As if it had to him bene sacrifide;
Wherewith all new-come guests he gratyfide[2]:
So did he eke Sir Guyon passing by;
But he his ydle curtesie defide,
And overthrew his bowle disdainfully,
And broke his staffe, with which he charmed semblants sly.

50 Thus being entred, they behold arownd
A large and spacious plaine, on every side
Strowed with pleasauns[3]; whose fayre grassy grownd
Mantled with greene, and goodly beautifide
With all the ornaments of Floraes pride,
Wherewith her mother Art, as halfe in scorne
Of niggard Nature, like a pompous bride
Did decke her, and too lavishly adorne,
When forth from virgin bowre she comes in th' early morne.

51 Thereto the heavens alwayes ioviall
Lookte on them lovely, still in stedfast state,
Ne suffred storme nor frost on them to fall,

1 *Mazer*, goblet.
2 *Gratyfide*, congratulated, welcomed.
3 *Pleasauns*, pleasantness.

Their tender buds or leaves to violate ;
Nor scorching heat, nor cold intemperate,
T' afflict the creatures which therein did dwell ;
But the milde ayre with season moderate
Gently attempred, and disposd so well,
That still it breathed forth sweet spirit[1] and holesom smell :

52 More sweet and holesome then the pleasaunt hill
Of Rhodope, on which the nimphe, that bore
A gyaunt babe, herselfe for griefe did kill ;
Or the Thessalian Tempe, where of yore
Fayre Daphne Phæbus hart with love did gore ;
Or Ida, where the gods lov'd to repayre,
Whenever they their heavenly bowres forlore[2] ;
Or sweet Parnasse, the haunt of Muses fayre ;
Or Eden selfe, if ought with Eden mote compayre.

53 Much wondred Guyon at the fayre aspéct
Of that sweet place, yet suffred no delight
To sincke into his sence, nor mind affect ;
But passed forth, and lookt still forward right,
Brydling his will and maystering his might,
Till that he came unto another gate :

1 *Spirit*, breath. 2 *Forlore*, forsook.

LII. 2. — *Of Rhodope.*] Rhodope was the wife of Hemus, king of Thrace, and was changed into the mountain of the same name. She had by Neptune the giant Athos, afterwards changed into a mountain of the same name. I presume that Rhodope is the "nimphe" mentioned in the text, but I can find no account of her killing herself for grief. H.

No gate, but like one, being goodly dight[1]
With bowes and braunches, which did broad dilate
Their clasping armes in wanton wreathings intricate:

54 So fashioned a porch with rare device,
Archt over head with an embracing vine,
Whose bounches hanging downe seemd to entice
All passers-by to taste their lushious wine,
And did themselves into their hands incline,
As freely offering to be gathered;
Some deepe empurpled as the hyacine,[2]
Some as the rubine laughing sweetely red,
Some like faire emeraudes, not yet well ripened:

55 And them amongst some were of burnisht gold,
So made by art to beautify the rest,
Which did themselves emongst the leaves enfold,
As lurking from the vew of covetous guest,
That the weake boughes with so rich load opprest
Did bow adowne as overburdened.
Under that porch a comely Dame did rest
Clad in fayre weedes[3] but fowle disordered,
And garments loose that seemd unmeet for womanhed.

56 In her left hand a cup of gold she held,
And with her right the riper fruit did reach,
Whose sappy liquor, that with fulnesse sweld,
Into her cup she scruzd[4] with daintie breach

1 *Dight*, covered.
2 *Hyacine*, hyacinth, or jacinth.
3 *Weedes*, clothes.
4 *Scruzd*, squeezed.

Of her fine fingers, without fowle empeach,[1]
That so faire winepresse made the wine more sweet:
Thereof she usd to give to drinke to each,
Whom passing by she happened to meet:
It was her guise all straungers goodly so to greet.

57 So she to Guyon offred it to tast;
Who, taking it out of her tender hond,
The cup to ground did violently cast,
That all in peeces it was broken fond,[2]
And with the liquor stained all the lond:
Whereat Excesse exceedingly was wroth,
Yet no'te[3] the same amend, ne yet withstond,
But suffered him to passe, all[4] were she loth;
Who, nought regarding her displeasure, forward goth.

58 There the most daintie paradise on ground
Itselfe doth offer to his sober eye,
In which all pleasures plenteously abownd,
And none does others happinesse envye;
The painted flowres; the trees upshooting hye;
The dales for shade; the hilles for breathing space;
The trembling groves; the christall running by;
And, that which all faire workes doth most aggrace,[5]
The art, which all that wrought, appeared in no place.

1 *Empeach*, impeachment (of offence).
2 *Fond*, found.
3 *No'te*, could not.
4 *All*, although.
5 *Aggrace*, give grace to.

59 One would have thought, (so cunningly the rude
And scorned partes were mingled with the fine,)
That Nature had for wantonesse ensude[1]
Art, and that Art at Nature did repine;
So striving each th' other to undermine,
Each did the others worke more beautify;
So diff'ring both in willes agreed in fine[2]:
So all agreed, through sweete diversity,
This gardin to adorne with all variety.

60 And in the midst of all a fountaine stood,
Of richest substance that on earth might bee,
So pure and shiny that the silver flood
Through every channell running one might see;
Most goodly it with curious ymageree
Was over-wrought, and shapes of naked boyes,
Of which some seemd with lively iollitee
To fly about playing their wanton toyes,
Whylest others did themselves embay[3] in liquid ioyes.

61 And over all of purest gold was spred
A trayle of yvie in his native hew;
For the rich metall was so coloured,
That wight, who did not well avis'd it vew,
Would surely deeme it to bee yvie trew:
Low his lascivious armes adown did creepe,
That, themselves dipping in the silver dew,
Their fleecy flowres they fearefully did steepe,
Which drops of christall seemd for wantones to weep.

1 *Ensude*, followed, or imitated.
2 *In fine*, in the end.
3 *Embay*, bathe.

62 Infinit streames continually did well
Out of this fountaine, sweet and faire to see,
The which into an ample laver fell,
And shortly grew to so great quantitie,
That like a litle lake it seemd to bee;
Whose depth exceeded not three cubits hight,
That through the waves one might the bottom see,
All pav'd beneath with iaspar shining bright,
That seemd the fountaine in that sea did sayle upright.

63 And all the margent round about was sett
With shady laurell trees, thence to defend[1]
The sunny beames which on the billowes bett,
And those which therein bathed mote offend.
As Guyon hapned by the same to wend,
Two naked Damzelles he therein espyde,
Which therein bathing seemed to contend
And wrestle wantonly, ne car'd to hyde
Their dainty partes from vew of any which them eyd.

64 Sometimes the one would lift the other quight
Above the waters, and then downe againe
Her plong, as over-maystered by might,
Where both awhile would covered remaine,
And each the other from to rise restraine;
The whiles their snowy limbes, as through a vele,
So through the christall waves appeared plaine:
Then suddeinly both would themselves unhele,[2]
And th' amarous sweet spoiles to greedy eyes revele.

1 *Defend*, keep off. 2 *Unhele*, uncover.

65 As that faire starre, the messenger of morne,
His deawy face out of the sea doth reare:
Or as the Cyprian goddesse, newly borne
Of th' oceans fruitfull froth, did first appeare:
Such seemed they, and so their yellow heare
Christalline humor dropped downe apace.
Whom such when Guyon saw, he drew him neare,
And somewhat gan relent[1] his earnest pace;
His stubborne brest gan secret pleasaunce to embrace.

66 The wanton maidens, him espying, stood
Gazing awhile at his unwonted guise;
Then th' one herselfe low ducked in the flood,
Abasht that her a straunger did avise[2]:
But th' other rather higher did arise,
And her two lilly paps aloft displayd,
And all, that might his melting hart entyse
To her delights, she unto him bewrayd;
The rest, hidd underneath, him more desirous made.

67 With that the other likewise up arose,
And her faire lockes, which formerly were bownd
Up in one knott, she low adowne did lose,
Which, flowing long and thick, her cloth'd arownd,
And th' yvorie in golden mantle gownd:
So that faire spectacle from him was reft,
Yet that which reft it no lesse faire was fownd:
So hidd in lockes and waves from lookers theft,
Nought but her lovely face she for his looking left.

1 *Relent*, slacken. 2 *Avise*, perceive.

68 Withall she laughed, and she blusht withall,
That blushing to her laughter gave more grace,
And laughter to her blushing, as did fall.[1]
Now when they spyde the Knight to slacke his pace
Them to behold, and in his sparkling face
The secrete signes of kindled lust appeare,
Their wanton meriments they did encreace,
And to him beckned to approch more neare,
And shewd him many sights that corage[2] cold could reare[3]:

69 On which when gazing him the Palmer saw,
He much rebukt those wandring eyes of his,
And counseld well him forward thence did draw.
Now are they come nigh to the Bowre of Blis,
Of her fond favorites so nam'd amis;
When thus the Palmer: "Now, Sir, well avise[4];
For here the end of all our traveill is:
Here wonnes[5] Acrasia, whom we must surprise,
Els she will slip away, and all our drift[6] despise."

70 Eftsoones they heard a most melodious sound,
Of all that mote delight a daintie eare,
Such as attonce might not on living ground,
Save in this paradise, be heard elswhere:
Right hard it was for wight which did it heare,
To read[7] what manner musicke that mote bee;

1 *Fall*, befall, or happen.
2 *Corage*, heart, mind.
3 *Reare*, raise, excite.
4 *Avise*, consider.
5 *Wonnes*, dwells.
6 *Drift*, aim, purpose.
7 *Read*, conceive.

For all that pleasing is to living eare
Was there consorted in one harmonee;
Birdes, voices, instruments, windes, waters, all agree.

71 The ioyous birdes, shrouded in chearefull shade,
Their notes unto the voice attempred sweet;
Th' angelicall soft trembling voyces made
To th' instruments divine respondence meet;
The silver-sounding instruments did meet
With the base murmure of the waters fall;
The waters fall, with difference discreet,
Now soft, now loud, unto the wind did call;
The gentle warbling wind low answered to all.

72 There, whence that musick seemed heard to bee,
Was the faire Witch herselfe now solacing
With a new lover, whom, through sorceree
And witchcraft, she from farre did thether bring:
There she had him now laid a slombering
In secret shade after long wanton ioyes;
Whilst round about them pleasauntly did sing
Many faire ladies and lascivious boyes,
That ever mixt their song with light licentious toyes.

73 And all that while right over him she hong
With her false eyes fast fixed in his sight,[1]
As seeking medicine whence she was stong,
Or greedily depasturing delight;
And oft inclining downe with kisses light,
For feare of waking him, his lips bedewd,

[1] *In his sight*, i. e. on his eyes.

And through his humid eyes did sucke his spright,
Quite molten into lust and pleasure lewd;
Wherewith she sighed soft, as if his case she rewd.[1]

74 The whiles some one did chaunt this lovely lay:
Ah, see, whoso fayre thing doest faine[2] *to see,*
In springing flowre the image of thy day[3]*!*
Ah, see the virgin rose, how sweetly shee
Doth first peepe foorth with bashfull modestee,
That fairer seemes the lesse ye see her may!
Lo! see soone after, how more bold and free
Her bared bosome she doth broad display!
Lo! see soone after how she fades and falls away!

[1] *Rewd*, pitied. [2] *Faine*, rejoice.
[3] *The image of thy day*, the emblem of thy life.

LXXIV., LXXV. — Subjoined are the corresponding stanzas in Fairfax's Tasso (xvi. 14, 15): —

"The gently-budding rose, quoth she, behold,
That first scant peeping forth with virgin beams,
Half ope, half shut, her beauties doth upfold
In their dear leaves, and less seen, fairer seems;
And after spreads them forth more broad and bold,
Then languisheth and dies in last extremes;
Nor seems the same, that decked bed and bower
Of many a lady, late, and paramour.

"So, in the passing of a day, doth pass,
The bud and blossom of the life of man,
Nor e'er doth flourish more, but like the grass
Cut down, becometh withered, pale and wan;
O gather then the rose while time thou has,
Short is the day, done when it scant began;
Gather the rose of love, while yet thou mayst,
Loving, be loved; embracing, be embraced."

75 *So passeth, in the passing of a day,*
Of mortall life the leafe, the bud, the flowre;
Ne more doth florish after first decay,
That[1] *earst was sought to deck both bed and bowre*
Of many a lady, and many a paramowre!
Gather therefore the rose whilest yet is prime,[2]
For soone comes age that will her pride deflowre:
Gather the rose of love whilest yet is time,
Whilest loving thou mayst loved be with equall crime.[3]

76 He ceast; and then gan all the quire of birdes
Their diverse notes t' attune unto his lay,
As in approvaunce of his pleasing wordes.
The constant[4] payre heard all that he did say,
Yet swarved not, but kept their forward way
Through many covert groves and thickets close,
In which they creeping did at last display[5]
That wanton Lady with her lover lose,[6]
Whose sleepie head she in her lap did soft dispose.

77 Upon a bed of roses she was layd,
As faint through heat, or dight[7] to pleasant sin;
And was arayd, or rather disarayd,
All in a vele of silke and silver thin,
That hid no whit her alablaster skin,
But rather shewd more white, if more might bee:
More subtile web Arachne cannot spin;

1 *That*, that which.
2 *Prime*, spring.
3 *With equall crime*, to an equal degree.
4 *Constant*, resolute.
5 *Display*, discover.
6 *Lose*, loose.
7 *Dight*, prepared.

Nor the fine nets, which oft we woven see
Of scorched deaw, do not in th' ayre more lightly flee.

78 Her snowy brest was bare to ready spoyle
Of hungry eies, which n'ote[1] therewith be fild;
And yet through languour of her late sweet toyle,
Few drops, more cleare then nectar, forth distild,
That like pure orient perles adowne it trild[2];
And her faire eyes, sweet smyling in delight,
Moystened their fierie beames, with which she thrild
Fraile harts, yet quenched not; like starry light,
Which, sparckling on the silent waves, does seeme more bright.

79 The young man, sleeping by her, seemd to be
Some goodly swayne of honorable place[3];
That certes it great pitty was to see
Him his nobility so fowle deface:
A sweet regard and amiable grace,
Mixed with manly sternesse, did appeare,
Yet sleeping, in his well-proportiond face;
And on his tender lips the downy heare
Did now but freshly spring, and silken blossoms beare.

80 His warlike armes, the ydle instruments
Of sleeping praise, were hong upon a tree;

[1] *N'ote*, might not. [2] *Trild*, flowed. [3] *Place*, rank.

LXXVII. 8.— *Fine nets.*] This alludes to the gossamer, which, when laden with dew-drops, falls to the ground, and is then observed from its sparkling in the sun. When it floats in the air, it is dry. Hence Spenser fancifully represents it as consisting of scorched or parched dew. H.

And his brave shield, full of old moniments,[1]
Was fowly ras't,[2] that none the signes might see;
Ne for them ne for honour cared hee,
Ne ought that did to his advauncement tend;
But in lewd loves, and wastfull luxuree,
His dayes, his goods, his bodie he did spend:
O horrible enchantment, that him so did blend.[3]

81 The noble Elfe and carefull Palmer drew
So nigh them, minding nought but lustfull game,
That suddein forth they on them rusht, and threw
A subtile net, which only for that same[4]
The skilfull Palmer formally did frame:
So held them under fast; the whiles the rest
Fled all away for feare of fowler shame.
The faire Enchauntresse, so unwares opprest,
Tryde all her arts and all her sleights thence out to
wrest[5];

82 And eke her lover strove; but all in vaine:
For that same net so cunningly was wound,
That neither guile nor force might it distraine.[6]
They tooke them both, and both them strongly bound
In captive bandes, which there they readie found:
But her in chaines of adamant he tyde;

[1] *Moniments*, marks, or memorials.
[2] *Ras't*, erased.
[3] *Blend*, blind.
[4] *That same*, i. e. purpose.
[5] *Wrest*, escape.
[6] *Distraine*, rend.

LXXXI. 5. — *Formally.*] That is, in a certain form. But we should probably read *formerly*. C.

For nothing else might keepe her safe and sound.
But Verdant (so he hight) he soone untyde,
And counsell sage in steed thereof to him applyde.

83 But all those pleasaunt bowres, and pallace brave,
Guyon broke downe with rigour pittilesse:
Ne ought their goodly workmanship might save
Them from the tempest of his wrathfulnesse,
But that their blisse he turn'd to balefulnesse,
Their groves he feld; their gardins did deface;
Their arbers spoyle; their cabinets[1] suppresse;
Their banket-houses burne; their buildings race;
And, of the fayrest late, now made the fowlest place.

84 Then led they her away, and eke that knight
They with them led, both sorrowfull and sad:
The way they came, the same retourn'd they right,
Till they arrived where they lately had
Charm'd those wild beasts that rag'd with furie mad;
Which, now awaking, fierce at them gan fly,
As in their mistresse reskew, whom they lad[2];
But them the Palmer soone did pacify.
Then Guyon askt, what meant those beastes which there did ly.

85 Sayd he: "These seeming beasts are men indeed,
Whom this Enchauntresse hath transformed thus;
Whylome her lovers, which her lustes did feed,
Now turned into figures hideous,
According to their mindes like monstruous."

1 *Cabinets*, cots. 2 *Lad*, led.

“Sad end,” quoth he, “of life intemperate,
And mournefull meed of ioyes delicious!
But, Palmer, if it mote thee so aggrate,[1]
Let them returned be unto their former state.”

86 Streightway he with his vertuous staffe them strooke,
And streight of beastes they comely men became;
Yet being men they did unmanly looke,
And stared ghastly; some for inward shame,
And some for wrath to see their captive Dame:
But one above the rest in speciall,
That had an hog beene late, hight Grylle by name,
Repyned greatly, and did him miscall[2]
That had from hoggish forme him brought to naturall.

87 Saide Guyon: “See the mind of beastly man,
That hath so soone forgot the excellence
Of his creation, when he life began,
That now he chooseth with vile difference
To be a beast, and lacke intelligence!”
To whom the Palmer thus: “The donghill kinde
Delightes in filth and fowle incontinence:
Let Gryll be Gryll, and have his hoggish minde;
But let us hence depart whilest wether serves and winde.”

[1] *Aggrate*, please. [2] *Miscall*, abuse.

LXXXVI. 7.—*Hight Grylle.*] In a dialogue by Plutarch, Gryllus, a companion of Ulysses, who had been changed into a swine by Circe, holds a conversation with him, and refuses to be restored to his human shape. H.

THE THIRDE BOOKE

OF

THE FAERIE QUEENE,

CONTAYNING

THE LEGEND OF BRITOMARTIS, OR OF CHASTITY.

1 It falls me here to write of Chastity,
That fayrest vertue, far above the rest:
For which what needes me fetch from Faëry
Forreine ensamples it to have exprest?
Sith it is shrined in my Soveraines brest,
And formd so lively in each perfect part,
That to all ladies, which have it profest,
Neede but behold the pourtraict of her hart;
If pourtrayd it might bee by any living art:

2 But living art may not least part expresse,
Nor life-resembling pencill it can paynt:
All[1] were it Zeuxis or Praxiteles,
His dædale[2] hand would faile and greatly faynt,

[1] *All*, although.

[2] *Dædale*, skilful.

And her perfections with his error taynt:
Ne poets witt, that passeth painter farre
In picturing the parts of beauty daynt,[1]
So hard a workemanship adventure darre,
For fear through want of words her excellence to marre.

3 How then shall I, apprentice of the skill
That whilome in divinest wits did rayne,
Presume so high to stretch mine humble quill?
Yet now my luckelesse lott doth me constrayne
Hereto perforce: but, O dredd Soverayne,
Thus far forth pardon, sith that choicest witt
Cannot your glorious pourtraict figure playne,
That I in colourd showes may shadow itt,
And antique praises unto present persons fitt.

4 But if in living colours, and right hew,
Thyselfe thou covet to see pictured,
Who can it doe more lively, or more trew,
Then that sweete verse, with nectar sprinckeled,
In which a gracious servaunt pictured
His Cynthia, his heavens fayrest light?
That with his melting sweetnes ravished,
And with the wonder of her beamës bright,
My sences lulled are in slomber of delight.

1 *Daynt*, dainty.

III. 4. — *Luckelesse lot.*] Luckless, because he apprehends he shall not do justice to the subject. H.

IV. 5. — *A gracious servaunt.*] Sir Walter Raleigh, in his poem called "Cynthia."

5 But let that same delitious poet lend
A little leave unto a rusticke Muse
To sing his Mistresse prayse; and let him mend,
If ought amis her liking may abuse:
Ne let his fayrest Cynthia refuse
In mirrours more then one herselfe to see;
But either Gloriana let her chuse,
Or in Belphœbe fashioned to bee;
In th' one her rule, in th' other her rare chastitee.

CANTO I.

Guyon encountreth Britomart:
Fayre Florimell is chaced:
Duessaes traines and Malecas-
taes[1] champions are defaced.

1 The famous Briton Prince and Faery Knight,
After long wayes and perilous paines endur'd,
Having their weary limbes to perfect plight
Restord, and sory wounds right well recur'd,
Of the faire Alma greatly were procur'd[2]
To make there lenger soiourne and abode;
But, when thereto they might not be allur'd
From seeking praise and deeds of armes abrode,
They courteous congé[3] tooke, and forth together yode.[4]

2 But the captív'd Acrasia he sent,
Because of traveill long, a nigher way,
With a strong gard, all reskew to prevent,
And her to Faery Court safe to convay;

[1] *Malecasta*, unchaste.
[2] *Procur'd*, entreated.
[3] *Congé*, leave.
[4] *Yode*, went.

I. 1. — *The famous Briton Prince.*] Prince Arthur remained in the house of Alma till the wounds he had received in his encounter with Maleger were healed. Sir Guyon, after destroying the Bower of Bliss, returned to the house of Alma, from which he and Prince Arthur now set forth. H.

That her for witnes of his hard assay
Unto his Faery Queene he might present:
But he himselfe betooke another way,
To make more triall of his hardiment,
And seeke adventures, as he with Prince Arthure went.

3 Long so they traveiled through wastefull wayes,
Where daungers dwelt, and perils most did wonne,[1]
To hunt for glory and renowmed prayse:
Full many countreyes they did overronne,
From the uprising to the setting sunne,
And many hard adventures did atchieve;
Of all the which they honour ever wonne,
Seeking the weake oppressed to relieve,
And to recover right for such as wrong did grieve.

4 At last, as through an open plaine they yode,
They spide a knight that towards pricked fayre;
And him beside an aged squire there rode,
That seemd to couch[2] under his shield three-square,
As if that age badd him that burden spare,
And yield it those that stouter could it wield:
He, them espying, gan himselfe prepare,
And on his arme addresse his goodly shield
That bore a lion passant in a golden field.

5 Which seeing, good Sir Guyon deare besought
The Prince, of grace, to let him ronne that turne.

1 *Wonne*, dwell. 2 *Couch*, bend.

IV. 9. — These are the legendary arms of Brute, from whom Britomartis is supposed to be descended.

He graunted : then the Faery quickly raught[1]
His poynant[2] speare, and sharply gan to spurne[3]
His fomy steed, whose fiery feete did burne
The verdant gras as he thereon did tread;
Ne did the other backe his foote returne,
But fiercely forward came withouten dread,
And bent his dreadful speare against the others head.

6 They beene ymett, and both theyr points arriv'd;
But Guyon drove so furious and fell,
That seemd both shield and plate it would have riv'd;
Nathelesse it bore his foe not from his sell,[4]
But made him stagger, as he were not well:
But Guyon selfe, ere well he was aware,
Nigh a speares length behind his crouper fell;
Yet in his fall so well himselfe he bare,
That mischievous mischaunce his life and limbs did spare.

7 Great shame and sorrow of that fall he tooke;
For never yet, sith warlike armes he bore
And shivering speare in bloody field first shooke,
He fownd himselfe dishonored so sore.
Ah! gentlest knight that ever armor bore,
Let not thee grieve dismounted to have beene,

1 *Raught*, reached.
2 *Poynant*, piercing, sharp.
3 *Spurne*, spur.
4 *Sell*, saddle.

VI. 6. — *But Guyon*, &c.] In this encounter between Guyon and Britomart, Upton discovers an historical allusion to the Earl of Essex's presuming to match himself with Queen Elizabeth, and adds, "And has not the poet with the finest art managed a very dangerous and secret piece of history?" H.

And brought to grownd, that never wast before;
For not thy fault, but secret powre unseene;
That speare enchaunted was which layd thee on the
greene!

8 But weenedst thou what wight thee overthrew,
Much greater griefe and shamefuller regrett
For thy hard fortune then thou wouldst renew,
That of a single damzell thou wert mett
On equall plaine, and there so hard besett:
Even the famous Britomart it was,
Whom straunge adventure did from Britayne fett[1]
To seeke her lover, (love far sought, alas!)
Whose image shee had seene in Venus looking-glas.

9 Full of disdainefull wrath, he fierce uprose
For to revenge that fowle reprochefull shame,
And, snatching his bright sword, began to close
With her on foot, and stoutly forward came;
Dye rather would he then[2] endure that same.
Which when his Palmer saw, he gan to feare
His toward[3] perill, and untoward blame,
Which by that new rencounter he should reare[4];
For death sate on the point of that enchaunted speare:

10 And hasting towards him gan fayre perswade
Not to provoke misfortune, nor to weene

1 *Fett*, fetch.
2 *Then*, than.
3 *Toward*, near at hand.
4 *Reare*, raise, bring upon himself.

VIII. 6. — Britomartis is one of the names of Diana, and is very happily employed by Spenser to denote a martial Britoness.

His speares default to mend with cruell blade;
For by his mightie science he had seene
The secrete vertue of that weapon keene,
That mortall puissaunce mote not withstond:
Nothing on earth mote alwaies happy[1] beene!
Great hazard were it, and adventure fond,[2]
To loose long-gotten honour with one evill hond.[3]

11 By such good meanes he him discounselled
From prosecuting his revenging rage:
And eke the Prince like treaty handeled,
His wrathfull will with reason to aswage;
And laid the blame, not to his carriage,
But to his starting steed that swarv'd asyde,
And to the ill purveyaunce of his page,
That had his furnitures[4] not firmely tyde:
So is his angry corage[5] fayrly pacifyde.

12 Thus reconcilement was betweene them knitt,
Through goodly temperaunce and affection chaste;
And either vowd with all their power and witt
To let not others honour be defaste
Of friend or foe, whoever it embaste,[6]
Ne armes to beare against the others syde:
In which accord[7] the Prince was also plaste,
And with that golden chaine of concord tyde:
So goodly all agreed, they forth yfere[8] did ryde.

1 *Happy*, successful.
2 *Fond*, foolish.
3 *Hond*, act, performance.
4 *Furnitures*, equipments.
5 *Corage*, heart.
6 *Embaste*, insulted.
7 *Accord*, agreement.
8 *Yfere*, together.

XI. 3. — *Like treaty handeled.*] Made use of the same reasoning.

13 O goodly usage of those antique tymes,
In which the sword was servaunt unto right!
When not for malice and contentious crymes,
But all for prayse, and proofe of manly might,
The martiall brood accustomed to fight:
Then honour was the meed of victory,
And yet the vanquished had no despight:
Let later age that noble use envý,
Vyle rancor to avoid and cruel surquedry[1]!

14 Long they thus traveiled in friendly wise,
Through countreyes waste, and eke well edifyde,[2]
Seeking adventures hard, to exercise
Their puissaunce, whylome full dernly[3] tryde.
At length they came into a forest wyde,
Whose hideous horror and sad trembling sownd
Full griesly[4] seemd: therein they long did ryde,
Yet tract of living creature none they fownd,
Save beares, lyons, and buls, which romed them arownd.

15 All suddenly out of the thickest brush,
Upon a milk-white palfrey all alone,
A goodly Lady did foreby[5] them rush,
Whose face did seeme as cleare as christall stone,
And eke, through feare, as white as whalës bone:
Her garments all were wrought of beaten gold,
And all her steed with tinsell trappings shone,

1 *Surquedry*, insolence.
2 *Edifyde*, built.
3 *Dernly*, sadly.
4 *Griesly*, grisly, terrible.
5 *Foreby*, by.

Which fledd so fast that nothing mote him hold,
And scarse them leasure gave her passing to behold.

16 Still as she fledd her eye she backward threw,
As fearing evill that poursewd her fast;
And her faire yellow locks behind her flew,
Loosely disperst with puff of every blast:
All as a blazing starre doth farre outcast
His hearie [1] beames, and flaming lockes dispredd,
At sight whereof the people stand aghast;
But the sage wisard telles, as he has redd,
That it impórtunes [2] death and dolefull dreryhedd.[3]

17 So as they gazed after her a whyle,
Lo! where a griesly foster [4] forth did rush,
Breathing out beastly lust her to defyle:
His tyreling [5] iade he fiersly forth did push
Through thicke and thin, both over banck and bush,
In hope her to attaine by hooke or crooke,
That from his gory sydes the blood did gush:
Large were his limbes, and terrible his looke,
And in his clownish hand a sharp bore-speare he shooke.

18 Which outrage when those gentle Knights did see,
Full of great envy and fell gealosy,

1 *Hearie*, hairy.
2 *Impórtunes*, portends.
3 *Dreryhedd*, sorrow.
4 *Foster*, forester.
5 *Tyreling*, hackney (?).

XVIII. 2.—*Full of great envy*, &c.] Both *envy* and *gealosy* are used here in the good sense of indignation. C.

They stayd not to avise[1] who first should bee,
But all spurd after, fast as they mote fly,
To reskew her from shamefull villany.
The Prince and Guyon equally bylive[2]
Herselfe pursewd, in hope to win thereby
Most goodly meede, the fairest dame alive:
But after the foule foster[3] Timias did strive.

19 The whiles faire Britomart, whose constant mind
Would not so lightly follow beauties chace,
Ne reckt of ladies love, did stay behynd;
And them awayted there a certaine space,
To weet if they would turne backe to that place
But, when she saw them gone, she forward went,
As lay her iourney, through that perlous[4] pace,[5]
With stedfast corage and stout hardiment;
Ne evil thing she feard, ne evill thing she ment.

20 At last, as nigh out of the wood she came,
A stately castle far away she spyde,
To which her steps directly she did frame.
That castle was most goodly edifyde,
And plaste for pleasure nigh that forrest syde:
But faire before the gate a spatious playne,

1 *Avise*, consider.
2 *Bylive*, quick.
3 *Foster*, forester.
4 *Perlous*, perilous.
5 *Pace*, pass.

XVIII. 6.— *The Prince and Guyon*, &c.] These adventures are resumed in Canto IV. Stanza 45, and Canto VI. Stanza 54.

XVIII. 9.— *Timias.*] Timias is Prince Arthur's squire, supposed to represent Sir Walter Raleigh. H.

Mantled with greene, itselfe did spredden[1] wyde,
On which she saw six knights, that did darrayne[2]
Fiers battaill against one with cruel might and mayne.

21 Mainely[3] they all attonce upon him laid,
And sore beset on every side arownd,
That nigh he breathlesse grew, yet nought dismaid,
Ne ever to them yielded foot of grownd,
All had he lost much blood through many a wownd;
But stoutly dealt his blowes, and every way,
To which he turned in his wrathfull stownd,[4]
Made them recoile, and fly from dredd decay,
That none of all the six before him durst assay[5]:

22 Like dastard curres, that, having at a bay
The salvage beast embost[6] in wearie chace,
Dare not adventure on the stubborne pray,
Ne byte before, but rome from place to place
To get a snatch when turned is his face.
In such distresse and doubtfull ieopardy
When Britomart him saw, she ran apace
Unto his reskew, and with earnest cry
Badd those same sixe forbeare that single enimy.

23 But to her cry they list not lenden eare,
Ne ought the more their mightie strokes surceasse;
But, gathering him rownd about more neare,
Their direfull rancour rather did encreasse;

1 *Spredden*, spread.
2 *Darrayne*, wage.
3 *Mainely*, strongly.
4 *Stownd*, moment, mood.
5 I. e. attack him in front.
6 *Embost*, tired out.

Till that she rushing through the thickest preasse
Perforce disparted their compacted gyre,[1]
And soone compeld to hearken unto peace:
Tho gan she myldly of them to inquyre
The cause of their dissention and outrageous yre.

24 Whereto that single Knight did answere frame:
"These six would me enforce, by oddes of might,
To chaunge my liefe,[2] and love another dame;
That death me liefer[3] were then such despight,
So unto wrong to yield my wrested right:
For I love one, the truest one on grownd,
Ne list me chaunge; she th' Errant Damzell hight;
For whose deare sake full many a bitter stownd
I have endurd, and tasted many a bloody wownd."

25 "Certes," said she, "then beene ye sixe to blame,
To weene your wrong by force to iustify:
For knight to leave his lady were great shame
That faithfull is; and better were to dy.
All losse is lesse, and lesse the infamy,
Then losse of love to him that loves but one:
Ne may Love be compeld by maistery[4];

1 *Gyre*, circle.
2 *Liefe*, love.
3 *Liefer*, preferable.
4 *Maistery*, superior power.

XXIV. 7. — *Th' Errant Damzell.*] Una, who is so called in Book II. Canto I. Stanza 19.

XXV. 7. — *Ne may Love*, &c.]

"Love wil nouht buen constreyned by maistré.
Whan maistré commeth, the god of love anon
Beteth his winges, and fare wel, he is gon."
Canterbury Tales (Wright) 11076-78.

For, soone as maistery comes, sweet Love anone
Taketh his nimble winges, and soone away is gone."

26 Then spake one of those six: "There dwelleth here
Within this castle wall a lady fayre,
Whose soveraine beautie hath no living pere;
Thereto so bounteous and so debonayre,[1]
That never any mote with her compayre:
She hath ordaind this law, which we approve,
That every knight which doth this way repayre,
In case he have no lady nor no love,
Shall doe unto her service, never to remove:

27 "But if he have a lady or a love,
Then must he her forgoe with fowle defame,[2]
Or els with us by dint of sword approve,
That she is fairer then our fairest Dame;
As did this Knight, before ye hether came."
"Perdy," said Britomart, "the choise is hard!
But what reward had he that overcame?"
"He should advaunced bee to high regard,"
Said they, "and have our Ladies love for his reward.

28 "Therefore aread,[3] Sir, if thou have a love."
"Love have I sure," quoth she, "but lady none;
Yet will I not fro mine owne love remove,
Ne to your Lady will I service done,[4]
But wreake your wronges wrought to this Knight alone,
And prove his cause." With that, her mortall speare

1 *Debonayre*, gracious.
2 *Defame*, dishonor.
3 *Aread*, declare.
4 *Done*, do.

She mightily aventred[1] towards one,
And downe him smot ere well aware he weare[2];
Then to the next she rode, and downe the next did beare.

29 Ne did she stay till three on ground she layd,
That none of them himselfe could reare againe:
The fourth was by that other Knight dismayd,
All were he wearie of his former paine;
That now there do but two of six remaine;
Which two did yield before she did them smight.
"Ah!" sayd she then, "now may ye all see plaine,
That Truth is strong, and trew Love most of might,
That for his trusty servaunts doth so strongly fight."

30 "Too well we see," saide they, "and prove too well
Our faulty weakenes, and your matchlesse might:
Forthy,[3] faire Sir, yours be the Damozell,
Which by her owne law to your lot doth light,
And we your liegemen faith unto you plight."
So underneath her feet their swords they mard,[4]
And, after, her besought, well as they might,
To enter in and reape the dew reward:
She graunted; and then in they all together far'd.

31 Long were it to describe the goodly frame
And stately port of Castle Ioyeous,

1 *Aventred*, adventured, aimed.
2 *Weare*, were.
3 *Forthy*, therefore.
4 *Mard*, marred, debased.

XXXI. 2.— *Castle Ioyeous.*] This is the name of Sir Lancelot's castle in the Morte d'Arthur. H.

(For so that castle hight by commun name,)
Where they were entertaynd with courteous
And comely glee of many gratious
Faire ladies, and of many a gentle knight;
Who, through a chamber long and spacious,
Eftsoones them brought unto their Ladies sight,
That of them cleeped[1] was the Lady of Delight.

32 But for to tell the sumptuous aray
Of that great chamber should be labour lost;
For living wit, I weene, cannot display
The roiall riches and exceeding cost
Of every pillour and of every post,
Which all of purest bullion framed were,
And with great perles and pretious stones embost,
That the bright glister of their beamës cleare
Did sparckle forth great light, and glorious did appeare.

33 These stranger Knights, through passing, forth were led
Into an inner rowme, whose royaltee
And rich purveyance[2] might uneath[3] be red[4];
Mote princes place beseeme so deckt to bee.
Which stately manner whenas they did see,
The image of superfluous riotize,[5]
Exceeding much the state of meane[6] degree,
They greatly wondred whence so sumpteous guize
Might be maintaynd, and each gan diversely devize.

1 *Cleeped*, called.
2 *Purveyance*, furniture.
3 *Uneath*, with difficulty.
4 *Red*, imagined.
5 *Riotize*, extravagance.
6 *Meane*, moderate.

34 The wals were round about appareiled
With costly clothes of Arras and of Toure;
In which with cunning hand was pourtrahed
The love of Venus and her paramoure,
The fayre Adonis, turned to a flowre;
A worke of rare device and wondrous wit.
First did it shew the bitter balefull stowre,[1]
Which her assayd with many a fervent fit,
When first her tender hart was with his beautie smit:

35 Then with what sleights and sweet allurements she
Entyst the boy, as well that art she knew,
And wooed him her paramoure to bee;
Now making girlonds of each flowre that grew,
To crowne his golden lockes with honour dew;
Now leading him into a secret shade
From his beauperes,[2] and from bright heavens vew,
Where him to sleepe she gently would perswade,
Or bathe him in a fountaine by some covert glade:

36 And, whilst he slept, she over him would spred
Her mantle colour'd like the starry skyes,
And her soft arme lay underneath his hed,
And with ambrosiall kisses bathe his eyes;
And, whilst he bath'd, with her two crafty spyes[3]
She secretly would search each daintie lim,
And throw into the well sweet rosemaryes,
And fragrant violets, and paunces[4] trim;
And ever with sweet nectar she did sprinkle him.

1 *Stowre*, distress.
2 *Beauperes*, fair companions.
3 *Spyes*, i. e. eyes.
4 *Paunces*, pansies.

37 So did she steale his heedelesse hart away,
And ioyd his love in secret unespyde :
But for she saw him bent to cruell play,
To hunt the salvage beast in forrest wyde,
Dreadfull[1] of daunger that mote him betyde,
She oft and oft adviz'd him to refraine
From chase of greater beastes, whose brutish pryde
Mote breede him scath unwares : but all in vaine ;
For who can shun the chance that dest'ny doth ordaine ?

38 Lo ! where beyond[2] he lyeth languishing,
Deadly engored of a great wilde bore ;
And by his side the goddesse groveling
Makes for him endlesse mone, and evermore
With her soft garment wipes away the gore
Which staynes his snowy skin with hatefull hew :
But, when she saw no helpe might him restore,
Him to a dainty flowre she did transmew,[3]
Which in that cloth was wrought, as if it lively grew.

39 So was that chamber clad in goodly wize :
And rownd about it many beds were dight,
As whylome was the antique worldës guize,
Some for untimely ease, some for delight,
As pleased them to use that use it might :
And all was full of damzels and of squyres,

1 *Dreadfull*, fearful.
2 *Beyond*, at a distance.
3 *Transmew*, change.

XXXVIII. 8. — *A dainty flowre.*] The anemone. H.

Dauncing and reveling both day and night,
And swimming deepe in sensuall desyres ;
And Cupid still emongest them kindled lustfull fyres.

40 And all the while sweet musicke did divide
Her looser notes with Lydian harmony ;
And all the while sweete birdes thereto applide
Their daintie layes and dulcet melody,
Ay caroling of love and iollity,
That wonder was to heare their trim consórt.[1]
Which when those Knights beheld, with scornefull eye
They sdeigned[2] such lascivious disport,
And loath'd the loose demeanure of that wanton sort.[3]

41 Thence they were brought to that great Ladies vew,
Whom they found sitting on a sumptuous bed
That glistred all with gold and glorious shew,
As the proud Persian queenes accustomed :
She seemd a woman of great bountihed
And of rare beautie, saving that askaunce
Her wanton eyes (ill signes of womanhed)
Did roll too lightly, and too often glaunce,
Without regard of grace or comely amenaunce.[4]

1 *Trim consórt*, pleasing concert.
2 *Sdeigned*, disdained.
3 *Sort*, company.
4 *Amenaunce*, behavior.

XL. 2. — *With Lydian harmony.*] The Lydian music was sup posed to be of a soft and voluptuous character. Thus Dryden

" Softly sweet, in Lydian measures,
Soon he soothed his soul to pleasures." H.

42 Long worke it were, and needlesse, to devize[1]
Their goodly entertainement and great glee:
She caused them be led in courteous wize
Into a bowre,[2] disarmed for to be,
And cheared well with wine and spiceree:
The Redcrosse Knight was soone disarmed there;
But the brave Mayd would not disarmed bee,
But onely vented up her umbriere,[3]
And so did let her goodly visage to appere.

43 As when fayre Cynthia, in darkesome night,
Is in a noyous cloud enveloped,
Where she may finde the substance thin and light,
Breakes forth her silver beames, and her bright hed
Discovers to the world discomfited,[4]
Of the poore traveiler that went astray
With thousand blessings she is heried[5];
Such was the beautie and the shining ray
With which fayre Britomart gave light unto the day.

44 And eke those six, which lately with her fought,
Now were disarmd, and did themselves present
Unto her vew, and company unsought;
For they all seemed courteous and gent,[6]
And all sixe brethren, borne of one parent,
Which had them traynd in all civilitee,
And goodly taught to tilt and turnament;

1 *Devize*, describe.
2 *Bowre*, chamber.
3 *Vented up her umbriere*, raised her visor.
4 *Discomfited*, dejected.
5 *Heried*, praised.
6 *Gent*, noble.

Now were they liegmen to this Ladie free,
And her knights-service ought,[1] to hold of her in fee.

45 The first of them by name Gardantè hight,
A iolly[2] person, and of comely vew;
The second was Parlantè, a bold knight;
And next to him Iocantè did ensew[3];
Basciantè did himselfe most courteous shew;
But fierce Bacchantè seemd too fell and keene;
And yett in armes Noctantè greater grew:
All were faire knights, and goodly well beseene[4];
But to faire Britomart they all but shadowes beene.

46 For shee was full of amiable grace
And manly terror mixed therewithall;
That as the one stird up affections bace,
So th' other did mens rash desires apall,
And hold them backe that would in error fall:
As hee that hath espide a vermeill rose,

1 *Ought*, owed.
2 *Iolly*, handsome.
3 *Ensew*, follow.
4 *Beseene*, appearing.

XLIV. 9. — *Knights-service ought.*] The tenure by knights-service was the most honorable one known to the English law. To constitute it, a determinate quantity of land, called a "knight's fee," was necessary; and the tenant was obliged to attend the lord of whom he held to the war forty days in every year, if called upon. H.

XLV. 1. — *The first of them*, &c.] The names of these six persons are appropriate to the attendants upon *Malecasta*, or Incontinence. *Gardantè* means a gazer, or ogler; *Parlantè*, a prattler; *Iocantè*, a jester; *Basciantè*, one who kisses; *Bacchantè*, a drinker of wine; and *Noctantè*, a reveller by night. H.

To which sharpe thornes and breres the way forstall,
Dare not for dread his hardy hand expose,
But, wishing it far off, his ydle wish doth lose.

47 Whom when the Lady saw so faire a wight,
All ignorant of her contrâry sex,
(For shee her weend a fresh and lusty knight,)
Shee greatly gan enamoured to wex,
And with vaine thoughts her falsed[1] fancy vex:
Her fickle hart conceived hasty fyre,
Like sparkes of fire which fall in sclender flex,[2]
That shortly brent[3] into extreme desyre,
And ransackt all her veines with passion entyre.

48 Eftsoones shee grew to great impatience,
And into termes of open outrage brust,[4]
That plaine discovered her incontinence;
Ne reckt shee who her meaning did mistrust;
For she was given all to fleshly lust,
And poured forth in sensuall delight,
That all regard of shame she had discust,[5]
And meet respect of honor putt to flight:
So shamelesse beauty soone becomes a loathly sight.

49 Faire Ladies, that to love captíved arre,
And chaste desires doe nourish in your mind,
Let not her fault your sweete affections marre;
Ne blott the bounty[6] of all womankind

1 *Falsed*, deceived.
2 *Flex*, flax.
3 *Brent*, burnt.
4 *Brust*, burst.
5 *Discust*, thrown off.
6 *Bounty*, goodness.

'Mongst thousands good, one wanton dame to find:
Emongst the roses grow some wicked weeds
For this was not to love, but lust, inclind;
For love does alwaies bring forth bounteous [1] deeds,
And in each gentle hart desire of honor breeds.

50 Nought so of love this looser dame did skill,[2]
But as a cole to kindle fleshly flame,
Giving the bridle to her wanton will,
And treading under foote her honest name:
Such love is hate, and such desire is shame.
Still did she rove[3] at her with crafty glaunce
Of her false eies, that at her hart did ayme,
And told her meaning in her countenaunce:
But Britomart dissembled it with ignoraunce.[4]

51 Supper was shortly dight,[5] and downe they satt;
Where they were served with all sumptuous fare,
Whiles fruitfull Ceres and Lyæus fatt
Pourd out their plenty, without spight[6] or spare;
Nought wanted there that dainty was and rare:
And aye the cups their bancks did overflow;
And aye betweene the cups she did prepare
Way to her love, and secret darts did throw;
But Britomart would not such guilfull message know.

1 *Bounteous*, virtuous.
2 *Skill*, understand.
3 *Rove*, shoot.
4 *Dissembled it with ignoraunce*, feigned not to understand her conduct.
5 *Dight*, prepared.
6 *Spight*, grudge.

LI. 3. — *Lyæus.*] A name of Bacchus, used here for wine, as Ceres is for food. H.

52 So, when they slaked had the fervent heat
Of appetite with meates of every sort,
The Lady did faire Britomart entreat
Her to disarme, and with delightfull sport
To loose her warlike limbs and strong effórt:
But when shee mote not thereunto be wonne,
(For shee her sexe under that straunge purpórt
Did use to hide, and plaine apparaunce shonne,)
In playner wise to tell her grievaunce she begonne;

53 And all attonce discovered her desire
With sighes, and sobs, and plaints, and piteous griefe,
The outward sparkes of her in-burning fire:
Which spent in vaine, at last she told her briefe,
That, but if she did lend her short reliefe
And doe her comfort, she mote algates [2] die.
But the chaste Damzell, that had never priefe [3]
Of such malengine [4] and fine forgerye, [5]
Did easely beleeve her strong extremitye.

54 Full easy was for her to have beliefe,
Who by self-feeling of her feeble sexe,
And by long triall of the inward griefe
Wherewith imperious love her hart did vexe,
Could iudge what paines doe loving harts perplexe.

1 *Purport*, disguise.
2 *Algates*, at all events.
3 *Priefe*, proof.
4 *Malengine*, guile.
5 *Forgerye*, deceit.

LII. 5.— *To loose*, &c.] To lay aside her arms, and relax the sternness of her demeanor. H.

Who meanes no guile, be guiled soonest shall,
And to faire semblaunce doth light[1] faith annexe:
The bird, that knowes not the false fowlers call,
Into his hidden nett full easely doth fall.

55 Forthy[2] she would not in discourteise wise
Scorne the faire offer of good will profest;
For great rebuke it is love to despise,
Or rudely sdeigne a gentle harts request;
But with faire countenaunce, as beseemed best,
Her entertaynd; nath'lesse shee inly deemd
Her love too light, to wooe a wandring guest;
Which she misconstruing, thereby esteemd
That from like inward fire that outward smoke had steemd.

56 Therewith awhile she her flit[3] fancy fedd,
Till she mote winne fit time for her desire;
But yet her wound still inward freshly bledd,
And through her bones the false instilled fire
Did spred itselfe, and venime close[4] inspire.
Tho were the tables taken all away;
And every knight, and every gentle 'squire,
Gan choose his dame with *bascimano*[5] gay,
With whom he ment to make his sport and courtly play.

57 Some fell to daunce; some fel to hazardry[6];
Some to make love; some to make meryment;

[1] *Light*, ready.
[2] *Forthy*, therefore.
[3] *Flit*, rapid.
[4] *Close*, secret.
[5] *Bascimano*, hand-kissing.
[6] *Hazardry*, gaming.

As diverse witts to diverse things apply:
And all the while faire Malecasta bent
Her crafty engins to her close intent.
By this th' eternall lampes, wherewith high Iove
Doth light the lower world, were halfe yspent,
And the moist daughters of huge Atlas strove
Into the ocean deepe to drive their weary drove.

58 High time it seemed then for everie wight
Them to betake unto their kindly rest:
Eftesoones long waxen torches weren light
Unto their bowres[1] to guyden every guest:
Tho, when the Britonesse saw all the rest
Avoided[2] quite, she gan herselfe despoile,
And safe committ to her soft fethered nest;
Wher through long watch, and late daies weary toile,
She soundly slept, and carefull thoughts did quite assoile.[3]

59 Now whenas all the world in silence deepe
Yshrowded was, and every mortall wight
Was drowned in the depth of deadly sleepe;
Faire Malecasta, whose engrieved spright
Could find no rest in such perplexed plight,
Lightly arose out of her wearie bed,
And, under the blacke vele of guilty night,

1 *Bowres*, chambers.
2 *Avoided*, departed.
3 *Assoile*, put off.

LVII. 8.—*And the moist daughters*, &c.] The Hyades, called moist because they set at twilight in the rainy months of August and November.

Her with a scarlott mantle covered
That was with gold and ermines faire enveloped.

60 Then panting softe, and trembling every ioynt,
Her fearfull feete towards the bowre she mov'd,
Where she for secret purpose did appoynt
To lodge the warlike Maide, unwisely loov'd;
And, to her bed approching, first she proov'd
Whether she slept or wakte: with her softe hand
She softely felt if any member moov'd,
And lent her wary eare to understand
If any puffe of breath or signe of sence shee fond.

61 Which whenas none she fond, with easy shifte,
For feare least her unwares she should abrayd,[1]
Th' embroderd quilt she lightly up did lifte,
And by her side herselfe she softly layd,
Of every finest fingers touch affrayd;
Ne any noise she made, ne word she spake,
But inly sigh'd. At last the royall Mayd
Out of her quiet slomber did awake,
And chaungd her weary side the better ease to take.

62 Where feeling one close couched by her side,
She lightly lept out of her filed[2] bedd,
And to her weapon ran, in minde to gride[3]
The loathed leachour: but the Dame, halfe dedd
Through suddeine feare and ghastly drerihedd,[4]
Did shrieke alowd, that through the hous it rong,

1 *Abrayd*, awake.
2 *Filed*, defiled.
3 *Gride*, pierce.
4 *Drerihedd*, horror.

And the whole family, therewith adredd,[1]
Rashly[2] out of their rouzed couches sprong,
And to the troubled chamber all in armes did throng.

63 And those sixe knights, that Ladies champions,
And eke the Redcrosse Knight ran to the stownd,[3]
Halfe armd and halfe unarmd, with them attons[4]:
Where when confusedly they came, they fownd
Their Lady lying on the sencelesse grownd:
On th' other side they saw the warlike Mayd
Al in her snow-white smocke, with locks unbownd,
Threatning the point of her avenging blaed;
That with so troublous terror they were all dismayd.

64 About their Ladye first they flockt arownd;
Whom having laid in comfortable couch,
Shortly they reard out of her frosen swownd;
And afterwardes they gan with fowle reproch
To stirre up strife, and troublous contecke[5] broch[6]:
But, by ensample of the last dayes losse,
None of them rashly durst to her approch,
Ne in so glorious spoile themselves embosse[7]:
Her succourd eke the Champion of the Bloody Crosse.

65 But one of those sixe knights, Gardantè hight,
Drew out a deadly bow and arrow keene,
Which forth he sent with felonous despight

1 *Adredd*, frightened.
2 *Rashly*, hastily.
3 *Stownd*, exigence, alarm.
4 *Attons*, together.
5 *Contecke*, contention.
6 *Broch*, broach.
7 *Embosse*, fatigue.

And fell intent against the Virgin sheene :
The mortall steele stayd not till it was seene
To gore her side ; yet was the wound not deepe,
But lightly rased her soft silken skin,
That drops of purple blood thereout did weepe,
Which did her lilly smock with staines of vermeil steep.

66 Wherewith enrag'd she fiercely at them flew,
And with her flaming sword about her layd,
That none of them foule mischiefe could eschew,
But with her dreadfull strokes were all dismayd:
Here, there, and every where, about her swayd
Her wrathfull steele, that none mote it abyde ;
And eke the Redcrosse Knight gave her good ayd,
Ay ioyning foot to foot, and syde to syde ;
That in short space their foes they have quite terrifyde.

67 Tho whenas all were put to shamefull flight,
The noble Britomartis her arayd,
And her bright armes about her body dight:
For nothing would she lenger there be stayd,
Where so loose life, and so ungentle trade,[1]
Was usd of knights and ladies seeming gent[2]:
So, earely, ere the grosse earthes gryesy[3] shade
Was all disperst out of the firmament,
They tooke their steeds, and forth upon their iourney went.

1 *Trade*, conduct.
2 *Gent*, high-bred.
3 *Gryesy*, moist, or foggy.

CANTO II.

The Redcrosse Knight to Britomart
 Describeth Artegall:
The wondrous Myrrhour, by which she
 In love with him did fall.

1 Here have I cause in men iust blame to find,
That in their proper praise too partiall bee,
And not indifferent[1] to woman kind,
To whom no share in armes and chevalree
They doe impart, ne maken memoree
Of their brave gestes[2] and prowesse martiall:
Scarse doe they spare to one, or two, or three,
Rowme in their writtes[3]; yet the same writing small
Does all their deedes deface, and dims their glories all.

2 But by recórd of antique times I finde
That wemen wont in warres to beare most sway,
And to all great exploites themselves inclind,
Of which they still the girlond bore away;
Till envious men, fearing their rules decay,[4]
Gan coyne streight lawes to curb their liberty:
Yet, sith they warlike armes have laide away,

1 *Indifferent*, impartial.
2 *Gestes*, deeds.
3 *Writtes*, writings.
4 I. e. the decline of their own authority.

They have exceld in artes and pollicy,
That now we foolish men that prayse gin eke t' envý.

3 Of warlike puissaunce in ages spent,[1]
Be thou, faire Britomart, whose prayse I wryte;
But of all wisedom bee thou precedent,
O soveraine Queene, whose prayse I would endyte,
Endite I would as dewtie doth excyte;
But ah! my rymes too rude and rugged arre,
When in[2] so high an obiect they doe lyte,
And, striving fit to make, I feare doe marre:
Thyselfe thy prayses tell, and make them knowen farre.

4 She, traveiling with Guyon, by the way
Of sondry thinges faire purpose[3] gan to find,
T' abridg their iourney long and lingring day:
Mongst which it fell into that Fairies mind
To aske this Briton Maid, what uncouth[4] wind
Brought her into those partes, and what inquest[5]
Made her dissemble her disguised kind[6]:
Faire lady she him seemd, like lady drest,
But fairest knight alive, when armed was her brest.

1 *Spent*, passed.
2 *In*, i. e. on.
3 *Purpose*, discourse.
4 *Uncouth*, strange.
5 *Inquest*, quest, or adventure.
6 *Kind*, sex.

III. 4. — *O soveraine Queene.*] This is an invocation to Queen Elizabeth. H.

IV. 1. — *Traveiling with Guyon.*] This is a mistake. Guyon went in quest of Florimel, in the first Canto, and Britomart is now in company with the Red-cross Knight. H.

5 Thereat she sighing softly had no powre
To speake awhile, ne ready answere make;
But with hart-thrilling throbs and bitter stowre,[1]
As if she had a fever fitt, did quake,
And every daintie limbe with horrour shake;
And ever and anone the rosy red
Flasht through her face, as it had beene a flake
Of lightning through bright heven fulmined:
At last, the passion past, she thus him answered:

6 "Faire Sir, I let you weete,[2] that from the howre
I taken was from nourses tender pap,
I have beene trained up in warlike stowre,
To tossen speare and shield, and to affrap[3]
The warlike ryder to his most mishap;
Sithence[4] I loathed have my life to lead,
As ladies wont, in pleasures wanton lap,
To finger the fine needle and nyce thread;
Me lever[5] were with point of foemans speare be dead.

7 "All my delight on deedes of armes is sett,
To hunt out perilles and adventures hard,
By sea, by land, whereso they may be mett,
Onely for honour and for high regard,
Without respect of richesse or reward:
For such intent into these partes I came,
Withouten compasse or withouten card,

1 *Stowre*, struggles, contentions.
2 *Let you weete*, inform you.
3 *Affrap*, strike.
4 *Sithence*, since.
5 *Me lever*, I would rather.

Far fro my native soyle, that is by name
The Greater Brytayne, here to seeke for praise and fame.

8 "Fame blazed hath, that here in Faery Lond
Doe many famous knightes and ladies wonne,[1]
And many straunge adventures to bee fond,
Of which great worth and worship[2] may be wonne:
Which to prove, I this voyage have begonne.
But mote I weet of you, right courteous Knight,
Tydings of one that hath unto me donne
Late foule dishonour and reprochfull spight,
The which I seeke to wreake, and Arthegall he hight."

9 The word gone out she backe againe would call,
As her repenting so to have missayd,
But that he, it uptaking ere the fall,[3]
Her shortly answered: "Faire martiall Mayd,
Certes ye misavised beene t' upbrayd
A gentle knight with so unknightly blame:
For weet ye well, of all that ever playd
At tilt or tourney, or like warlike game,
The noble Arthegall hath ever borne the name.[4]

1 *Wonne*, dwell. 2 *Worship*, honor.
3 I. e. before the words had fallen from her mouth.
4 I. e. of "gentle knight."

VII. 9. — *The Greater Brytayne.*] Church says that this means Wales, and is so called to distinguish it from Lesser Brittany, in France. Fairy Land is England proper. H.

10 "Forthy[1] great wonder were it, if such shame
Should ever enter in his bounteous[2] thought,
Or ever doe that mote deserven blame:
The noble corage[3] never weeneth ought
That may unworthy of itselfe be thought.
Therefore, faire Damzell, be ye well aware,
Least that too farre ye have your sorrow sought:
You and your countrey both I wish welfare,
And honour both; for each of other worthy are."

11 The royall maid woxe inly wondrous glad,
To heare her Love so highly magnifyde;
And ioyd that ever she affixed had
Her hart on knight so goodly glorifyde,
However finely she it faind to hyde.
The loving mother, that nine monethes did beare
In the deare closett of her painefull syde
Her tender babe, it seeing safe appeare,
Doth not so much reioyce as she reioyced theare.

12 But to occasion him to further talke,
To feed her humor with his pleasing style,
Her list[4] in stryfull[5] termes with him to balke,[6]
And thus replyde: "However, Sir, ye fyle
Your courteous tongue his prayses to compyle,[7]

1 *Forthy*, therefore.
2 *Bounteous*, good, noble.
3 *Corage*, heart.
4 *Her list*, it pleased her.
5 *Stryfull*, contentious.
6 *Balke*, deal in cross purposes.
7 *Compyle*, heap up.

X. 7.—Lest you have already gone too far in pursuit of undeserved revenge upon him who is the cause of your sorrow. C.

It ill beseemes a knight of gentle sort,
Such as ye have him boasted, to beguyle
A simple maide, and worke so hainous tort,[1]
In shame of knighthood, as I largely can report.

13 "Let bee therefore my vengeaunce to disswade,
And read,[2] where I that faytour[3] false may find."
"Ah! but if reason faire might you perswade
To slake your wrath, and mollify your mind,"
Said he, "perhaps ye should it better find:
For hardie thing it is, to weene by might
That man to hard conditions to bind;
Or ever hope to match in equall fight,
Whose prowesse paragone[4] saw never living wight.

14 "Ne soothlich[5] is it easie for to read
Where now on earth, or how, he may be fownd;
For he ne wonneth[6] in one certeine stead,[7]
But restlesse walketh all the world arownd,
Ay doing thinges that to his fame redownd,
Defending ladies cause and orphans right,
Whereso he heares that any doth confownd
Them comfortlesse, through tyranny or might;
So is his soveraine honour raisde to hevens hight."

15 His feeling wordes her feeble sence much pleased,
And softly sunck into her molten hart:
Hart, that is inly hurt, is greatly eased

1 *Tort*, wrong.
2 *Read*, declare.
3 *Faytour*, deceiver.
4 I. e. the like of whose prowesse.
5 *Soothlich*, truly.
6 *Wonneth*, dwelleth.
7 *Stead*, place.

With hope of thing that may allegge[1] his smart;
For pleasing wordes are like to magick art,
That doth the charmed snake in slomber lay:
Such secrete ease felt gentle Britomart,
Yet list the same efforce[2] with faind gainesay:—
So dischord ofte in musick makes the sweeter lay:—

16 And sayd: "Sir Knight, these ydle termes forbeare;
And, sith it is uneath[3] to finde his haunt,
Tell me some markes by which he may appeare,
If chaunce I him encounter paravaunt[4];
For perdy one shall other slay, or daunt:
What shape, what shield, what armes, what steed, what stedd,[5]
And whatso else his person most may vaunt."
All which the Redcrosse Knight to point aredd,[6]
And him in everie part before her fashioned.

17 Yet him in everie part before she knew,
However list her now her knowledge fayne,
Sith him whylome in Brytayne she did vew,
To her revealed in a mirrhour playne;
Whereof did grow her first engraffed payne,
Whose root and stalke so bitter yet did taste,
That, but the fruit more sweetnes did[7] contayne,
Her wretched dayes in dolour[8] she mote waste,
And yield the pray of love to lothsome death at last.

1 *Allegge*, allay.
2 *Efforce*, extort.
3 *Uneath*, hard.
4 *Paravaunt*, peradventure.
5 *Stedd*, place.
6 *To point aredd*, exactly described.
7 I. e. should.
8 *Dolour*, grief.

18 By straunge occasion she did him behold,
And much more straungely gan to love his sight,
As it in bookes hath written beene of old.
In Deheubarth, that now South-Wales is hight,
What time King Ryence raign'd and dealed right,
The great Magitien Merlin had deviz'd,
By his deepe science and hell-dreaded might,
A looking-glasse, right wondrously aguiz'd,[1]
Whose vertues through the wyde worlde soone were solemniz'd.[2]

19 It vertue had to shew in perfect sight
Whatever thing was in the world contaynd,
Betwixt the lowest earth and hevens hight,
So that it to the looker appertaynd:
What ever foe had wrought, or frend had faynd,
Therein discovered was, ne ought mote pas,
Ne ought in secret from the same remaynd;
Forthy[3] it round and hollow shaped was,
Like to the world itselfe, and seemd a world of glas.

20 Who wonders not, that reades so wonderous worke?
But who does wonder, that has red the towre

1 *Aguiz'd*, fashioned.
2 *Solemniz'd*, celebrated.
3 *Forthy*, therefore.

XX. — The story of this tower is apparently derived from some mediæval legend about the Pharos of Ptolemy Philadelphus, in which, perhaps, Phao took the place of the historical Arsinoe. The king was, no doubt, confounded with Ptolemy the Astronomer, who, says Warton, "was famous among the Eastern writers and their followers for his skill in operations of glass." C.

Wherein th' Aegyptian Phao long did lurke
From all mens vew, that none might her discoure,[1]
Yet she might all men vew out of her bowre [2]?
Great Ptolomæe it for his lemans sake
Ybuilded all of glasse, by magicke powre,
And also it impregnable did make;
Yet, when his Love was false, he with a peaze [3] it brake.

21 Such was the glassy globe that Merlin made,
And gave unto King Ryence for his gard,[4]
That never foes his kingdome might invade,
But he it knew at home before he hard [5]
Tydings thereof, and so them still debar'd:
It was a famous present for a Prince,
And worthy worke of infinite reward,
That treasons could bewray, and foes convince [6]:
Happy this realme, had it remayned ever since!

22 One day it fortuned fayre Britomart
Into her fathers closet to repayre;
For nothing he from her reserv'd apart,
Being his onely daughter and his hayre;
Where when she had espyde that mirrhour fayre,

1 *Discoure*, discover.
2 *Bowre*, chamber.
3 *Peaze*, blow.
4 *Gard*, protection.
5 *Hard*, heard.
6 *Convince*, discover.

XXI. — Similar to this glassy globe were the mirror sent to Cambuscan by the king of Arabie and Inde (Canterbury Tales, v. 10446), the mirror erected by Virgil in Rome, described by Gower, and many others mentioned in romantic poetry. — See Warton's History, Vol. II. p. 178. C.

Herselfe awhile therein she vewd in vaine:
Tho, her avizing[1] of the vertues rare
Which thereof spoken were, she gan againe
Her to bethinke of that mote to herselfe pertaine.

23 But as it falleth, in the gentlest harts
Imperious Love hath highest set his throne,
And tyrannizeth in the bitter smarts
Of them, that to him buxome[2] are and prone:
So thought this mayd (as maydens use to done)
Whom fortune for her husband would allot;
Not that she lusted after any one,
For she was pure from blame of sinfull blott;
Yet wist her life at last must lincke in that same knot.

24 Eftsoones there was presented to her eye
A comely knight, all arm'd in complete wize,[3]
Through whose bright ventayle,[4] lifted up on hye,
His manly face, that did his foes agrize[5]
And frends to termes of gentle truce entize,
Lookt foorth, as Phœbus face out of the east
Betwixt two shady mountaynes doth arize:
Portly[6] his person was, and much increast
Through his heroicke grace and honorable gest.[7]

1 *Avizing*, bethinking.
2 *Buxome*, yielding.
3 *Wize*, manner.
4 *Ventayle*, beaver, the part of the helmet which lifted up.
5 *Agrize*, terrify.
6 *Portly*, stately.
7 *Gest*, carriage.

XXII. 6.—*In vaine.*] Because, looking into it without any definite purpose, she saw nothing but her own image. H.

25 His crest was covered with a couchant hownd,
And all his armour seemd of antique mould,
But wondrous massy and assured sownd,
And round about yfretted all with gold,
In which there written was, with cyphres old,
Achilles armes which Arthegall did win:
And on his shield enveloped sevenfold
He bore a crowned litle ermilin,[1]
That deckt the azure field with her fayre pouldred[2] skin.

26 The Damzell well did vew his personage,
And liked well ; ne further fastned not,
But went her way ; ne her unguilty age
Did weene, unwares, that her unlucky lot
Lay hidden in the bottome of the pot:
Of hurt unwist most daunger doth redound:
But the false archer, which that arrow shot
So slyly that she did not feele the wound,
Did smyle full smoothly at her weetlesse[3] wofull stound.[4]

27 Thenceforth the fether in her lofty crest,
Ruffed[5] of Love, gan lowly to availe[6];

1 *Ermilin*, ermine.
2 *Pouldred*, spotted.
3 *Weetlesse*, unconscious.
4 *Stound*, plight.
5 *Ruffed*, ruffled.
6 *Availe*, sink.

XXV. 6. — Arthegall (Arthur's peer) is meant for Arthur, Lord Grey of Wilton, and the arms seem to be devised in allusion to his name. UPTON.

XXVI. 2. — *Ne further fastned not.*] Her thoughts dwelt no more upon it. H.

And her prowd portaunce[1] and her princely gest,
With which she earst tryúmphed, now did quaile:
Sad, solemne, sowre, and full of fancies fraile,
She woxe; yet wist she nether how, nor why;
She wist not, silly Mayd, what she did aile,
Yet wist she was not well at ease perdy;
Yet thought it was not love, but some meláncholy.

28 So soone as Night had with her pallid hew
Defaste[2] the beautie of the shyning skye,
And reft from men the worldes desired vew,
She with her nourse adowne to sleepe did lye;
But sleepe full far away from her did fly:
In stead thereof sad sighes and sorrowes deepe
Kept watch and ward about her warily,
That nought she did but wayle, and often steepe
Her dainty couch with teares which closely[3] she did weepe.

29 And if that any drop of slombring rest
Did chaunce to still[4] into her weary spright,
When feeble nature felt herselfe opprest,
Streightway with dreames, and with fantastick sight
Of dreadfull things, the same was put to flight;
That oft out of her bed she did astart,
As one with vew of ghastly feends affright:
Tho gan she to renew her former smart,
And thinke of that fayre visage written in her hart.

1 *Portaunce*, port.
2 *Defaste*, defaced.
3 *Closely*, secretly.
4 *Still*, drop, flow.

30 One night, when she was tost with such unrest,
Her aged nourse, whose name was Glaucè hight,
Feeling her leape out of her loathed nest,
Betwixt her feeble armes her quickly keight,[1]
And downe againe her in her warme bed dight[2]:
"Ah! my deare daughter, ah! my dearest dread,
What uncouth fit," sayd she, "what evill plight,
Hath thee opprest, and with sad drearyhead[3]
Chaunged thy lively cheare, and living made thee dead?

31 "For not of nought these suddein ghastly feares
All night afflict thy naturall repose;
And all the day, whenas thine equall peares
Their fit disports with faire delight doe chose,
Thou in dull corners doest thyselfe inclose;
Ne tastest princes pleasures, ne doest spred
Abroad thy fresh youths fayrest flowre, but lose
But leafe and fruite, both too untimely shed,
As one in wilfull bale[4] for ever buried.

32 "The time that mortall men their weary cares
Do lay away, and all wilde beastes do rest,
And every river eke his course forbeares,
Then doth this wicked evill thee infest,
And rive with thousand throbs thy thrilled[5] brest:
Like an huge Aetn' of deepe engulfed gryefe,
Sorrow is heaped in thy hollow chest,

[1] *Keight*, caught.
[2] *Dight*, disposed, placed.
[3] *Drearyhead*, sorrow.
[4] *Bale*, sorrow.
[5] *Thrilled*, pierced.

Whence foorth it breakes in sighes and anguish ryfe,
As smoke and sulphure mingled with confused stryfe.

33 "Ay me! how much I feare least love it bee!
But if that love it be, as sure I read
By knowen signes and passions which I see,
Be it worthy of thy race and royall sead,
Then I avow, by this most sacred head
Of my deare foster childe, to ease thy griefe
And win thy will. Therefore away doe dread;
For death nor daunger from thy dew reliefe
Shall me debarre: tell me, therefore, my liefest liefe[1]!"

34 So having sayd, her twixt her armës twaine
Shee streightly[2] straynd, and colled[3] tenderly;
And every trembling ioynt and every vaine
Shee softly felt, and rubbed busily,
To doe the frosen cold away to fly;
And her faire deawy eies with kisses deare
Shee ofte did bathe, and ofte againe did dry:
And ever her impórtund not to feare
To let the secret of her hart to her appeare.

35 The Damzell pauzd; and then thus fearfully:
"Ah! nurse, what needeth thee to eke[4] my paine?
Is not enough that I alone doe dye,
But it must doubled bee with death of twaine?
For nought for me but death there doth remaine!"
"O daughter deare," said she, "despeire no whit:
For never sore but might a salve obtaine:

1 *Liefest liefe*, dearest dear.
2 *Streightly*, closely.
3 *Colled*, clasped round the neck.
4 *Eke*, increase.

That blinded god, which hath ye blindly smit,
Another arrow hath your lovers hart to hit."

36 "But mine is not," quoth she, "like other wownd;
For which no reason can finde remedy."
"Was never such, but mote the like be fownd,"
Said she; "and though no reason may apply
Salve to your sore, yet Love can higher stye[1]
Then Reasons reach, and oft hath wonders donne."
"But neither god of love nor god of skye
Can doe," said she, "that which cannot be donne."
"Things ofte impossible," quoth she, "seeme, ere begonne."

37 "These idle wordes," said she, "doe nought aswage
My stubborne smart, but more annoiaunce breed:
For no, no usuall fire, no usuall rage
Yt is, O nourse, which on my life doth feed,
And sucks the blood which from my hart doth bleed.
But since thy faithfull zele lets me not hyde
My crime, (if crime it be,) I will it reed.[2]
Nor prince nor pere it is, whose love hath gryde[3]
My feeble brest of late, and launched this wound wyde:

38 "Nor man it is, nor other living wight;
For then some hope I might unto me draw;
But th' only shade and semblant[4] of a knight,
Whose shape or person yet I never saw,
Hath me subiected to Loves cruell law:
The same one day, as me misfortune led,

1 *Stye*, mount.
2 *Reed*, declare.
3 *Gryde*, pierced.
4 *Semblant*, appearance.

I in my fathers wondrous mirrhour saw,
And, pleased with that seeming goodlyhed,[1]
Unwares the hidden hooke with baite I swallowed.

39 "Sithens[2] it hath infixed faster hold
Within my bleeding bowells, and so sore
Now ranckleth in this same fraile fleshly mould,
That all mine entrailes flow with poisnous gore,
And th' ulcer groweth daily more and more;
Ne can my ronning sore finde remedee,
Other then my hard fortune to deplore,
And languish as the leafe faln from the tree,
Till death make one end of my daies and miseree!"

40 "Daughter," said she, "what need ye be dismayd?
Or why make ye such monster of your minde?
Of much more uncouth[3] thing I was affrayd;
Of filthy lust, contrâry unto kinde[4]:
But this affection nothing straunge I finde;
For who with reason can you aye reprove
To love the semblaunt pleasing most your minde,
And yield your heart whence ye cannot remove?
No guilt in you, but in the tyranny of Love.

41 "Not so th' Arabian Myrrhe did sett her mynd;
Nor so did Biblis spend her pining hart;

1 *Goodlyhed*, goodliness.
2 *Sithens*, since that time.
3 *Uncouth*, strange.
4 *Kinde*, nature.

XL. 2.— *Or why make*, &c.] Why speak of your passion as if it were monstrous or unnatural? H.

XLI. 1.— *Th' Arabian Myrrhe*, &c.] Myrrha and Byblis are names associated with classical tales of incestuous passion. H.

But lov'd their native flesh against al kynd,
And to their purpose used wicked art:
Yet playd Pasiphaë a more monstrous part,
That lov'd a bul, and learnd a beast to bee:
Such shamefull lusts who loaths not, which depart
From course of nature and of modestee?
Swete Love such lewdnes bands [1] from his faire companee.

42 "But thine, my deare, (wel fare thy heart, my deare!)
Though straunge beginning had, yet fixed is
On one that worthy may perhaps appeare;
And certes seemes bestowed not amis:
Ioy thereof have thou and eternall blis!"
With that, upleaning on her elbow weake,
Her alablaster brest she soft did kis,
Which all that while shee felt to pant and quake,
As it an earth-quake were: at last she thus bespake:

43 "Beldame,[2] your words doe worke me litle ease;
For though my love be not so lewdly bent
As those ye blame, yet may it nought appease
My raging smart, ne ought my flame relent,
But rather doth my helpelesse griefe augment.
For they, however shamefull and unkinde,[3]
Yet did possesse their horrible intent:
Short end of sorowes they therby did finde;
So was their fortune good, though wicked were their minde.

1 *Bands*, banishes.
2 *Beldame*, (here) grandmother, or good mother.
3 *Unkinde*, unnatural.

44 "But wicked fortune mine, though minde be good,
Can have no end nor hope of my desire,
But feed on shadowes whiles I die for food,
And like a shadow wexe, whiles with entire
Affection I doe languish and expire.
I, fonder then Cephisus foolish chyld,[1]
Who, having vewed in a fountaine shere[2]
His face, was with the love thereof beguyld;
I, fonder, love a shade, the body far exyld."

45 "Nought like," quoth shee; "for that same wretched boy
Was of himselfe the ydle paramoure,
Both Love and Lover, without hope of ioy;
For which he faded to a watry flowre.
But better fortune thine, and better howre,[3]
Which lov'st the shadow of a warlike knight;
No shadow, but a body hath in powre:
That body, wheresoever that it light,
May learned be by cyphers, or by magicke might.

46 "But if thou may with reason yet represse
The growing evill, ere it strength have gott,
And thee abandond wholy doe possesse;
Against it strongly strive, and yield thee nott
Til thou in open fielde adowne be smott:
But if the passion mayster thy fraile might,

1 I. e. Narcissus.
2 *Shere*, clear.
3 *Howre*, i. e. lot.

XLV. 7.— *No shadow*, &c.] "There is no shadow which has not a body belonging to it." H.

So that needs love or death must bee thy lott,
Then I avow to thee, by wrong or right,
To compas thy desire, and find that loved knight."

47 Her chearefull words much cheard the feeble spright
Of the sicke Virgin, that her downe she layd
In her warme bed to sleepe, if that she might;
And the old-woman carefully displayd[1]
The clothes about her round with busy ayd;
So that at last a litle creeping sleepe
Surprisd her sence. Shee, therewith well apayd,[2]
The dronken lamp down in the oyl did steepe,
And sett her by to watch, and sett her by to weepe.

48 Earely, the morrow next, before that day
His ioyous face did to the world revele,
They both uprose and tooke their ready way
Unto the church, their praiers to appele,[3]
With great devotion, and with litle zele:
For the faire Damzel from the holy herse[4]
Her love-sicke hart to other thoughts did steale;
And that old Dame said many an idle verse,
Out of her daughters hart fond fancies to reverse.[5]

1 *Displayd*, spread.
2 *Apayd*, satisfied.
3 *Appele*, i. e. prefer.
4 *Herse*, rehearsal (of the service).
5 *Reverse*, cause to return or depart.

XLVII. 8. — *The dronken lamp*, &c.] The lamp is called *dronken*, because it drinks or consumes the oil. Upton says that she does not blow out the lamp because that was ill-ominous. H.

49 Retourned home, the royall Infant fell
Into her former fitt; for why? no powre
Nor guidaunce of herselfe in her did dwell.
But th' aged nourse, her calling to her bowre,[1]
Had gathered rew, and savine, and the flowre
Of camphora, and calamint, and dill;
All which she in a earthen pot did poure,
And to the brim with coltwood did it fill,
And many drops of milk and blood through it did spill.

50 Then, taking thrise three heares from of her head,
Them trebly breaded in a threefold lace,
And round about the pots mouth bound the thread;
And, after having whispered a space
Certein sad words with hollow voice and bace,[2]
Shee to the Virgin sayd, thrise sayd she itt:
"Come, daughter, come; come, spit upon my face;
Spitt thrise upon me, thrise upon me spitt;
Th' uneven nomber for this busines is most fitt."

51 That sayd, her rownd about she from her turnd,
She turned her contrâry to the sunne;
Thrise she her turnd contrâry, and returnd
All cóntrary; for she the right did shunne;
And ever what she did was streight[3] undonne.
So thought she to undoe her daughters love:

[1] *Bowre*, chamber.
[2] *Bace*, low.
[3] *Streight*, immediately.

L. 1.— *Then, taking*, &c.] The classic poets, especially Theocritus and Virgil, have supplied Spenser with the various processes of Glauce's incantation. H.

But love, that is in gentle brest begonne,
No ydle charmes so lightly may remove;
That well can witnesse, who by tryall it does prove.

52 Ne ought it mote the noble Mayd avayle,
Ne slake the fury of her cruell flame,
But that shee still did waste, and still did wayle,
That through long languour and hart-burning brame[1]
She shortly like a pyned ghost became
Which long hath waited by the Stygian strond.
That when old Glaucè saw, for feare least blame
Of her miscarriage should in her be fond,
She wist not how t' amend, nor how it to withstond.

[1] *Brame*, desire, Ital. *brama* (?).

LII. 6. — *Hath waited.*] Because the body had not been buried. H.

CANTO III.

Merlin bewrayes to Britomart
  The state of Arthegall:
And shews the famous progeny,
  Which from them springen shall.

1 MOST sacred fyre, that burnest mightily
In living brests, ykindled first above
Emongst th' eternall spheres and lamping [1] sky,
And thence pourd into men, which men call Love;
Not that same which doth base affections move
In brutish mindes, and filthy lust inflame;
But that sweete fit [2] that doth true beautie love,
And choseth Vertue for his dearest dame,
Whence spring all noble deedes and never-dying fame:

2 Well did antiquity a god thee deeme,
That over mortall mindes hast so great might,
To order them as best to thee doth seeme,
And all their actions to direct aright:
The fatall [3] purpose of divine foresight
Thou doest effect in destined descents,
Through deepe impression of thy secret might,
And stirredst up th' heroës high intents,
Which the late world admyres for wondrous moniments.

1 *Lamping*, shining.
2 *Fit*, passion.
3 *Fatall*, foreordained.

3 But thy dredd dartes in none doe triumph more,
Ne braver proofe in any of thy powre
Shewd'st thou, then in this royall maid of yore,
Making her seeke an unknowne paramoure,
From the worlds end, through many a bitter stowre[1]:
From whose two loynes thou afterwardes did rayse
Most famous fruites of matrimoniall bowre,
Which through the earth have spredd their living prayse,
That fame in tromp of gold eternally displayes.

4 Begin then, O my dearest sacred Dame,
Daughter of Phœbus and of Memorye,
That doest ennoble with immortall name
The warlike worthies, from antiquitye,
In thy great volume of eternitye;
Begin, O Clio, and recount from hence
My glorious Soveraines goodly auncestrye,
Till that by dew degrees, and long protense,[2]
Thou have it lastly brought unto her excellence.

5 Full many wayes within her troubled mind
Old Glaucè cast to cure this ladies griefe;
Full many waies she sought, but none could find,
Nor herbes, nor charmes, nor counsel that is chiefe
And choisest med'cine for sick harts reliefe:
Forthy[3] great care she tooke,[4] and greater feare,
Least that it should her turne to fowle repriefe

1 *Stowre*, peril.
2 *Protense*, extension.
3 *Forthy*, therefore.
4 I. e. she felt great concern.

And sore reproch, whenso her father deare
Should of his dearest daughters hard misfortune heare.

6 At last she her avisde,[1] that he which made
That mirrhour, wherein the sicke damosell
So straungely vewed her straunge lovers shade,
To weet, the learned Merlin, well could tell
Under what coast of heaven the man did dwell,
And by what means his love might best be wrought:
For, though beyond the Africk Ismaël
Or th' Indian Peru he were, she thought
Him forth through infinite endevour to have sought.

7 Forthwith themselves disguising both in straunge
And base atyre, that none might them bewray,
To Maridunum, that is now by chaunge
Of name Cayr-Merdin cald, they tooke their way:
There the wise Merlin whylome wont (they say)
To make his wonne,[2] low underneath the ground
In a deepe delve,[3] farre from the vew of day,
That of no living wight he mote be found,
Whenso he counseld with his sprights encompast round.

8 And, if thou ever happen that same way
To traveill, go to see that dreadfull place:

1 *Avisde*, bethought.
2 *Wonne*, dwelling.
3 *Delve*, dell.

VI. 7.— *The Africk Ismaël.*] The Moors, Bedouin Arabs, &c., inhabiting the northern parts of Africa, are supposed to be descendants of Ishmael. H.

VII. 4.— *Cayr-Merdin*, that is, city of Merdin or Merlin, is Caermarthen, in South Wales. C.

It is an hideous hollow cave (they say)
Under a rock that lyes, a litle space
From the swift Barry, tombling downe apace
Emongst the woody hilles of Dynevowre:
But dare thou not, I charge, in any cace,
To enter into that same balefull bowre,[1]
For feare the cruell feendes should thee unwares devowre:

9 But, standing high aloft, low lay thine eare,
And there such ghastly noyse of yron chaines
And brasen caudrons thou shalt rombling heare,
Which thousand sprights with long enduring paines
Doe tosse, that it will stonn thy feeble braines;
And oftentimes great grones, and grievous stownds,[2]
When too huge toile and labour them constraines;
And oftentimes loud strokes and ringing sowndes
From under that deepe rock most horribly rebowndes.

10 The cause, some say, is this: A litle whyle
Before that Merlin dyde, he did intend
A brasen wall in compas to compyle[3]
About Cairmardin, and did it commend
Unto these sprights to bring to perfect end:
During which worke the Lady of the Lake,
Whom long he lov'd, for him in hast did send;
Who, thereby forst his workemen to forsake,
Them bownd, till his retourne, their labour not to slake.

1 *Bowre*, chamber.
2 *Stownds*, (strictly) times.
3 *Compyle*, pile together, construct.

11 In the meane time, through that false ladies traine[1]
He was surprisd, and buried under beare,
Ne ever to his worke returnd againe:
Nath'lesse those feends may not their work forbeare,
So greatly his commandëment they feare,
But there doe toyle and traveile day and night,
Untill that brasen wall they up doe reare:
For Merlin had in magick more insight
Then ever him before or after living wight:

12 For he by wordes could call out of the sky
Both sunne and moone, and make them him obay,
The land to sea, and sea to maineland dry,
And darksom night he eke could turne to day;
Huge hostes of men he could alone dismay,
And hostes of men of meanest thinges could frame,
Whenso him list his enimies to fray[2]:
That to this day, for terror of his fame,
The feends do quake when any him to them does name.

1 *Traine*, artifice. 2 *Fray*, terrify.

XI. 2. — One day when Merlin and the Lady of the Lake were together in a cave in the forest of Arvantes where he had made a dwelling and a tomb, the wizard told the lady, in answer to an inquiry, that he would die before her, and desired that she would cause herself to be buried in the same tomb with him after her death. The lady, under pretence of a wish to see if the tomb were large enough for both, induced Merlin to lie down in it, and when she saw him stretched out in the tomb, she put down the lid, and closed it so, within and without, that no man could open it. — This account, taken from the Prophecies of Merlin, differs from that given in the Romance. See Southey's Kyng Arthur, Vol. II. p. 463. C.

13 And, sooth, men say that he was not the sonne
Of mortall syre or other living wight,
But wondrously begotten, and begonne
By false illusion of a guilefull spright
On a faire lady nonne, that whilome hight
Matilda, daughter to Pubidius
Who was the lord of Mathraval by right,
And coosen unto King Ambrosius;
Whence he indued was with skill so merveilous.

14 They, here ariving, staid a while without,
Ne durst adventure rashly in to wend,
But of their first intent gan make new dout
For dread of daunger, which it might portend:
Untill the hardy Mayd (with love to frend)
First entering, the dreadfull Mage[1] there fownd
Deepe busied 'bout worke of wondrous end,
And writing straunge charácters in the grownd,
With which the stubborne feendes he to his service bownd.

15 He nought was moved at their entraunce bold,
For of their comming well he wist afore;
Yet list them bid their businesse to unfold,
As if ought in this world in secrete store

1 *Mage*, magician.

XIII. 8. — *Wondrously begotten.*] According to one account, the father of Merlin was a demon, or spirit, and his mother a daughter of the king of Dimetia (South Wales). The king of Dimetia would have been lord of Dinevwr, not of Mathraval, which was the capital of Powys. For the names, Matilda and Pubidius, I know of no authority besides Spenser's. C.

Were from him hidden, or unknowne of yore.
Then Glaucè thus: "Let not it thee offend,
That we thus rashly through thy darksom dore
Unwares have prest; for either fatall end,[1]
Or other mightie cause, us two did hether send."

16 He bad tell on; and then she thus began:
"Now have three moones with borrowd brothers light
Thrise shined faire, and thrise seemd dim and wan,
Sith a sore evill, which this Virgin bright
Tormenteth and doth plonge in dolefull plight,
First rooting tooke; but what thing it mote bee,
Or whence it sprong, I can not read aright:
But this I read, that, but if remedee
Thou her afford, full shortly I her dead shall see."

17 Therewith th' Enchaunter softly gan to smyle
At her smooth speeches, weeting inly well
That she to him dissembled womanish guyle,
And to her said: "Beldame, by that ye tell
More neede of leach-crafte hath your damozell,
Then of my skill: who helpe may have elswhere,
In vaine seekes wonders out of magick spell."
Th' old woman wox half blanck those wordes to heare;
And yet was loth to let her purpose plaine appeare;

18 And to him said: "Yf any leaches skill,
Or other learned meanes, could have redrest

[1] *Fatall end*, some purpose of the Fates.

This my deare daughters deepe-engraffed ill,
Certes I should be loth thee to molest:
But this sad evill, which doth her infest,
Doth course of naturall cause farre exceed,
And housed is within her hollow brest,
That either seemes some cursed witches deed,
Or evill spright, that in her doth such torment breed."

19 The Wisard could no lenger beare her bord,[1]
But, brusting forth in laughter, to her sayd:
"Glaucè, what needes this colourable word
To cloke the cause that hath itselfe bewrayd?
Ne ye, fayre Britomartis, thus arayd,
More hidden are then sunne in cloudy vele;
Whom thy good fortune, having fate obayd,
Hath hether brought for succour to appele;
The which the Powres to thee are pleased to revele."

20 The doubtfull Mayd, seeing herselfe descryde,
Was all abasht, and her pure yvory
Into a cleare carnation suddeine dyde;
As fayre Aurora, rysing hastily,
Doth by her blushing tell that she did lye
All night in old Tithonus frosen bed,
Whereof she seemes ashamed inwardly:
But her olde nourse was nought dishartened,
But vauntage made of that which Merlin had ared[2];

21 And sayd: "Sith then thou knowest all our griefe,
(For what doest not thou knowe?) of grace I pray,

[1] *Bord*, trifling. [2] *Ared*, declared.

Pitty our playnt, and yield us meet reliefe!"
With that the Prophet still awhile did stay,
And then his spirite thus gan foorth display:
"Most noble Virgin, that by fatall lore
Hast learn'd to love, let no whit thee dismay
The hard beginne that meetes thee in the dore,
And with sharpe fits thy tender hart oppresseth sore:

22 "For so must all things excellent begin;
And eke enrooted deepe must be that tree,
Whose big embodied braunches shall not lin[1]
Till they to hevens hight forth stretched bee.
For from thy wombe a famous progenee
Shall spring out of the auncient Troian blood,
Which shall revive the sleeping memoree
Of those same antique peres, the hevens brood,
Which Greeke and Asian rivers stayned with their blood.

23 "Renowmed kings, and sacred emperours,
Thy fruitfull ofspring, shall from thee descend;
Brave captaines, and most mighty warriours,
That shall their conquests through all lands extend,
And their decayed kingdomes shall amend:
The feeble Britons, broken with long warre,
They shall upreare, and mightily defend
Against their forren foe that commes from farre,
Till universall peace compound all civill iarre.

24 "It was not, Britomart, thy wandring eye
Glauncing unwares in charmed looking-glas,

[1] *Lin*, stop.

But the streight course of hevenly destiny,
Led with Eternall Providence, that has
Guyded thy glaunce, to bring His will to pas.
Ne is thy fate, ne is thy fortune ill,
To love the prowest knight that ever was:
Therefore submit thy wayes unto His will,
And doe, by all dew meanes, thy destiny fulfill."

25 "But read," saide Glaucè, "thou Magitian,
What meanes shall she out-seeke, or what waies take?
How shall she know, how shall she finde the man?
Or what needes her to toyle, sith fates can make
Way for themselves, their purpose to pertake?"
Then Merlin thus: "Indeede the fates are firme,
And may not shrinck, though all the world do shake:
Yet ought mens good endevours them confirme,
And guyde the heavenly causes to their constant terme.[1]

26 "The man, whom heavens have ordaynd to bee
The spouse of Britomart, is Arthegall:
He wonneth[2] in the land of Fayeree,
Yet is no Fary borne, ne sib[3] at all
To Elfes, but sprong of seed terrestriall,
And whylome by false Faries stolne away,

1 *Constant terme*, fixed conclusion.
2 *Wonneth*, dwelleth.
3 *Sib*, kinsman.

XXV. 5.— *Their purpose to pertake.*] To obtain a share in the happiness which they purpose to bring to pass. C.

XXVI. 1.— *The man*, &c.] The fabulous chronicle of British kings is here resumed from the tenth canto of the second book, stanza 68. H.

Whyles yet in infant cradle he did crall;
Ne other to himselfe is knowne this day,
But that he by an Elfe was gotten of a Fay:

27 "But sooth he is the sonne of Gorloïs,
And brother unto Cador, Cornish king;
And for his warlike feates renowmed is,
From where the day out of the sea doth spring,
Untill the closure of the evening:
From thence him, firmely bound with faithfull band,
To this his native soyle thou backe shalt bring,
Strongly to ayde his countrey to withstand
The powre of forreine Paynims which invade thy land.

28 "Great ayd thereto his mighty puissaunce
And dreaded name shall give in that sad day;
Where also proofe of thy prow[1] valiaunce
Thou then shalt make, t' increase thy lovers pray:
Long time ye both in armes shall beare great sway,
Till thy wombes burden thee from them do call,
And his last fate him from thee take away;

[1] *Prow* (*preux*), brave.

XXVII. 1.—*Gorloïs.*] This Gorlois was the Duke of Cornwall. Uther Pendragon, the king of Britain, became enamored of his wife Igerna, and having, by Merlin's held, assumed the person of Gorlois, he became by her the father of Arthur; and after the death of Gorlois he married her. By Gorlois she had also a son Cador. So far the chronicles and romances. Spenser represents her as having another son by Gorlois, that is, Arthegall. H.

XXVII. 6.—*From thence.*] From Fairy land.

Too rathe[1] cut off by practise criminall
Of secrete foes, that him shall make in mischiefe fall.

29 "With thee yet shall he leave, for memory
Of his late puissaunce, his ymage dead,
That living him in all activity
To thee shall represent. He from the head
Of his coosen Constantius, without dread,
Shall take the crowne that was his fathers right,
And therewith crowne himselfe in th' others stead:
Then shall he issew forth with dreadfull might
Against his Saxon foes in bloody field to fight.

30 "Like as a lyon that in drowsie cave
Hath long time slept, himselfe so shall he shake;
And, comming forth, shall spred his banner brave
Over the troubled South, that it shall make
The warlike Mertians for feare to quake:
Thrise shall he fight with them, and twise shall win;
But the third time shall fayre accordaunce make:
And, if he then with victorie can lin,[2]
He shall his dayes with peace bring to his earthly in.[3]

31 "His sonne, hight Vortipore, shall him succeede
In kingdome, but not in felicity:

1 *Rathe*, early.
2 *Lin*, stop.
3 *Earthly in*, i. e. the grave.

XXIX. 5. — Arthur, being mortally wounded in battle, gave up the crown to Constantine, the son of Cador. Spenser pretends that the rightful successor of Arthur would have been Arthegall, who, in that case, should be older than Cador. C.

Yet shall he long time warre with happy speed,
And with great honour many batteills try;
But at the last to th' importunity
Of froward fortune shall be forst to yield:
But his sonne Malgo shall full mightily
Avenge his fathers losse with speare and shield,
And his proud foes discomfit in victorious field.

32 "Behold the man! and tell me, Britomart,
If ay more goodly creature thou didst see?
How like a gyaunt in each manly part
Beares he himselfe with portly maiestee,
That one of th' old heroës seemes to bee!
He the six Islands, comprovinciall
In auncient times unto great Britainee,
Shall to the same reduce, and to him call
Their sondry kings to doe their homage severall.

33 "All which his sonne Careticus awhile
Shall well defend, and Saxons powre suppresse;
Untill a straunger king, from unknowne soyle
Arriving, him with multitude oppresse;
Great Gormond, having with huge mightinesse
Ireland subdewd, and therein fixt his throne,
Like a swift otter, fell through emptinesse,[1]

[1] *Fell through emptinesse*, cruel through hunger.

XXXII. 6. — *The six Islands.*] These islands are Ireland, Iceland, Gothland, the Orkneys, Norway, and Dacia (Denmark). C.

XXXIII. 5. — *Great Gormond.*] Gormond was the son of an African king, and might have inherited his father's throne. But he despised to rule over a kingdom that he had not conquered. He accordingly issued an invitation to the brave youth of all heathendom

Shall overswim the sea with many one
Of his Norveyses,[1] to assist the Britons fone.[2]

34 "He in his furie all shall over-ronne,
And holy church with faithlesse handes deface,
That thy sad people, utterly fordonne,[3]
Shall to the utmost mountaines fly apace:
Was never so great waste in any place,
Nor so fowle outrage doen by living men;
For all thy citties they shall sacke and race,
And the greene grasse that groweth they shall bren,[4]
That even the wilde beast shall dy in starved den.

35 "Whiles thus thy Britons doe in languour pine,
Proud Etheldred shall from the North arise,
Serving th' ambitious will of Augustine,
And, passing Dee, with hardy enterprise,
Shall backe repulse the valiaunt Brockwell twise,
And Bangor with massácred martyrs fill;
But the third time shall rew his fool-hardise:
For Cadwan, pittying his peoples ill,
Shall stoutly him defeat, and thousand Saxons kill.

1 *Norveyses*, Norwegians.
2 *Fone*, foes.
3 *Fordonne*, undone.
4 *Bren*, burn.

to join him in a piratical expedition, and by their help made himself king of Ireland. The Norveyses (v. 9) may be regarded as a general name for his freebooting allies. According to some, Gormond was himself a Dane. C.

XXXV. 2.—*Proud Etheldred.*] In this stanza we have a glimmering of authentic history. In the beginning of the seventh century, Ethelfrith, the king of Bernicia, defeated the Welsh under Cadvan and Brocmail, near Bangor, with great slaughter. But this was not until after the death of St. Augustine, who introduced Christianity among the Anglo-Saxons. H.

36 "But, after him, Cadwallin mightily
On his sonne Edwin all those wrongs shall wreake;
Ne shall availe the wicked sorcery
Of false Pellite his purposes to breake,
But him shall slay, and on a gallowes bleak
Shall give th' enchaunter his unhappy hire:
Then shall the Britons, late dismayd and weake,
From their long vassallage gin to respire,
And on their Paynim foes avenge their ranckled ire.

37 "Ne shall he yet his wrath so mitigate,
Till both the sonnes of Edwin he have slayne,
Offricke and Osricke, twinnes unfortunate,
Both slaine in battaile upon Layburne playne,
Together with the king of Louthiane,
Hight Adin, and the king of Orkeny,
Both ioynt partakers of their fatall payne:
But Penda, fearefull of like desteny,
Shall yield himselfe his liegeman, and sweare fëalty:

38 "Him shall he make his fatall instrument
T' afflict the other Saxons unsubdewd:
He marching forth with fury insolent
Against the good King Oswald, who, indewd
With heavenly powre, and by angels reskewd,

XXXVI. 1. — *Cadwallin mightily.*] In 633, Edwin, the king of Northumbria, was defeated by Cadwallon, king of North Wales, and slain. H.

XXXVI. 4. — Pellitus was a Spanish soothsayer, who gave Edwin intelligence of Cadwallon's designs.

XXXVIII. 4. — *King Oswald.*] In 634, Cadwallon was totally defeated by Oswald, king of Northumbria, and slain in battle. H.

Al holding crosses in their hands on hye,
Shall him defeate withouten blood imbrewd:
Of which that field for endlesse memory
Shall Hevenfield be cald to all posterity.

39 "Whereat Cadwallin wroth shall forth issew,
And an huge hoste into Northumber lead,
With which he godly Oswald shall subdew,
And crowne with martiredome his sacred head:
Whose brother Oswin, daunted with like dread,
With price of silver shall his kingdome buy;
And Penda, seeking him adowne to tread,
Shall tread adowne, and doe him fowly dye;
But shall with guifts his lord Cadwallin pacify.

40 "Then shall Cadwallin die; and then the raine
Of Britons eke with him attonce shall dye;
Ne shall the good Cadwallader, with paine
Or powre, be hable it to remedy,
When the full time, prefixt by destiny,
Shal be expird of Britons regiment[1]:
For Heven itselfe shall their successe envy,
And them with plagues and murrins pestilent
Consume, till all their warlike puissaunce be spent.

41 "Yet after all these sorrowes, and huge hills
Of dying people, during eight yeares space,
Cadwallader, not yielding to his ills,
From Armoricke, where long in wretched cace
He liv'd, retourning to his native place,
Shal be by vision staide from his intent:

[1] *Regiment*, government.

For th' Heavens have decreëd to displace
The Britons for their sinnes dew punishment,
And to the Saxons over-give their government.

42 "Then woe, and woe, and everlasting woe,
Be to the Briton babe that shal be borne
To live in thraldome of his fathers foe!
Late king, now captive; late lord, now forlorne;
The worlds reproch; the cruell victors scorne;
Banisht from princely bowre to wasteful wood!
O, who shall helpe me to lament and mourne
The royall seed, the antique Troian blood,
Whose empire lenger here then ever any stood!"

43 The Damzell was full deepe empassioned
Both for his griefe, and for her peoples sake,
Whose future woes so plaine he fashioned;
And, sighing sore, at length him thus bespake:
"Ah! but will Hevens fury never slake,
Nor vengeaunce huge relent itselfe at last?
Will not long misery late mercy make,
But shall their name for ever be defaste,
And quite from of the earth their memory be raste?"

44 "Nay, but the terme," sayd he, "is limited,
That in this thraldome Britons shall abide;
And the iust revolution measured
That they as straungers shal be notifide[1]:
For twise fowre hundreth yeares shal be supplide,[2]
Ere they to former rule restor'd shal bee,
And their impórtune fates all satisfide:

[1] *Notifide*, marked, branded. [2] *Supplide*, fulfilled.

Yet, during this their most obscuritee,
Their beames shall ofte breake forth, that men them
faire may see.

45 "For Rhodoricke, whose surname shal be Great,
Shall of himselfe a brave ensample shew,
That Saxon kings his frendship shall intreat;
And Howell Dha shall goodly well indew
The salvage minds with skill of iust and trew:
Then Griffyth Conan also shall upreare
His dreaded head, and the old sparkes renew
Of native corage, that his foes shall feare
Least backe againe the kingdom he from them should
beare.

46 "Ne shall the Saxons selves all peaceably
Enioy the crowne, which they from Britons wonne
First ill, and after ruled wickedly:
For, ere two hundred yeares be full outronne,
There shall a Raven, far from rising sunne,
With his wide wings upon them fiercely fly,
And bid his faithlesse chickens[1] overonne
The fruitfull plaines, and with fell cruelty
In their avenge tread downe the victors surquedry.[2]

47 "Yet shall a Third both these and thine subdew:
There shall a Lion from the sea-bord wood

[1] *Faithlesse chickens*, heathen brood. [2] *Surquedry*, insolence.

XLV. — Roderic the Great succeeded to the principality of Wales about 843, and reigned some thirty years. Howel Dha died about 948, and Griffyth Conan in 1136. C.

XLVI. 5. — *A Raven.*] This refers to the invasion of the Danes.

XLVII. 2. — *A Lion.*] This is William of Normandy. *Neustria* was the ancient name of the northwest part of France. H.

Of Neustria come roring, with a crew
Of hungry whelpes, his battailous bold brood,
Whose clawes were newly dipt in cruddy[1] blood.
That from the Daniske tyrants head shall rend
Th' usurped crowne, as if that he were wood,[2]
And the spoile of the countrey conquered
Emongst his young ones shall divide with bountyhed.

48 "Tho, when the terme is full accomplishid,
There shall a sparke of fire, which hath longwhile
Bene in his ashes raked up and hid,
Bee freshly kindled in the fruitfull ile
Of Mona, where it lurked in exíle;
Which shall breake forth into bright burning flame,
And reach into the house that beares the stile
Of roiall maiesty and soveraine name:
So shall the Briton blood their crowne agayn reclame.

49 "Thenceforth eternall union shall be made
Betweene the nations different afore,
And sacred Peace shall lovingly persuade
The warlike minds to learne her goodly lore,
And civile armes to exercise no more:

1 *Cruddy*, curdled. 2 *Wood*, mad.

XLVIII. 2.— *There shall*, &c.] Llewellyn, the last of the native Welsh princes, made an unsuccessful resistance to Edward I., and was defeated and slain. Edward soon after created his own infant son Prince of Wales. H.

XLVIII. 9.—By the accession of Henry of Richmond to the crown. Henry, descended from the Tudors, was born in Mona, now called Anglesey. UPTON.

Then shall a royall Virgin raine, which shall
Stretch her white rod over the Belgicke shore,
And the great Castle smite so sore withall,
That it shall make him shake, and shortly learn[1] to fall:

50 "But yet the end is not ——" There Merlin stayd,
As overcomen of the spirites powre,
Or other ghastly spectacle dismayd,
That secretly he saw, yet note discoure[2]:
Which suddein fitt and halfe extatick stoure[3]
When the two fearefull wemen saw, they grew
Greatly confused in behaveoure:
At last, the fury past, to former hew
Hee turnd againe, and chearfull looks as earst did shew.

51 Then, when themselves they well instructed had
Of all that needed them to be inquird,
They both, conceiving hope of comfort glad,
With lighter hearts unto their home retird;
Where they in secret counsell close conspird,
How to effect so hard an enterprize,
And to possesse the purpose they desird:
Now this, now that, twixt them they did devize,
And diverse plots did frame to maske in strange dis guise.

1 Qu. *lean?*
2 *Note discoure*, might not discover.
3 *Stoure*, paroxysm.

XLIX. 6. — *A royall Virgin.*] This is Queen Elizabeth, who assisted the Belgian provinces, and shook the power of the king of *Castile* (v. 8).

52 At last the nourse in her fool-hardy wit
Conceivd a bold devise, and thus bespake:
"Daughter, I deeme that counsel aye most fit,
That of the time doth dew advauntage take:
Ye see that good King Uther now doth make
Strong warre upon the Paynim brethren, hight
Octa and Oza, whome hee lately brake
Beside Cayr Verolame in victorious fight,
That now all Britany doth burne in armës bright.

53 "That therefore nought our passage may empeach,[1]
Let us in feigned armes ourselves disguize,
And our weake hands (need makes good schollers) teach
The dreadful speare and shield to exercize:
Ne certes, daughter, that same warlike wize,
I weene, would you misseeme; for ye beene tall
And large of limbe t' atchieve an hard emprize;
Ne ought ye want but skil, which practize small
Wil bring, and shortly make you a mayd martiall.

54 "And, sooth, it ought your corage much inflame
To heare so often, in that royall hous,
From whence to none inferior ye came,
Bards tell of many wemen valorous,
Which have full many feats adventurous
Performd, in paragone[2] of proudest men:
The bold Bunduca, whose victorious

1 *Empeach*, prevent. 2 *Paragone*, rivalry.

LII. 5. — Uther died shortly after the battle at Verulam. The date of this enterprise would therefore be about 470, when Arthur begins to make his appearance in history.

Exployts made Rome to quake; stout Guendolen;
Renowmed Martia; and redoubted Emmilen;—

55 "And, that which more then all the rest may sway,
Late dayes ensample, which these eyes beheld:
In the last field before Menevia,
Which Uther with those forrein Pagans held,
I saw a Saxon virgin, the which feld
Great Ulfin thrise upon the bloody playne;
And, had not Carados her hand withheld
From rash revenge, she had him surely slayne;
Yet Carados himselfe from her escapt with payne."

56 "Ah! read," quoth Britomart, "how is she hight?"
"Fayre Angela," quoth she, "men do her call,
No whit lesse fayre then terrible in fight:
She hath the leading of a martiall
And mightie people, dreaded more then all
The other Saxons, which doe, for her sake
And love, themselves of her name *Angles* call.
Therefore, faire Infant, her ensample make
Unto thyselfe, and equall corage to thee take."

57 Her harty wordes so deepe into the mynd
Of the yong damzell sunke, that great desire
Of warlike armes in her forthwith they tynd,[1]

[1] *Tynd*, kindled.

LIV. 8, 9.—Guendolen is the wife of Locrine (Book II. Canto X. St. 17); Martia, the lawgiver (St. 42 of the same Canto). Who Emmilen is, is uncertain. C.

LV. 5.—*A Saxon virgin.*] "This Saxon virgin is, I believe, entirely of Spenser's own feigning."—UPTON.

And generous stout courage did inspyre,
That she resolv'd, unweeting[1] to her syre,
Advent'rous knighthood on herselfe to don;
And counseld with her nourse her maides attyre
To turne into a massy habergeon[2];
And bad her all things put in readinesse anon.

58 Th' old woman nought that needed did omit;
But all thinges did conveniently purvay.
It fortuned (so time their turne did fitt)
A band of Britons, ryding on forray
Few dayes before, had gotten a great pray
Of Saxon goods; emongst the which was seene
A goodly armour, and full rich aray,
Which long'd to Angela, the Saxon queene,
All fretted round with gold, and goodly wel beseene.[3]

59 The same, with all the other ornaments,
King Ryence caused to be hanged hy
In his chiefe church, for endlesse moniments
Of his successe and gladfull victory:
Of which herselfe avising[4] readily,
In th' evening late old Glaucè thether led
Faire Britomart, and, that same armory
Downe taking, her therein appareled
Well as she might, and with brave bauldrick garnished.

60 Beside those armes there stood a mightie speare,
Which Bladud made by magick art of yore,

1 *Unweeting*, unknown.
2 *Habergeon*, coat of mail.
3 *Beseene*, appearing.
4 *Avising*, bethinking.

LX. 2. — *Bladud.*] Of Bladud, see Book II. Canto X. Stanza 25.

And usd the same in batteill aye to beare;
Sith which it had beene here preserv'd in store,
For his great vertues proved long afore:
For never wight so fast in sell[1] could sit,
But him perforce unto the ground it bore:
Both speare she tooke and shield which hong by it;
Both speare and shield of great powre, for her purpose fit.

61 Thus when she had the Virgin all arayd,
Another harnesse which did hang thereby
About herselfe she dight,[2] that the yong mayd
She might in equall armes accompany,
And as her Squyre attend her carefully:
Tho to their ready steedes they clombe full light;
And through back waies, that none might them espy,
Covered with secret cloud of silent night,
Themselves they forth convaid, and passed forward right.

62 Ne rested they, till that to Faery lond
They came, as Merlin them directed late:
Where, meeting with this Redcrosse Knight, she fond
Of diverse thinges discourses to dilate,
But most of Arthegall and his estate.
At last their wayes so fell, that they mote part:
Then each to other, well affectionate,
Frendship professed with unfained hart:
The Redcrosse Knight diverst[3]; but forth rode Britomart.

1 *Sell*, saddle.
2 *Dight*, disposed.
3 *Diverst*, diverged, turned off.

CANTO IV.

Bold Marinell of Britomart
  Is throwne on the Rich Strond:
Faire Florimell of Arthure is
  Long followed, but not fond.

1 Where is the antique glory now become,
  That whylome wont in wemen to appeare?
  Where be the brave atchievements doen by some?
  Where be the batteilles, where the shield and speare,
  And all the conquests which them high did reare,
  That matter made for famous poets verse,
  And boastfull men so oft abasht to heare?
  Beene they all dead, and laide in dolefull herse?
Or doen they onely sleepe, and shall againe reverse[1]?

2 If they be dead, then woe is me therefore;
  But if they sleepe, O let them soone awake!
  For all too long I burne with envy sore
  To heare the warlike feates which Homere spake
  Of bold Penthesilee, which made a lake
  Of Greekish blood so ofte in Troian plaine;

[1] *Reverse*, return.

II. 5. — *Bold Penthesilee.*] Penthesilea is not mentioned by Homer. She came to the assistance of Priam during the latter years of the Trojan war. H.

But when I reade, how stout Debora strake
Proud Sisera, and how Camill' hath slaine
The huge Orsilochus, I swell with great disdaine.

3 Yet these, and all that els had puissaunce,
Cannot with noble Britomart compare,
As well for glorie of great valiaunce,
As for pure chastitie and vertue rare,
That all her goodly deedes doe well declare.
Well worthie stock, from which the branches sprong
That in late yeares so faire a blossome bare,
As thee, O Queene, the matter of my song,
Whose lignage from this Lady I derive along!

4 Who when, through speaches with the Redcrosse
Knight,
She learned had th' estate of Arthegall,
And in each point herselfe informd aright,
A frendly league of love perpetuall
She with him bound, and congé tooke withall.
Then he forth on his iourney did proceede,
To seeke adventures which mote him befall,
And win him worship through his warlike deed,
Which alwaies of his paines he made the chiefest meed.

5 But Britomart kept on her former course,
Ne ever dofte her armes; but all the way
Grew pensive through that amarous discourse,

II. 7. — *Stout Debora strake.*] This was done by Jael, and not Deborah. See Judges iv. 21. — 9. *Orsilochus*, a huge Trojan killed by Camilla, Æneid, XI. 690.

III. 8. — *O Queene.*] Queen Elizabeth.

By which the Redcrosse Knight did earst display
Her lovers shape and chevalrous aray:
A thousand thoughts she fashiond in her mind;
And in her feigning fancie did pourtray
Him, such as fittest she for love could find,
Wise, warlike, personable,[1] courteous, and kind.

6 With such selfe-pleasing thoughts her wound she fedd,
And thought so to beguile her grievous smart;
But so her smart was much more grievous bredd,
And the deepe wound more deep engord her hart,
That nought but death her dolour mote depart.[2]
So forth she rode, without repose or rest,
Searching all lands and each remotest part,
Following the guydaunce of her blinded guest,[3]
Till that to the sea-coast at length she her addrest.

7 There she alighted from her light-foot beast,
And, sitting downe upon the rocky shore,
Badd her old Squyre unlace her lofty creast:
Tho, having vewd a while the surges hore
That gainst the craggy clifts did loudly rore,
And in their raging surquedry[4] disdaynd
That the fast earth affronted[5] them so sore,
And their devouring covetize restraynd;
Thereat she sighed deepe, and after thus complaynd:

8 " Huge sea of sorrow and tempestuous griefe,
Wherein my feeble barke is tossed long,

1 *Personable*, handsome.
2 *Depart*, remove.
3 I. e. Love.
4 *Surquedry*, insolence.
5 *Affronted*, confronted.

Far from the hoped haven of reliefe,
Why doe thy cruel billowes beat so strong,
And thy moyst mountaines each on others throng,
Threatning to swallow up my fearefull lyfe?
O, doe thy cruell wrath and spightfull wrong
At length allay, and stint[1] thy stormy stryfe,
Which in these troubled bowels raignes and rageth ryfe!

9 "For els my feeble vessell, crazd and crackt
Through thy strong buffets and outrageous blowes,
Cannot endure, but needes it must be wrackt
On the rough rocks, or on the sandy shallówes,
The whiles that Love it steres, and Fortune rowes:
Love, my lewd[2] pilott, hath a restlesse minde;
And Fortune, boteswaine, no assuraunce[3] knowes;
But saile withouten starres gainst tyde and winde:
How can they other doe, sith both are bold and blinde!

10 "Thou god of windes, that raignest in the seas,
That raignest also in the continent,
At last blow up some gentle gale of ease,
The which may bring my ship, ere it be rent,
Unto the gladsome port of her intent!
Then, when I shall myselfe in safety see,
A table, for eternall moniment

1 *Stint*, stop.
2 *Lewd*, ignorant.
3 *Assuraunce*, steadiness.

X. 7.—*A table*, &c.] It was the custom among the Romans for any one who escaped shipwreck to express his gratitude by hanging up, in the temple of Neptune, a tablet or picture representing the circumstances of his danger and escape. H.

Of thy great grace and my great ieopardee,
Great Neptune, I avow to hallow unto thee!"

11 Then sighing softly sore, and inly deepe,
She shut up all her plaint in privy griefe;
(For her great courage would not let her weepe;)
Till that old Glaucè gan with sharpe repriefe
Her to restraine, and give her good reliefe
Through hope of those which Merlin had her told
Should of her name and nation be chiefe,
And fetch their being from the sacred mould
Of her immortall womb, to be in heaven enrold.

12 Thus as she her recomforted, she spyde
Where far away one, all in armour bright,
With hasty gallop towards her did ryde:
Her dolour soone she ceast, and on her dight[1]
Her helmet, to her courser mounting light:
Her former sorrow into suddein wrath
(Both coosen[2] passions of distroubled spright)
Converting, forth she beates the dusty path:
Love and despight attonce her courage kindled hath.

13 As when a foggy mist hath overcast
The face of heven and the cleare ayre engroste,[3]
The world in darkenes dwels; till that at last
The watry southwinde, from the seabord coste
Upblowing, doth disperse the vapour lo'ste,[4]
And poures itselfe forth in a stormy showre;

1 *Dight*, put.
2 *Coosen*, kindred.
3 *Engroste*, made thick.
4 *Lo'ste*, dissolved.

So the fayre Britomart, having disclo'ste[1]
Her clowdy care into a wrathfull stowre,[2]
The mist of griefe dissolv'd did into vengeance powre.

14 Eftsoones, her goodly shield addressing[3] fayre,
That mortall speare she in her hand did take,
And unto battaill did herselfe prepayre.
The Knight, approching, sternely her bespake:
"Sir Knight, that doest thy voyage rashly make
By this forbidden way in my despight,
Ne doest by others death ensample take,
I read[4] thee soone retyre, whiles thou hast might,
Least afterwards it be too late to take thy flight."

15 Ythrild with deepe disdaine of his proud threat,
She shortly thus: "Fly they, that need to fly;
Wordes fearen[5] babes: I meane not thee entreat
To passe; but maugre thee will passe or dy":
Ne lenger stayd for th' other to reply,
But with sharpe speare the rest made dearly knowne.
Strongly the straunge knight ran, and sturdily
Strooke her full on the brest, that made her downe
Decline her head, and touch her crouper with her crown.

1 I. e. developed, transmuted.
2 *Stowre*, fury.
3 *Addressing*, adjusting.
4 *Read*, advise.
5 *Fearen*, frighten.

XIV. 6. — *This forbidden way.*] In the romances of chivalry, it is not unfrequent for a knight to station himself at some particular spot, and to compel every one who passes to joust with him. H.

16 But she againe him in the shield did smite
With so fierce furie and great puissaunce,
That, through his three-square scuchin[1] percing quite
And through his mayled hauberque,[2] by mischaunce
The wicked steele through his left side did glaunce:
Him so transfixed she before her bore
Beyond his croupe, the length of all her launce;
Till, sadly soucing[3] on the sandy shore,
He tombled on[4] an heape, and wallowd in his gore.

17 Like as the sacred oxe that carelesse stands
With gilden hornes and flowry girlonds crownd,
Proud of his dying honor and deare bandes,
Whiles th' altars fume with frankincense arownd,
All suddeinly with mortall stroke astownd
Doth groveling fall, and with his streaming gore
Distaines the pillours and the holy grownd,
And the faire flowres that decked him afore:
So fell proud Marinell upon the Pretious Shore.

18 The martiall Mayd stayd not him to lament,
But forward rode, and kept her ready way
Along the strond; which, as she over-went,
She saw bestrowed all with rich aray
Of pearles and pretious stones of great assay,[5]
And all the gravell mixt with golden owre:
Whereat she wondred much, but would not stay

1 *Scuchin*, shield.
2 *Hauberque*, coat of mail.
3 *Sadly soucing*, falling heavily.
4 *On*, i. e. in.
5 *Assay*, proof, value.

For gold, or perles, or pretious stones, an howre,
But them despised all, for[1] all was in her powre.

19 Whiles thus he lay in deadly stonishment,
Tydings hereof came to his mothers eare;
His mother was the blacke-browd Cymoënt,
The daughter of great Nereus, which did beare
This warlike sonne unto an earthly peare,
The famous Dumarin; who on a day
Finding the nymph asleepe in secret wheare,[2]
As he by chaunce did wander that same way,
Was taken with her love, and by her closely lay.

20 There he this knight of her begot, whom borne,
She, of his father, Marinell did name;
And in a rocky cave as wight forlorne
Long time she fostred up, till he became
A mighty man at armes, and mickle fame
Did get through great adventures by him donne:
For never man he suffred by that same
Rich Strond to travell, whereas he did wonne,[3]
But that he must do battail with the Sea-nymphes sonne.

21 An hundred knights of honorable name
He had subdew'd, and them his vassals made:

1 *For*, notwithstanding.
2 *Wheare*, place (as in *everywhere*).
3 *Wonne*, dwell.

XX. 2.—*Marinell.*] Upton conjectures that Lord Howard, the Lord High Admiral of England, is imaged under the character of Marinell, and that there is, in Stanza 22, an allusion to the rich prizes taken by him from the Spaniards. H.

That through all Farie Lond his noble fame
Now blazed was, and feare did all invade,
That none durst passen through that perilous glade:
And, to advaunce his name and glory more,
Her sea-god syre she dearely did perswade
T' endow her sonne with threasure and rich store
Bove all the sonnes that were of earthly wombes ybore.

22 The god did graunt his daughters deare demaund,
To doen his nephew[1] in all riches flow:
Eftsoones his heaped waves he did commaund
Out of their hollow bosome forth to throw
All the huge threasure, which the sea below
Had in his greedy gulfe devoured deepe,
And him enriched through the overthrow
And wreckes of many wretches, which did weepe
And often wayle their wealth which he from them did keepe.

23 Shortly upon that shore there heaped was
Exceeding riches and all pretious things,
The spoyle of all the world; that it did pas
The wealth of th' East, and pompe of Persian kings:
Gold, amber, yvorie, perles, owches,[2] rings,
And all that els was pretious and deare,
The sea unto him voluntary brings;
That shortly he a great lord did appeare,
As was in all the lond of Faery, or else wheare.

24 Thereto he was a doughty dreaded knight,
Tryde often to the scath of many deare,[3]

[1] *Nephew*, grandson. [2] *Owches*, jewels. [3] *Deare*, dearly.

That none in equall armes him matchen might:
The which his mother seeing gan to feare
Least his too haughtie hardines might reare
Some hard mishap in hazard of his life:
Forthy[1] she oft him counseld to forbeare
The bloody batteill, and to stirre up strife,
But after all his warre to rest his wearie knife:

25 And, for his more assuraunce, she inquir'd
One day of Proteus by his mighty spell
(For Proteus was with prophecy inspir'd)
Her deare sonnes destiny to her to tell,
And the sad end of her sweet Marinell:
Who, through foresight of his eternall skill,
Bad her from womankind to keepe him well;
For of a woman he should have much ill;
A Virgin straunge and stout him should dismay[2] or kill.

26 Forthy she gave him warning every day
The love of women not to entertaine;
A lesson too too[3] hard for living clay,
From love in course of nature to refraine!
Yet he his mothers lore did well retaine,
And ever from fayre ladies love did fly;
Yet many ladies fayre did oft complaine,
That they for love of him would algates[4] dy:
Dy who so list for him, he was Loves enimy.

1 *Forthy*, therefore.
2 *Dismay*, deprive of strength, overpower.
3 *Too too*, exceeding.
4 *Algates*, by all means, absolutely.

27 But ah! who can deceive his destiny,
Or weene by warning to avoyd his fate?
That, when he sleepes in most security
And safest seemes, him soonest doth amate,[1]
And findeth dew effect or soone or late;
So feeble is the powre of fleshly arme!
His mother bad him wemens love to hate,
For she of womans force did feare no harme;
So weening to have arm'd him, she did quite dis-
arme.

28 This was that woman, this that deadly wownd,
That Proteus prophecide should him dismay;
The which his mother vainely did expownd
To be hart-wownding love, which should assay
To bring her sonne unto his last decay.
So ticle[2] be the termes of mortall state
And full of subtile sophismes, which doe play
With double sences, and with false debate,
T' approve the unknowen purpose of eternall fate.

29 Too trew the famous Marinell it fownd;
Who, through late triall, on that Wealthy Strond
Inglorious now lies in sencelesse swownd,
Through heavy stroke of Britomartis hond.
Which when his mother deare did understond,
And heavy tidings heard, whereas she playd
Amongst her watry sisters by a pond,
Gathering sweete daffadillyes, to have made
Gay girlonds from the sun their forheads fayr to shade,

[1] *Amate*, confound. [2] *Ticle*, unstable.

30 Eftesoones[1] both flowres and girlonds far away
Shee flong, and her faire deawy locks yrent;
To sorrow huge she turnd her former play,
And gamesom merth to grievous dreriment[2]:
Shee threw herselfe downe on the continent,[3]
Ne word did speake, but lay as in a swowne,
Whiles al her sisters did for her lament
With yelling outcries, and with shrieking sowne;
And every one did teare her girlond from her crowne.

31 Soone as shee up out of her deadly fitt
Arose, shee bad her charett to be brought;
And all her sisters, that with her did sitt,
Bad eke attonce their charetts to be sought:
Tho, full of bitter griefe and pensife thought,
She to her wagon clombe; clombe all the rest,
And forth together went, with sorow fraught:
The waves obedient to theyr beheast
Them yielded ready passage, and their rage surceast.

32 Great Neptune stoode amazed at their sight,
Whiles on his broad rownd backe they softly slid,
And eke himselfe mournd at their mournfull plight,
Yet wist not what their wailing ment, yet did,
For great compassion of their sorow, bid
His mighty waters to them buxome[4] bee:
Eftesoones the roaring billowes still abid,[5]
And all the griesly monsters of the see
Stood gaping at their gate,[6] and wondred them to see.

1 *Eftesoones*, immediately.
2 *Dreriment*, sorrow.
3 *Continent*, land.
4 *Buxome*, yielding.
5 *Abid*, abode.
6 *Gate*, procedure.

33 A teme of dolphins raunged in aray
Drew the smooth charett of sad Cymoënt;
They were all taught by Triton to obay
To the long raynes at her commaundëment:
As swifte as swallowes on the waves they went,
That their brode flaggy finnes no fome did reare,
Ne bubling rowndell[1] they behinde them sent;
The rest, of other fishes drawen weare,
Which with their finny oars the swelling sea did
sheare.

34 Soone as they bene arriv'd upon the brim
Of the Rich Strond, their charets they forlore,[2]
And let their temed fishes softly swim
Along the margent of the fomy shore,
Least they their finnes should bruze, and surbate[3]
sore
Their tender feete upon the stony grownd:
And coming to the place, where all in gore
And cruddy[4] blood enwallowed they fownd
The lucklesse Marinell lying in deadly swownd,

35 His mother swowned thrise, and the third time
Could scarce recovered bee out of her paine;
Had she not beene devoide of mortall slime,
Shee should not then have bene relyv'd[5] againe:
But, soone as life recovered had the raine,
Shee made so piteous mone and deare wayment,[6]

1 *Rowndell*, globule.
2 *Forlore*, left.
3 *Surbate*, batter.
4 *Cruddy*, curdled.
5 *Relyv'd*, brought to life.
6 *Wayment*, lamentation.

That the hard rocks could scarse from tears refraine:
And all her sister nymphes with one consent
Supplide her sobbing breaches[1] with sad complement.

36 "Deare image of my selfe," she sayd, "that is
The wretched sonne of wretched mother borne,
Is this thine high advauncement? O, is this
Th' immortall name, with which thee yet unborne
Thy gransire Nereus promist to adorne?
Now lyest thou of life and honor refte;
Now lyest thou a lumpe of earth forlorne;
Ne of thy late life memory is lefte;
Ne can thy irrevocable desteny be wefte[2]!

37 "Fond Proteus, father of false prophecis!
And they more fond that credit to thee give!
Not this the worke of womans hand ywis,[3]
That so deepe wound through these deare members drive.
I feared love; but they that love doe live;
But they that dye doe nether love nor hate:
Nath'lesse to thee thy folly I forgive;
And to myselfe, and to accursed fate,
The guilt I doe ascribe: deare wisedom bought too late!

38 "O! what availes it of immortall seed
To beene ybredd and never borne to dye?

[1] I. e. the intervals of her sobbing.
[2] *Wefte*, waived, or avoided.
[3] *Ywis*, surely.

Farre better I it deeme to die with speed,
Then waste in woe and waylfull miserye:
Who dyes, the utmost dolor doth abye[1];
But who that lives is lefte to waile his losse:
So life is losse, and death felicity:
Sad life worse then glad death; and greater crosse
To see frends grave, then dead the grave self to engrosse.[2]

39 "But if the heavens did his dayes envíe,
And my short blis maligne,[3] yet mote they well
Thus much afford me, ere that he did die,
That the dim eies of my deare Marinell
I mote have closed, and him bed farewell,
Sith other offices for mother meet
They would not graunt ———
Yett, maulgre them, farewell, my sweetest sweet!
Farewell, my sweetest sonne, sith we no more shall meet!"

40 Thus when they all had sorowed their fill,
They softly gan to search his griesly wownd:
And, that they might him handle more at will,
They him disarmd; and, spredding on the grownd
Their watchet[4] mantles frindgd with silver rownd,
They softly wipt away the gelly blood
From th' orifice; which having well upbownd,

1 *Abye*, abide.
2 *Engrosse*, occupy.
3 *Maligne*, grudge.
4 *Watchet*, pale blue.

XXXIX. 9. — So the Second Edition. First Edition, "till we againe may meet," — an expression not appropriate to a Pagan.

They pourd in soveraine balme and nectar good,
Good both for erthly med'cine and for hevenly food.

41 Tho, when the lilly-handed Liagore
(This Liagore whilome had learned skill
In leaches craft, by great Apolloes lore,
Sith her whilome upon high Pindus hill
He loved, and at last her wombe did fill
With hevenly seed, whereof wise Pæon sprong)
Did feele his pulse, shee knew there staied still
Some litle life his feeble sprites emong;
Which to his mother told, despeyre she from her flong.

42 Tho, up him taking in their tender hands,
They easely unto her charett beare:
Her teme at her commaundement quiet stands,
Whiles they the corse into her wagon reare,
And strowe with flowres the lamentable beare:
Then all the rest into their coches clim,
And through the brackish waves their passage shear[1];
Upon great Neptunes necke they softly swim,
And to her watry chamber swiftly carry him.

43 Deepe in the bottome of the sea, her bowre[2]
Is built of hollow billowes heaped hye,
Like to thicke clouds that threat a stormy showre,
And vauted[3] all within like to the skye,
In which the gods doe dwell eternally:

1 *Shear*, cut.
2 *Bowre*, chamber, dwelling.
3 *Vauted*, vaulted.

There they him laide in easy couch well dight,[1]
And sent in haste for Tryphon, to apply
Salves to his wounds, and medicines of might:
For Tryphon of sea-gods the soveraine leach is hight.

44 The whiles the nymphes sitt all about him rownd,
Lamenting his mishap and heavy plight;
And ofte his mother, vewing his wide wownd,
Cursed the hand that did so deadly smight
Her dearest sonne, her dearest harts delight:
But none of all those curses overtooke
The warlike Maide, th' ensample[2] of that might;
But fairely well shee thryvd, and well did brooke[3]
Her noble deeds, ne her right course for ought forsooke.

45 Yet did false Archimage her still pursew,
To bring to passe his mischievous intent,
Now that he had her singled from the crew
Of courteous knights, the Prince and Fary gent,[4]
Whom late in chace of beauty excellent
Shee lefte, pursewing that same foster[5] strong;
Of whose fowle outrage they impatient,

1 *Dight*, arranged.
2 I. e. who had given this specimen of her power.
3 I. e. she suffered no evil in consequence of her exploit.
4 *Gent*, noble.
5 *Foster*, forester.

XLIII. 9. — *For Tryphon of sea-gods*, &c.] Tryphon's medical diploma is of Spenser's own conferring. There is no "leech of the sea-gods" in classical mythology. H.

XLIV. 5. — *Her dearest harts delight.*] This portion of the narrative is continued in Book IV. Canto XI. H.

XLV. 4. — *The Prince and Fary gent.*] Prince Arthur and Sir Guyon. The narrative is resumed from Canto I. Stanza 18. H.

And full of firy zele, him followed long,
To reskew her from shame, and to revenge her wrong.

46 Through thick and thin, through mountains and
through playns,
Those two gret champions did attonce pursew
The fearefull Damzell with incessant payns;
Who from them fled, as light-foot hare from vew
Of hunter swifte and sent[1] of howndës trew.
At last they came unto a double way;
Where, doubtfull which to take, her to reskéw,
Themselves they did dispart, each to assay
Whether more happy were to win so goodly pray.

47 But Timias, the Princes gentle squyre,
That Ladies love unto his lord forlent,[2]
And with proud envy and indignant yre
After that wicked foster fiercely went.
So beene they three three sondry wayes ybent:
But fayrest fortune to the Prince befell;
Whose chaunce it was, that soone he did repent,
To take that way in which that Damozell
Was fledd afore, affraid of him as feend of hell.

48 At last of her far of he gained vew:
Then gan he freshly pricke his fomy steed,
And ever as he nigher to her drew,
So evermore he did increase his speed,
And of each turning still kept wary heed;
Alowd to her he oftentimes did call,

[1] *Sent*, scent. [2] *Forlent*, gave up.

To doe away vaine doubt and needlesse dreed:
Full myld to her he spake, and oft let fall
Many meeke wordes to stay and comfort her withall.

49 But nothing might relent[1] her hasty flight;
So deepe the deadly feare of that foule swaine
Was earst impressed in her gentle spright:
Like as a fearefull dove, which through the raine[2]
Of the wide ayre her way does cut amaine,
Having farre off espyde a tassell gent,
Which after her his nimble winges doth straine,
Doubleth her hast for feare to bee for-hent,[3]
And with her pineons cleaves the liquid firmament.

50 With no lesse hast, and eke with no lesse dreed,
That fearefull Ladie fledd from him that ment
To her no evill thought nor evill deed;
Yet former feare of being fowly shent[4]
Carried her forward with her first intent:
And though, oft looking backward, well she vewde
Herselfe freed from that foster insolent,
And that it was a knight which now her sewde,
Yet she no lesse the Knight feard then that Villein rude.

1 *Relent*, slacken. 2 *Raine*, realm.
3 *For-hent*, taken, to her destruction. (Folios, *fore*-hent.)
4 *Shent*, outraged.

XLIX. 6. — *Tassell gent.*] The tassel or tercel is the male of the goshawk. The *tassel-gent* is commonly said to be so called on account of its tractability; but it more probably receives the name from those qualities which distinguish it from the base, unserviceable breed of kestrels and stannels. C.

51 His uncouth[1] shield and straunge armes her dismayd,
Whose like in Faery Lond were seldom seene;
That fast she from him fledd, no lesse afrayd
Then of wilde beastes if she had chased beene:
Yet he her followd still with corage keene
So long, that now the golden Hesperus
Was mounted high in top of heaven sheene,
And warnd his other brethren ioyeous
To light their blessed lamps in Ioves eternall hous.

52 All suddeinly dim wox the dampish ayre,
And griesly shadowes covered heaven bright,
That now with thousand starres was decked fayre:
Which when the Prince beheld, a lothfull sight,
And that perforce, for want of lenger light,
He mote surceasse his suit and lose the hope
Of his long labour; he gan fowly wyte[2]
His wicked fortune that had turnd aslope,
And cursed Night that reft from him so goodly scope.[3]

53 Tho, when her wayes he could no more descry,
But to and fro at disaventure strayd;
Like as a ship, whose lodestar suddeinly
Covered with cloudes her pilott hath dismayd;
His wearisome pursuit perforce he stayd,
And from his loftie steed dismounting low

1 *Uncouth*, unknown, strange.
2 *Wyte*, reproach.
3 *Scope*, i. e. prospect.

LI. 1.—*His uncouth shield.*] Prince Arthur's shield was covered with a veil.

Did let him forage: downe himselfe he layd
Upon the grassy ground to sleepe a throw[1];
The cold earth was his couch, the hard steele his pillów.

54 But gentle Sleepe envyde him any rest;
Instead thereof sad sorow and disdaine
Of his hard hap did vexe his noble brest,
And thousand fancies bett his ydle brayne
With their light wings, the sights of semblants[2] vaine:
Oft did he wish that Lady faire mote bee
His Faery Queene, for whom he did complaine;
Or that his Faery Queene were such as shee:
And ever hasty Night he blamed bitterlie:

55 "Night! thou foule mother of annoyaunce sad,
Sister of heavie Death, and nourse of Woe,
Which wast begot in heaven, but for thy bad
And brutish shape thrust downe to hell below,
Where, by the grim floud of Cocytus slow,
Thy dwelling is in Herebus black hous,
(Black Herebus, thy husband, is the foe
Of all the gods,) where thou ungratious
Halfe of thy dayes doest lead in horrour hideous:

56 "What had th' Eternall Maker need of thee
The world in his continuall course to keepe,
That doest all thinges deface, ne lettest see
The beautie of his worke? Indeed, in sleepe

[1] *Throw*, a while. [2] *Semblants*, phantoms.

The slouthfull body that doth love to steep
His lustlesse[1] limbes, and drowne his baser mind,
Doth praise thee oft, and oft from Stygian deepe
Calles thee, his goddesse, in his errour blind,
And great dame Natures handmaide chearing every
kind.

57 " But well I wote that to an heavy hart
Thou art the roote and nourse of bitter cares,
Breeder of new, renewer of old smarts:
Instead of rest thou lendest rayling[2] teares;
Instead of sleepe thou sendest troublous feares
And dreadfull visions, in the which alive
The dreary image of sad Death appeares:
So from the wearie spirit thou doest drive
Desired rest, and men of happinesse deprive.

58 " Under thy mantle black there hidden lye
Light-shonning Thefte, and Traiterous Intent,
Abhorred Bloodshed, and vile Felony,
Shamefull Deceipt, and Daunger imminent,
Fowle Horror, and eke hellish Dreriment[3]:
All these I wote in thy protection bee,
And light doe shonne, for feare of being shent[4]:
For light ylike is loth'd of them and thee:
And all, that lewdnesse[5] love, doe hate the light to see.

59 " For day discovers all dishonest wayes,
And sheweth each thing as it is in deed:

1 *Lustlesse*, listless.
2 *Rayling*, trickling.
3 *Dreriment*, sorrow.
4 *Shent*, shamed.
5 *Lewdnesse*, wickedness generally.

The prayses of High God he faire displayes,
And His large bountie rightly doth areed[1]:
Dayes dearest children be the blessed seed
Which Darknesse shall subdue and heaven win:
Truth is his daughter; he her first did breed
Most sacred virgin without spot of sinne:
Our life is day; but death with darknesse doth begin.

60 "O, when will Day then turne to me againe,
And bring with him his long-expected light!
O Titan! hast to reare thy ioyous waine;
Speed thee to spred abroad thy beamës bright,
And chace away this too long lingring Night;
Chace her away, from whence she came, to hell:
She, she it is, that hath me done despight:
There let her with the damned spirits dwell,
And yield her rowme to Day, that can it governe well."

61 Thus did the Prince that wearie night outweare
In restlesse anguish and unquiet paine;
And earely, ere the Morrow did upreare
His deawy head out of the ocean maine,
He up arose, as halfe in great disdaine,
And clombe unto his steed. So forth he went
With heavy looke and lumpish pace, that plaine
In him bewraid great grudge and maltalent[2]:
His steed eke seemd t' apply[3] his steps to his intent.

[1] *Areed*, set forth.
[2] *Maltalent*, ill-will, spleen.
[3] *Apply*, ply; to accommodate his pace.

CANTO V.

Prince Arthur heares of Florimell:
Three fosters[1] Timias wound;
Belphebe findes him almost dead,
And reareth out of swownd.

1 WONDER it is to see in diverse mindes
How diversly Love doth his pageaunts play,
And shewes his powre in variable kindes[2]:
The baser wit, whose ydle thoughts alway
Are wont to cleave unto the lowly clay,
It stirreth up to sensuall desire,
And in lewd slouth to wast his carelesse day;
But in brave sprite it kindles goodly fire,
That to all high desert and honour doth aspire.

2 Ne suffereth it uncomely Idlenesse
In his free thought to build her sluggish nest;
Ne suffereth it thought of ungentlenesse
Ever to creepe into his noble brest;
But to the highest and the worthiest
Lifteth it up that els would lowly fall:
It lettes not fall, it lettes it not to rest;
It lettes not scarse this Prince to breath at all,
But to his first poursuit him forward still doth call.

[1] *Fosters*, foresters. [2] *Variable kindes*, various sorts of men.

II. 9. — *But to his first poursuit*, &c.] See Book I. Canto IX. Stanza 15.

3 Who long time wandred through the forest wyde
To finde some issue thence ; till that at last
He met a Dwarfe that seemed terrifyde
With some late perill which he hardly past,
Or other accident which him aghast[1];
Of whom he asked, whence he lately came,
And whether now he traveiled so fast:
For sore he swat, and, ronning through that same
Thicke forest, was bescracht, and both his feet nigh lame.

4 Panting for breath, and almost out of hart,
The Dwarfe him answerd: "Sir, ill mote I stay
To tell the same. I lately did depart
From Faery Court, where I have many a day
Served a gentle lady of great sway
And high accompt throughout all Elfin Land,
Who lately left the same, and tooke this way:
Her now I seeke ; and if ye understand
Which way she fared hath, good Sir, tell out of hand."[2]

5 "What mister wight,"[3] saide he, "and how arayd?"
"Royally clad," quoth he, "in cloth of gold,
As meetest may beseeme a noble mayd;
Her faire lockes in rich circlet be enrold,
A fayrer wight did never sunne behold;

[1] *Aghast*, terrified.
[2] *Out of hand*, immediately.
[3] *Mister wight*, sort of person.

III. 3. — *He met a Dwarfe.*] Who this dwarf was is told us in Book V. Canto II. Stanza 3.

And on a palfrey rydes more white then snow,
Yet she herselfe is whiter manifold;
The surest signe, whereby ye may her know,
Is, that she is the fairest wight alive, I trow."

6 "Now certes, Swaine," saide he, "such one, I weene,
Fast flying through this forest from her fo,
A foule, ill-favoured foster, I have seene;
Herselfe, well as I might, I reskewd tho,
But could not stay; so fast she did foregoe,[1]
Carried away with wings of speedy feare."
"Ah! dearest God," quoth he, "that is great woe,
And wondrous ruth to all that shall it heare:
But can ye read,[2] Sir, how I may her finde, or where?"

7 "Perdy, me lever were[3] to weeten that,"
Saide he, "then ransome of the richest knight,
Or all the good that ever yet I gat:
But froward fortune, and too forward[4] night,
Such happinesse did, maulgre,[5] to me spight,[6]
And fro me reft both life and light attone.[7]
But, Dwarfe, aread what is that Lady bright
That through this forrest wandreth thus alone;
For of her errour[8] straunge I have great ruth and mone."

1 *Foregoe*, go forward.
2 *Read*, say.
3 *Me lever were*, I would rather.
4 I. e. coming on too fast.
5 *Maulgre*, curse on it.
6 *Spight*, grudge.
7 *Attone*, at once.
8 *Errour*, wandering.

8 "That Ladie is," quoth he, "whereso she bee,
The bountiest[1] virgin and most debonaire
That ever living eye, I weene, did see:
Lives none this day that may with her compare
In stedfast chastitie and vertue rare,
The goodly ornaments of beautie bright;
And is ycleped Florimell the Fayre,
Faire Florimell belov'd of many a knight,
Yet she loves none but one, that Marinell is hight.

9 "A Sea-nymphes sonne, that Marinell is hight,
Of my deare dame is loved dearely well;
In other none, but him, she sets delight;
All her delight is set on Marinell;
But he sets nought at all by Florimell:
For[2] ladies love his mother long ygoe
Did him, they say, forwarne through sacred spell:
But fame now flies, that of a forreine foe
He is yslaine, which is the ground of all our woe.

10 "Five daies there be since he (they say) was slaine,
And fowre since Florimell the court forwent,[3]
And vowed never to returne againe
Till him alive or dead she did invent.[4]
Therefore, faire Sir, for love of knighthood gent[5]
And honour of trew ladies, if ye may
By your good counsell, or bold hardiment,[6]
Or succour her, or me direct the way,
Do one or other good, I you most humbly pray:

1 *Bountiest*, best.
2 *For*, against.
3 *Forwent*, left.
4 *Invent*, find.
5 *Gent*, noble.
6 *Hardiment*, courage.

11 "So may ye gaine to you full great renowme
Of all good ladies through the world so wide,
And haply in her hart finde highest rowme[1]
Of whom ye seeke to be most magnifide!
At least eternall meede shall you abide."
To whom the Prince: "Dwarfe, comfort to thee take;
For, till thou tidings learne what her betide,
I here avow thee never to forsake:
Ill weares he armes, that nill[2] them use for ladies sake."

12 So with the Dwarfe he backe retourn'd againe,
To seeke his Lady, where he mote her finde;
But by the way he greatly gan complaine
The want of his good Squire late left behinde,
For whom he wondrous pensive grew in minde,
For doubt of daunger which mote him betide;
For him he loved above all mankinde,
Having him trew and faithfull ever tride,[3]
And bold, as ever squyre that waited by knights side:

13 Who all this while full hardly was assayd
Of deadly daunger which to him betidd:
For, whiles his Lord pursewd that noble Mayd,
After that foster fowle he fiercely ridd,
To bene avenged of the shame he did
To that faire Damzell. Him he chaced long

1 *Rowme*, place.
2 *Nill*, will not.
3 *Tride*, proved.

XII. 4. — *Late left behinde.*] See Canto IV. Stanza 47.

Through the thicke woods wherein he would have hid
His shamefull head from his avengement strong,
And oft him threatned death for his outrageous wrong.

14 Nathlesse the villein sped himselfe so well,
Whether through swiftnesse of his speedie beast,
Or knowledge of those woods where he did dwell,
That shortly he from daunger was releast,
And out of sight escaped at the least;
Yet not escaped from the dew reward
Of his bad deedes, which daily he increast,
Ne ceased not, till him oppressed hard
The heavie plague that for such leachours is prepard.

15 For, soone as he was vanisht out of sight,
His coward courage gan emboldned bee,
And cast t' avenge him of that fowle despight
Which he had borne of his bold enimee:
Tho to his brethren came, (for they were three
Ungratious children of one gracelesse syre,)
And unto them complayned how that he
Had used beene of that foole-hardie Squyre:
So them with bitter words he stird to bloodie yre.

16 Forthwith themselves with their sad instruments
Of spoyle and murder they gan arme bylive,[1]
And with him foorth into the forrest went
To wreake the wrath, which he did earst revive
In their sterne brests, on him which late did drive

[1] *Bylive*, quickly.

Their brother to reproch and shamefull flight:
For they had vow'd that never he alive
Out of that forest should escape their might;
Vile rancour their rude harts had fild with such despight.

17 Within that wood there was a covert glade,
Foreby[1] a narrow foord, to them well knowne,
Through which it was uneath[2] for wight to wade,
And now by fortune it was overflowne:
By that same way they knew that Squyre unknowne
Mote algates[3] passe; forthy[4] themselves they set
There in await with thicke woods overgrowne,
And all the while their malice they did whet
With cruell threats his passage through the ford to let.[5]

18 It fortuned, as they devized had,
The gentle Squyre came ryding that same way,
Unweeting of their wile and treason bad,
And through the ford to passen did assay;
But that fierce foster, which late fled away,
Stoutly foorth stepping on the further shore,
Him boldly bad his passage there to stay,
Till he had made amends, and full restore
For all the damage which he had him doen afore.

19 With that, at him a quiv'ring dart he threw
With so fell force, and villeinous despite,
That through his haberieon[6] the forkehead flew,

1 *Foreby*, near to.
2 *Uneath*, not easy.
3 *Algates*, at all events.
4 *Forthy*, therefore.
5 *Let*, hinder.
6 *Haberieon*, coat of mail.

And through the linked mayles empierced quite,
But had no powre in his soft flesh to bite:
That stroke the hardy Squire did sore displease,
But more that him he could not come to smite;
For by no meanes the high banke he could sease,
But labour'd long in that deepe ford with vaine disease.[1]

20 And still the foster with his long bore-speare
Him kept from landing at his wished will:
Anone one sent out of the thicket neare
A cruell shaft headed with deadly ill,
And fethered with an unlucky quill;
The wicked steele stayd not till it did light
In his left thigh, and deepely did it thrill[2];
Exceeding griefe that wound in him empight,[3]
But more that with his foes he could not come to fight.

21 At last, through wrath and vengeaunce making way,
He on the bancke arryvd with mickle payne;
Where the third brother him did sore assay,
And drove at him with all his might and mayne
A forest-bill, which both his hands did strayne;
But warily he did avoide the blow,
And with his speare requited him agayne,
That both his sides were thrilled with the throw,[4]
And a large streame of blood out of the wound did flow.

[1] *Disease*, uneasiness.
[2] *Thrill*, pierce.
[3] *Empight*, infixed.
[4] *Throw*, thrust.

22 He, tombling downe, with gnashing teeth did bite
The bitter earth, and bad to lett him in
Into the balefull house of endlesse night,
Where wicked ghosts doe waile their former sin.
Tho gan the battaile freshly to begin;
For nathëmore for that spectăcle bad
Did th' other two their cruell vengeaunce blin,[1]
But both attonce on both sides him bestad,[2]
And load upon him layd, his life for to have had.

23 Tho when that villayn he aviz'd,[3] which late
Affrighted had the fairest Florimell,
Full of fiers fury and indignant hate
To him he turned, and with rigor fell
Smote him so rudely on the pannikell,[4]
That to the chin he clefte his head in twaine:
Downe on the ground his carkas groveling fell;
His sinfull sowle with desperate disdaine
Out of her fleshly ferme [5] fled to the place of paine.

24 That seeing now the only last of three,
Who [6] with that wicked shafte him wounded had,
Trembling with horror, (as that did foresee
The fearefull end of his avengement sad,
Through which he follow should his brethren bad,)
His bootelesse bow in feeble hand upcaught,

1 *Blin*, cease.
2 *Bestad*, beset.
3 *Aviz'd*, perceived.
4 *Pannikell*, brain-pan, skull.
5 *Ferme*, lodging.
6 I. e. he who.

XXII. 9.—*And load*, &c.] Laid a load or weight of blows upon him in order to take his life. H.

And therewith shott an arrow at the lad;
Which, fayntly fluttring, scarce his helmet raught,
And glauncing fel to ground, but him annoyed naught.

25 With that he would have fled into the wood;
But Timias him lightly overhent,[1]
Right as he entring was into the flood,
And strooke at him with force so violent,
That headlesse him into the foord he sent;
The carcas with the streame was carried downe,
But th' head fell backeward on the continent.[2]
So mischief fel upon the meaners crowne[3]:
They three be dead with shame; the Squire lives with renowne:

26 He lives, but takes small ioy of his renowne;
For of that cruell wound he bled so sore,
That from his steed he fell in deadly swowne;
Yet still the blood forth gusht in so great store,
That he lay wallowd all in his owne gore.
Now God thee keepe! thou gentlest Squire alive,
Els shall thy loving lord thee see no more;
But both of comfort him thou shalt deprive,
And eke thyselfe of honor which thou didst atchive.

27 Providence hevenly passeth living thought,
And doth for wretched mens reliefe make way;
For loe! great grace or fortune thether brought
Comfort to him that comfortlesse now lay.

1 *Overhent*, overtook. 2 *Continent*, dry land.
3 I. e. upon the head of those that meant it.

In those same woods ye well remember may
How that a noble hunteresse did wonne,[1]
Shee, that base Braggadochio did affray,
And made him fast out of the forest ronne;
Belphœbe was her name, as faire as Phæbus sunne.

28 She on a day, as shee pursewd the chace
Of some wilde beast, which with her arrowes keene
She wounded had, the same along did trace
By tract of blood, which she had freshly seene
To have besprinckled all the grassy greene;
By the great pérsue which she there perceav'd,
Well hoped shee the beast engor'd[2] had beene,
And made more haste the life to have bereav'd:
But ah! her expectation greatly was deceav'd.

29 Shortly she came whereas that woefull Squire
With blood deformed lay in deadly swownd;
In whose faire eyes, like lamps of quenched fire,
The christall humor stood congealed rownd;
His locks, like faded leaves fallen to grownd,
Knotted with blood in bounches rudely ran;
And his sweete lips, on which before that stownd[3]

1 *Wonne*, dwell.
2 *Engor'd*, shot through.
3 *Stownd*, (sad) hour.

XXVII. 5. — *Ye well remember may.*] See Book II. Canto III. Stanza 21.

XXVIII. 6. — *Pérsue.*] If this word is allowed to stand, it must be explained *pursuit*, i. e. the trampling of dogs. But it is not improbably a misprint for *issue*, the *per* being caught by the printer's eye from *perceav'd*. C.

The bud of youth to blossome faire began,
Spoild of their rosy red, were woxen pale and wan.

30 Saw never living eie more heavy sight,
That could have made a rocke of stone to rew,[1]
Or rive in twaine: which when that Lady bright,
Besides [2] all hope, with melting eies did vew,
All suddeinly abasht shee chaunged hew,
And with sterne horror backward gan to start:
But, when shee better him beheld, shee grew
Full of soft passion and unwonted smart:
The point of pitty perced through her tender hart.

31 Meekely shee bowed downe, to weete if life
Yett in his frosen members did remaine;
And, feeling by his pulses beating rife [3]
That the weake sowle her seat did yett retaine,
She cast to comfort him with busy paine:
His double-folded necke she reard upright,
And rubd his temples and each trembling vaine;
His mayled haberieon [4] she did undight,
And from his head his heavy burganet [5] did light.

32 Into the woods thenceforth in haste shee went,
To seeke for hearbes that mote him remedy;
For shee of herbes had great intendiment,[6]
Taught of the nymphe which from her infancy
Her nourced had in trew nobility:

1 *Rew*, pity.
2 *Besides*, without.
3 *Rife*, frequently.
4 *Haberieon*, coat of mail.
5 *Burganet*, helmet.
6 *Intendiment*, knowledge.

There, whether yt divine Tobacco were,
Or Panachæa, or Polygony,
Shee fownd, and brought it to her patient deare,
Who al this while lay bleding out his hart-blood neare.

33 The soveraine weede betwixt two marbles plaine[1]
Shee pownded small, and did in peeces bruze;
And then atweene her lilly handës twaine
Into his wound the iuice thereof did scruze[2];
And round about, as she could well it uze,
The flesh therewith shee suppled[3] and did steepe,
T' abate all spasme and soke the swelling bruze;
And, after having searcht the intuse[4] deepe,
She with her scarf did bind the wound, from cold to keepe.

34 By this he had sweet life recur'd[5] agayne,
And, groning inly deepe, at last his eies,
His watry eies, drizling like deawy rayne,
He up gan lifte toward the azure skies,
From whence descend all hopelesse[6] remedies:
Therewith he sigh'd; and, turning him aside,
The goodly Maide full of divinities
And gifts of heavenly grace he by him spide,
Her bow and gilden quiver lying him beside.

1 *Plaine*, smooth.
2 *Scruze*, squeeze.
3 *Suppled*, softened.
4 *Intuse*, contusion.
5 *Recur'd*, recovered.
6 *Hopelesse*, unexpected.

XXXII. 6.—*Divine Tobacco.*] Warton conjectures that this honorable mention of tobacco was intended as a compliment to Sir Walter Raleigh, by whom it had shortly before been introduced into England. H.

35 "Mercy! deare Lord," said he, "what grace is this
That thou hast shewed to me, sinfull wight,
To send thine angell from her bowre of blis
To comfort me in my distressed plight!
Angell, or goddesse, doe I call thee right?
What service may I doe unto thee meete,
That hast from darkenes me returnd to light,
And with thy hevenly salves and med'cines sweete
Hast drest my sinfull wounds! I kisse thy blessed
feete."

36 Thereat she blushing said: "Ah! gentle Squire,
Nor goddesse I, nor angell, but the mayd
And daughter of a woody nymphe, desire
No service but thy safëty and ayd;
Which if thou gaine, I shal be well apayd.[1]
Wee mortall wights, whose lives and fortunes bee
To commun accidents stil open layd,
Are bownd with commun bond of fraïltee,
To succor wretched wights whom we captíved see."

37 By this her damzells, which the former chace
Had undertaken after her, arryv'd,
As did Belphœbe, in the bloody place,
And thereby deemd the beast had bene depriv'd
Of life, whom late their ladies arrow ryv'd[2]:
Forthy[3] the bloody tract they followd fast,
And every one to ronne the swiftest stryv'd;
But two of them the rest far overpast,
And where their lady was arrived at the last.

[1] *Apayd*, satisfied.
[2] *Ryv'd*, pierced.
[3] *Forthy*, therefore.

38 Where when they saw that goodly boy with blood
Defowled, and their lady dresse his wownd,
They wondred much; and shortly understood
How him in deadly case theyr lady fownd,
And reskewed out of the heavy stownd.[1]
Eftsoones his warlike courser, which was strayd
Farre in the woodes whiles that he lay in swownd,
She made those damzels search; which being stayd,
They did him set theron, and forth with them convayd.

39 Into that forest farre they thence him led
Where was their dwelling; in a pleasant glade
With mountaines rownd about environed
And mightie woodes, which did the valley shade,
And like[2] a stately theatre it made,
Spreading itselfe into a spatious plaine;
And in the midst a little river plaide
Emongst the pumy[3] stones, which seemd to plaine
With gentle murmure that his cours they did restraine.

40 Beside the same a dainty place there lay,
Planted with mirtle trees and laurells greene,
In which the birds song many a lovely lay
Of Gods high praise, and of their loves sweet teene,[4]
As it an earthly paradize had beene:
In whose enclosed shadow there was pight[5]
A faire pavilion, scarcely to be seene,
The which was al within most richly dight,
That greatest princes living it mote well delight.

1 *Stownd*, exigence, situation.
2 *Like*, as it were.
3 *Pumy*, porous.
4 *Teene*, pain.
5 *Pight*, placed.

41 Thether they brought that wounded Squyre, and
 layd
In easie couch his feeble limbes to rest.
He rested him awhile; and then the Mayd
His readie wound with better salves new drest:
Daily she dressed him, and did the best,
His grievous hurt to guarish,[1] that she might;
That shortly she his dolour hath redrest,
And his foule sore reduced to faire plight:
It she reduced, but himselfe destroyed quight.

42 O foolish physick, and unfruitfull paine,[2]
That heales up one, and makes another wound!
She his hurt thigh to him recurd againe,
But hurt his hart, the which before was sound,
Through an unwary dart which did rebownd
From her faire eyes and gratious countenaunce.
What bootes it him from death to be unbownd,
To be captíved in endlésse duraúnce
Of sorrow and despeyre without aleggeaunce[3]!

43 Still as his wound did gather, and grow hole,
So still his hart woxe sore, and health decayd:
Madnesse to save a part, and lose the whole!
Still whenas he beheld the heavenly Mayd,
Whiles dayly playsters to his wownd she layd,
So still his malady the more increast,
The whiles her matchlesse beautie him dismayd.[4]
Ah God! what other could he doe at least,
But love so fayre a lady that his life releast!

1 *Guarish*, heal.
2 *Paine*, labor.
3 *Alleggeaunce*, alleviation.
4 *Dismayd*, overpowered.

44 Long while he strove in his corageous brest
With reason dew the passion to subdew,
And love for to dislodge out of his nest:
Still when her excellencies he did vew,
Her soveraine bountie[1] and celestiall hew,
The same to love he strongly was constraynd:
But, when his meane estate he did revew,
He from such hardy boldnesse was restraynd,
And of his lucklesse lott and cruell love thus playnd:

45 "Unthankfull wretch," said he, "is this the meed,
With which her soverain mercy thou doest quight?
Thy life she saved by her gratious deed;
But thou doest weene with villeinous despight
To blott her honour and her heavenly light:
Dye rather, dye, then so disloyally
Deeme of her high desert, or seeme so light:
Fayre death it is, to shonne more shame, to dy:
Dye rather, dy, then ever love disloyally.

46 "But if to love disloyalty it bee,
Shall I then hate her that from deathës dore
Me brought? ah! farre be such reproch fro mee!
What can I lesse doe then her love therefóre,
Sith I her dew reward cannot restore?
Dye rather, dye, and dying doe her serve;
Dying her serve, and living her adore;
Thy life she gave, thy life she doth deserve:
Dye rather, dye, then ever from her service swerve.

1 *Bountie*, goodness.

47 "But, foolish boy, what bootes thy service bace
To her, to whom the hevens doe serve and sew[1]?
Thou, a meane squyre, of meeke and lowly place;
She, hevenly borne and of celestiall hew.
How then? of all Love taketh equall vew:
And doth not Highest God vouchsafe to take
The love and service of the basest crew?
If she will not, dye meekly for her sake:
Dye rather, dye, then ever so faire love forsake!"

48 Thus warreid[2] he long time against his will;
Till that through weaknesse he was forst at last
To yield himselfe unto the mightie ill;
Which, as a victour proud, gan ransack fast
His inward partes, and all his entrayles wast,
That neither blood in face nor life in hart
It left, but both did quite drye up and blast;
As percing levin, which the inner part
Of every thing consumes and calcineth by art.

49 Which seeing, fayre Belphœbe gan to feare
Least that his wound were inly well not heald,
Or that the wicked steele empoysned were:
Litle shee weend that love he close conceald.
Yet still he wasted, as the snow congeald

1 *Sew*, follow, obey. 2 *Warreid*, contended.

XLVII. 2.—An allusion to the destruction of the Spanish fleet by storms. Timias's affection for Belphœbe is thought to signify Raleigh's admiration for the Queen.

XLVIII. 9.—*Calcineth by art.*] This expression occasions some trouble if *levin* be explained lightning. *By art* would most naturally signify, in a wonderful or mysterious way. C.

When the bright sunne his beams theron doth beat
Yet never he his hart to her reveald;
But rather chose to dye for sorow great,
Then with dishonorable termes her to entreat.

50 She, gracious lady, yet no paines did spare
To doe him ease, or doe him remedy:
Many restoratives of vertues rare
And costly cordialles she did apply,
To mitigate his stubborne malady:
But that sweet cordiall, which can restore
A love-sick hart, she did to him envý[1];
To him, and to all th' unworthy world forlore,
She did envý that soveraine salve in secret store.

51 That daintie rose, the daughter of her morne,
More deare then life she tendered, whose flowre
The girlond of her honour did adorne:
Ne suffred she the middayes scorching powre,
Ne the sharp northerne wind thereon to showre;
But lapped up her silken leaves most chayre,[2]
Whenso the froward skye began to lowre;
But, soone as calmed was the christall ayre,
She did it fayre dispred and let to florish fayre.

52 Eternall God, in his almightie powre,
To make ensample of his heavenly grace,
In paradize whylome did plant this flowre;
Whence he it fetcht out of her native place,
And did in stocke of earthly flesh enrace,[3]

1 *Envý*, grudge, deny. 2 *Chayre*, chary.
3 *Enrace*, implant.

That mortall men her glory should admyre.
In gentle ladies breste and bounteous race
Of woman-kind it fayrest flowre doth spyre,[1]
And beareth fruit of honour and all chast desyre.

53 Fayre ympes[2] of beautie, whose bright shining beames
Adorne the world with like to heavenly light,
And to your willes both royalties and reames[3]
Subdew, through conquest of your wondrous might,
With this fayre flowre your goodly girlonds dight[4]
Of chastity and vertue virginall,
That shall embellish more your beautie bright,
And crowne your heades with heavenly coronall,
Such as the Angels weare before Gods tribunall!

54 To youre faire selves a faire ensample frame
Of this faire virgin, this Belphebe fayre;
To whom, in perfect love and spotlesse fame
Of chastitie, none living may compayre:
Ne poysnous envy iustly can empayre
The prayse of her fresh-flowring maydenhead;
Forthy she standeth on the highest stayre
Of th' honorable stage of womanhead,
That ladies all may follow her ensample dead.

55 In so great prayse of stedfast chastity
Nathlesse she was so courteous and kynde,
Tempred with grace and goodly modesty,

1 *Spyre*, shoot forth.
2 *Ympes*, daughters.
3 *Reames*, realms.
4 *Dight*, adorn.

That seemed those two vertues strove to fynd
The higher place in her heroick mynd :
So striving each did other more augment,
And both encreast the prayse of womankynde,
And both encreast her beautie excellent :
So all did make in her a perfect complement.[1]

[1] *Complement*, complete character.

CANTO VI.

The Birth of fayre Belphœbe and
Of Amorett is told:
The Gardins of Adonis fraught
With pleasures manifold.

1 WELL may I weene, faire Ladies, all this while
Ye wonder how this noble Damozell
So great perfections did in her compile,[1]
Sith that in salvage forests she did dwell,
So farre from court and royall citadell,
The great schoolmaistresse of all courtesy:
Seemeth that such wilde woodes should far expell
All civile usage and gentility,
And gentle sprite deforme with rude rusticity.

2 But to this faire Belphœbe in her berth
The hevens so favorable were and free,
Looking with myld aspéct upon the earth
In th' horoscope of her nativitee,
That all the gifts of grace and chastitee
On her they poured forth of plenteous horne:
Iove laught on Venus from his soverayne see,[2]
And Phœbus with faire beames did her adorne,
And all the Graces rockt her cradle being borne.

1 *Compile*, combine. 2 *See*, seat.

3 Her berth was of the wombe of morning dew,
And her conception of the ioyous Prime;
And all her whole creation did her shew
Pure and unspotted from all loathly crime
That is ingenerate in fleshly slime:
So was this Virgin borne, so was she bred;
So was she trayned up from time to time
In all chaste vertue and true bountihed,
Till to her dew perfection she were ripened.

4 Her mother was the faire Chrysogonee,
The daughter of Amphisa, who by race
A Faerie was, yborne of high degree:
She bore Belphæbe; she bore in like cace
Fayre Amoretta in the second place:
These two were twinnes, and twixt them two did share
The heritage of all celestiall grace;
That all the rest it seemd they robbed bare
Of bounty, and of beautie, and all vertues rare.

5 It were a goodly storie to declare
By what straunge accident faire Chrysogone

III. 1, 2. — That is, she was begotten by Spring of the morning dew. The expression in the first line is caught from the 3d verse of the 110th Psalm: "The dew of thy birth is of the womb of the morning" (Coverdale), — a sentence without meaning. The original signifies, "Thy youth shall come forth like dew from the womb of the morning" (Noyes), — a notion quite different from what Spenser intends. C.

IV. 1. — *The faire Chrysogonee.*] This pedigree is entirely fanciful, and though Belphœbe is Queen Elizabeth, Chrysogonee is not Anne Boleyn. H.

Conceiv'd these infants, and how them she bare
In this wilde forrest wandring all alone,
After she had nine moneths fulfild and gone:
For not as other wemens commune brood
They were enwombed in the sacred throne
Of her chaste bodie; nor with commune food,
As other wemens babes, they sucked vitall blood:

6 But wondrously they were begot and bred,
Through influence of th' hevens fruitfull ray,
As it in antique bookes is mentioned.
It was upon a sommers shinie day,
When Titan faire his beames did display,
In a fresh fountaine, far from all mens vew,
She bath'd her brest the boyling heat t' allay;
She bath'd with roses red and violets blew,
And all the sweetest flowres that in the forrest grew:

7 Till, faint through yrkesome wearines, adowne
Upon the grassy ground herselfe she layd
To sleepe, the whiles a gentle slombring swowne
Upon her fell all naked bare displayd:
The sunbeames bright upon her body playd,
Being through former bathing mollifide,
And pierst into her wombe; where they embayd[1]
With so sweet sence and secret power unspide,
That in her pregnant flesh they shortly fructifide.

8 Miraculous may seeme to him that reades
So straunge ensample of conception;

[1] *Embayd*, bathed.

But reason teacheth that the fruitfull seades
Of all things living, through impression
Of the sunbeames in moyst complexion,[1]
Doe life conceive and quickned are by kynd[2]:
So, after Nilus inundation,
Infinite shapes of creatures men doe fynd
Informed[3] in the mud on which the sunne hath shynd.

9 Great father he of generation
Is rightly cald, th' authour of life and light;
And his faire sister for creation
Ministreth matter fit, which, tempred right
With heate and humour, breedes the living wight.
So sprong these twinnes in womb of Chrysogone;
Yet wist she nought thereof, but, sore affright,
Wondred to see her belly so upblone,
Which still increast till she her terme had full outgone.

10 Whereof conceiving shame and foule disgrace,
Albe her guiltlesse conscience her cleard,
She fled into the wildernesse a space,
Till that unweeldy burden she had reard,[4]
And shund dishonor which as death she feard:
Where, wearie of long traveill, downe to rest
Herselfe she set, and comfortably cheard;
There a sad cloud of sleepe her overkest,
And seized every sence with sorrow sore opprest.

1 *Complexion*, condition, or constitution. 2 *Kynd*, nature.
3 *Informed*, shapeless (a Latinism).
4 *Reard*, discharged (cf. IV. VI. 6).

VIII. 7.—*So, after Nilus*, &c.] This story has already been alluded to, Book I. Canto I. Stanza 21.

11 It fortuned, faire Venus having lost
Her little sonne, the winged God of Love,
Who for some light displeasure, which him crost,
Was from her fled as flit[1] as ayery dove,
And left her blisfull bowre of ioy above;
(So from her often he had fled away,
When she for ought him sharpely did reprove,
And wandred in the world in straunge aray,
Disguiz'd in thousand shapes, that none might him bewray;)

12 Him for to seeke, she left her heavenly hous,
The house of goodly formes and faire aspéct,
Whence all the world derives the glorious
Features of beautie, and all shapes select,
With which High God his workmanship hath deckt;
And searched everie way through which his wings
Had borne him, or his tract she mote detect:
She promist kisses sweet, and sweeter things,
Unto the man that of him tydings to her brings.

13 First she him sought in Court, where most he us'd
Whylome to haunt, but there she found him not;
But many there she found which sore accus'd
His falshood, and with fowle infámous blot
His cruell deedes and wicked wyles did spot:
Ladies and lordes she every where mote heare
Complayning, how with his empoysned shot

[1] *Flit*, fleet.

XI. 1. — *Venus having lost*, &c.] This incident was suggested by a very pretty idyl of Moschus, called "Love a Fugitive." H.

Their wofull harts he wounded had whyleare,[1]
And so had left them languishing twixt hope and feare.

14 She then the cities sought from gate to gate,
And everie one did aske, Did he him see?
And everie one her answerd, that too late
He had him seene, and felt the crueltee
Of his sharpe dartes and whot artilleree:
And every one threw forth reproches rife
Of his mischiévous deedes, and sayd that hee
Was the disturber of all civill life,
The enimy of peace, and authour of all strife.

15 Then in the countrey she abroad him sought,
And in the rurall cottages inquir'd;
Where also many plaintes to her were brought,
How he their heedelesse harts with love had fir'd,
And his false venim through their veines inspir'd;
And eke the gentle shepheard swaynes, which sat
Keeping their fleecy flockes, as they were hyr'd,
She sweetly heard complaine both how and what
Her sonne had to them doen; yet she did smile thereat.

16 But, when in none of all these she him got,
She gan avize[2] where els he mote him hyde:
At last she her bethought that she had not
Yet sought the salvage woods and forests wyde,
In which full many lovely nymphes abyde;
Mongst whom might be that he did closely[3] lye,
Or that the love of some of them him tyde:

1 *Whyleare*, some time before.
2 *Avize*, consider.
3 *Closely*, secretly.

Forthy[1] she thether cast her course t' apply,
To search the secret haunts of Dianes company.

17 Shortly unto the wastefull woods she came,
Whereas she found the goddesse with her crew,
After late chace of their embrewed[2] game,
Sitting beside a fountaine in a rew[3];
Some of them washing with the liquid dew
From of their dainty limbs the dusty sweat
And soyle, which did deforme their lively hew;
Others lay shaded from the scorching heat;
The rest upon her person gave attendance great.

18 She, having hong upon a bough on high
Her bow and painted quiver, had unlaste
Her silver buskins from her nimble thigh,
And her lanck loynes[4] ungirt, and brests unbraste,
After her heat the breathing cold to taste;
Her golden lockes, that late in tresses bright
Embreaded were for hindring of her haste,
Now loose about her shoulders hong undight,
And were with sweet ambrosia all besprinckled light.

19 Soone as she Venus saw behinde her backe,
She was asham'd to be so loose surpriz'd;
And woxe halfe wroth against her damzels slacke,
That had not her thereof before aviz'd,
But suffred her so carelesly disguiz'd
Be overtaken. Soone her garments loose

1 *Forthy*, therefore.
2 *Embrewed*, wet with blood.
3 *Rew*, row.
4 *Lanck loynes*, slender waist.

Upgath'ring, in her bosome she compriz'd[1]
Well as she might, and to the goddesse rose;
Whiles all her nymphes did like a girlond her enclose.

20 Goodly she gan faire Cytherea greet,
And shortly asked her what cause her brought,
Into that wildernesse for her unmeet,
From her sweete bowres and beds with pleasures fraught:
That suddein chaung she straung adventure thought.
To whom halfe weeping she thus answered:
That she her dearest sonne Cupido sought,
Who in his frowardnes from her was fled;
That she repented sore to have him angered.

21 Thereat Diana gan to smile, in scorne
Of her vaine playnt, and to her scoffing sayd:
"Great pitty sure that ye be so forlorne[2]
Of your gay sonne, that gives ye so good ayd
To your disports; ill mote ye bene apayd!"[3]
But she was more engrieved, and replide:
"Faire sister, ill beseemes it to upbrayd
A dolefull heart with so disdainfull pride;
The like that mine may be your paine another tide.[4]

22 "As you in woods and wanton wildernesse
Your glory sett, to chace the salvage beasts,
So my delight is all in ioyfulnesse,
In beds, in bowres, in banckets, and in feasts:

[1] I. e. she concealed her bosom.
[2] *Forlorne*, bereft.
[3] I. e. you must be sadly discontented.
[4] *Tide*, time.

And ill becomes you, with your lofty creasts,
To scorne the ioy that Iove is glad to seeke:
We both are bownd to follow heavens beheasts,
And tend our charges with obeisaunce meeke:
Spare, gentle sister, with reproch my paine to eeke[1];

23 "And tell me if that ye my sonne have heard
To lurke emongst your nimphes in secret wize,
Or keepe their cabins: much I am affeard
Least he like one of them himselfe disguize,
And turne his arrowes to their exercize:
So may he long himselfe full easie hide;
For he is faire, and fresh in face and guize
As any nimphe; let not it be envide."[2]
So saying, every nimph full narrowly shee eide.

24 But Phœbe therewith sore was angered,
And sharply saide: "Goe, Dame; goe, seeke your boy,
Where you him lately lefte, in Mars his bed:
He comes not here: we scorne his foolish ioy,
Ne lend we leisure to his idle toy:
But, if I catch him in this company,
By Stygian lake I vow, whose sad annoy
The gods doe dread, he dearly shall abye[3]:
Ile clip his wanton wings that he no more shall flye."

25 Whom whenas Venus saw so sore displeasd,
Shee inly sory was, and gan relent[4]

1 *Eeke*, increase.
2 I. e. do not grudge him that praise.
3 *Abye*, abide, pay for it.
4 *Relent*, soften, qualify.

What shee had said: so her she soone appeasd
With sugred words and gentle blandishment,
Which as a fountaine from her sweete lips went
And welled goodly forth, that in short space
She was well pleasd, and forth her damzells sent
Through all the woods, to search from place to place,
If any tract of him or tidings they mote trace.

26 To search the God of Love, her nimphes she sent
Throughout the wandring forest every where:
And after them herselfe eke with her went
To seeke the fugitive both farre and nere.
So long they sought, till they arrived were
In that same shady covert whereas lay
Faire Crysogone in slombry traunce whilere;
Who in her sleepe (a wondrous thing to say)
Unwares had borne two babes as faire as springing day.

27 Unwares she them conceivd, unwares she bore:
She bore withouten paine, that she conceiv'd
Withouten pleasure; ne her need implore
Lucinaes aide. Which when they both perceiv'd,
They were through wonder nigh of sence berev'd,
And, gazing each on other, nought bespake:
At last they both agreed, her seeming griev'd
Out of her heavie swowne not to awake,
But from her loving side the tender babes to take.

28 Up they them tooke, each one a babe uptooke,
And with them carried to be fostered:

Dame Phæbe to a nymphe her babe betooke[1]
To be upbrought in perfect maydenhed,
And, of herselfe, her name Belphœbe red[2]:
But Venus hers thence far away convayd,
To be upbrought in goodly womanhed;
And, in her litle Loves stead which was strayd,
Her Amoretta cald, to comfort her dismayd.[3]

29 Shee brought her to her ioyous paradize
Wher most she wonnes, when she on earth does dwell:
So faire a place as Nature can devize:
Whether in Paphos, or Cytheron hill,
Or it in Gnidas bee, I wote not well;
But well I wote by triall, that this same
All other pleasaunt places doth excell,
And called is, by her lost lovers name,
The Gardin of Adonis, far renowmd by fame.

30 In that same gardin all the goodly flowres
Wherewith Dame Nature doth her beautify,
And decks the girlonds of her paramoures,
Are fetcht: there is the first semínary
Of all things that are borne to live and dye,
According to their kynds.[4] Long worke it were
Here to account the endlesse progeny

1 *Betooke*, committed.
2 *Red*, declared.
3 *Dismayd*, dejected.
4 *Kynds*, natures.

XXX. 1. — *In that same gardin*, &c.] In the fable of Venus and Adonis, Adonis represents the sun, which quickens the growth of all things.

Of all the weeds[1] that bud and blossome there;
But so much as doth need must needs be counted[2] here.

31 It sited was in fruitfull soyle of old,
And girt in with two walls on either side,
The one of yron, the other of bright gold,
That none might thorough breake, nor overstride:
And double gates it had which opened wide,
By which both in and out men moten pas;
Th' one faire and fresh, the other old and dride:
Old Genius the porter of them was,
Old Genius, the which a double nature has.

32 He letteth in, he letteth out to wend
All that to come into the world desire:
A thousand thousand naked babes attend
About him day and night, which doe require
That he with fleshly weeds would them attire:
Such as him list, such as eternall fate
Ordained hath, he clothes with sinfull mire,
And sendeth forth to live in mortall state,
Till they agayn returne backe by the hinder gate.

1 *Weeds*, plants. 2 *Counted*, recounted.

XXXI. 8. — *Old Genius.*] Warton observes that the Genius here spoken of (who is the same as the Agdistes of Book II. XII. 48) seems to be that which is represented in the *Picture* of Cebes. "First you must know that this place is called Life. And the great crowd which is standing by the gate are those who are just about to enter into Life. The Old Man who stands above, holding a paper in one hand and apparently pointing with the other, is called Dæmon (Genius). He assigns to every person as he comes in what he is to do," etc. C.

33 After that they againe retourned beene,
They in that gardin planted bee agayne,
And grow afresh, as they had never seene
Fleshly corruption nor mortall payne :
Some thousand yeares so doen they there remayne,
And then of him are clad with other hew,
Or sent into the chaungefull world agayne,
Till thether they retourne where first they grew :
So, like a wheele, arownd they ronne from old to new

34 Ne needs there gardiner to sett or sow,
To plant or prune ; for of their owne accord
All things, as they created were, doe grow,
And yet remember well the mighty word
Which first was spoken by th' Almighty Lord,
That bad them to increase and multiply :
Ne doe they need, with water of the ford
Or of the clouds, to moysten their roots dry ;
For in themselves eternall moisture they imply.[1]

35 Infinite shapes of creatures there are bred,
And uncouth formes, which none yet ever knew :
And every sort is in a sondry bed
Sett by itselfe, and ranckt in comely rew[2] ;
Some fitt for reasonable sowles t' indew ;
Some made for beasts, some made for birds to weare ;
And all the fruitfull spawne of fishes hew

[1] *Imply*, wrap up, contain. [2] *Rew*, row.

XXXIII. 1.—*After that*, &c.] In this and the following stanzas, the Pythagorean and Platonic doctrines of metempsychosis are expounded. H.

In endlesse rancks along enraunged were,
That seemd the ocean could not containe them there.

36 Daily they grow, and daily forth are sent
Into the world, it to replenish more;
Yet is the stocke not lessened nor spent,
But still remaines in everlasting store
As it at first created was of yore:
For in the wide wombe of the world there lyes,
In hatefull darknes and in deep horróre,
An huge eternal chaos, which supplyes
The substaunces of Natures fruitfull progenyes.

37 All things from thence doe their first being fetch,
And borrow matter whereof they are made;
Which, whenas forme and feature it does ketch,
Becomes a body, and doth then invade[1]
The state of life out of the griesly shade.
That substaunce is eterne, and bideth so;
Ne, when the life decayes and forme does fade,
Doth it consume and into nothing goe,
But chaunged is and often altred to and froe.

38 The substaunce is not chaungd nor altered,
But th' only forme and outward fashion;
For every substaunce is conditioned
To chaunge her hew, and sondry formes to don,
Meet for her temper and complexion:
For formes are variable, and decay
By course of kinde[2] and by occasion;

[1] *Invade*, come into. [2] *Kinde*, nature.

And that faire flowre of beautie fades away,
As doth the lilly fresh before the sunny ray.

39 Great enimy to it, and to all the rest
That in the Gardin of Adonis springs,
Is wicked Tyme; — who, with his scyth addrest,[1]
Does mow the flowring herbes and goodly things,
And all their glory to the ground downe flings,
Where they do wither and are fowly mard:
He flyes about, and with his flaggy winges
Beates downe both leaves and buds without regard,
Ne ever pitty may relent[2] his malice hard.

40 Yet pitty often did the gods relent,
To see so faire thinges mard and spoiled quight:
And their great mother Venus did lament
The losse of her deare brood, her deare delight:
Her hart was pierst with pitty at the sight,
When walking through the gardin them she spyde,[3]
Yet no'te[4] she find redresse for such despight:
For all that lives is subiect to that law:
All things decay in time, and to their end doe draw.

41 But were it not that Time their troubler is,
All that in this delightfull gardin growes
Should happy bee, and have immortall blis:
For here all plenty and all pleasure flowes;
And sweete Love gentle fitts emongst them throwes,
Without fell rancor or fond gealosy:

[1] *Addrest*, prepared, furnished.
[2] *Relent*, soften.
[3] The rhyme requires *saw*.
[4] *No'te*, could not.

Franckly each paramor his leman knowes;
Each bird his mate; ne any does envý
Their goodly meriment and gay felicity.

42 There is continuall spring, and harvest there
Continuall, both meeting at one tyme:
For both the boughes doe laughing blossoms beare,
And with fresh colours decke the wanton pryme,[1]
And eke attonce the heavy trees they clyme,
Which seeme to labour under their fruites lode:
The whiles the ioyous birdes make their pastyme
Emongst the shady leaves, their sweet abode,
And their trew loves without suspition tell abrode.

43 Right in the middest of that paradise
There stood a stately mount, on whose round top
A gloomy grove of mirtle trees did rise,
Whose shady boughes sharp steele did never lop,
Nor wicked beastes their tender buds did crop,
But like a girlond compassed the hight,
And from their fruitfull sydes sweet gum did drop,
That all the ground, with pretious deaw bedight,[2]
Threw forth most dainty odours and most sweet delight.

44 And in the thickest covert of that shade
There was a pleasaunt arber, not by art
But of the trees owne inclination made,
Which knitting their rancke[3] braunches part to part,

1 *Pryme*, spring.
2 *Bedight*, covered.
3 *Rancke*, luxuriant.

With wanton yvie twyne entrayld[1] athwart,
And eglantine and caprifole[2] emong,
Fashiond above within their inmost part,
That nether Phoebus beams could through them
throng,
Nor Aeolus sharp blast could worke them any wrong.

45 And all about grew every sort of flowre,
To which sad lovers were transformde of yore;
Fresh Hyacinthus, Phœbus paramoure
And dearest love;
Foolish Narcisse, that likes the watry shore;
Sad Amaranthus, made a flowre but late,
Sad Amaranthus, in whose purple gore
Me seemes I see Amintas wretched fate,
To whom sweet poets verse hath given endlesse
date.

46 There wont fayre Venus often to enioy
Her deare Adonis ioyous company,
And reape sweet pleasure of the wanton boy:
There yet, some say, in secret he does ly,
Lapped in flowres and pretious spycery,
By her hid from the world, and from the skill
Of Stygian gods, which doe her love envý;
But she herselfe, whenever that she will,
Possesseth him, and of his sweetnesse takes her fill:

[1] *Entrayld*, twisted. [2] *Caprifole*, woodbine.

XLV. 8. — *Amintas wretched fate.*] This is supposed to allude to the untimely death of Sir Philip Sidney. H.

47 And sooth, it seemes, they say; for he may not
For ever dye, and ever buried bee
In balefull night where all thinges are forgot;
All be he subiect to mortalitie,
Yet is eterne in mutabilitie,
And by succession made perpetuall,
Transformed oft, and chaunged diverslie:
For him the father of all formes they call;
Therfore needs mote he live, that living gives to all.

48 There now he liveth in eternall blis,
Ioying his goddesse, and of her enioyd;
Ne feareth he henceforth that foe of his,
Which with his cruell tuske him deadly cloyd[1]:
For that wilde bore, the which him once annoyd,
She firmely hath emprisoned for ay,
(That her sweet Love his malice mote avoyd,)
In a strong rocky cave, which is, they say,
Hewen underneath that mount, that none him losen[2] may.

49 There now he lives in everlasting ioy,
With many of the gods in company
Which thether haunt, and with the winged boy,
Sporting himselfe in safe felicity:
Who when he hath with spoiles and cruelty

[1] *Cloyd*, clawed. [2] *Losen*, loosen.

XLVIII. 5.—*For that wilde bore.*] Adonis representing the productive energy of nature, the wild boar is a type of winter, during which that energy is suspended. H.

Ransackt the world, and in the wofull harts
Of many wretches set his triumphes hye,
Thether resortes, and, laying his sad dartes
Asyde, with faire Adonis playes his wanton partes.

50 And his trew Love, faire Psyche, with him playes,
Fayre Psyche to him lately reconcyld,
After long troubles and unmeet upbrayes,[1]
With which his mother Venus her revyld,
And eke himselfe her cruelly exyld:
But now in stedfast love and happy state
She with him lives, and hath him borne a chyld,
Pleasure, that doth both gods and men aggrate,[2]
Pleasure, the daughter of Cupid and Psyche late.

51 Hether great Venus brought this infant fayre,
The yonger daughter of Chrysogonee,
And unto Psyche with great trust and care
Committed her, yfostered to bee,
And trained up in trew feminitee[3]:
Who no lesse carefully her tendered
Then her owne daughter Pleasure, to whom shee
Made her companion, and her lessoned
In all the lore of love and goodly womanhead.

52 In which when she to perfect ripenes grew,
Of grace and beautie noble paragone,
She brought her forth into the worldës vew,
To be th' ensample of true love alone,

1 *Upbrayes*, upbraidings.
2 *Aggrate*, please.
3 *Feminitee*, womanhood.

And lodestarre of all chaste affection
To all fayre ladies that doe live on grownd.
To Faery Court she came; where many one
Admyrd her goodly haveour, and fownd
His feeble hart wide launched with loves cruel wownd.

53 But she to none of them her love did cast,
Save to the noble knight, Sir Scudamore,
To whom her loving hart she linked fast
In faithfull love, t' abide for evermore;
And for his dearest sake endured sore,
Sore trouble of an hainous enimy,
Who her would forced have to have forlore[1]
Her former love and stedfast loialty,
As ye may elswhere reade that ruefull history.

54 But well I weene ye first desire to learne
What end unto that fearefull damozell,
Which fledd so fast from that same foster stearne
Whom with his brethren Timias slew, befell:
That was, to weet, the goodly Florimell;
Who, wandring for to seeke her lover deare,
Her lover deare, her dearest Marinell,
Into misfortune fell, as ye did heare,
And from Prince Arthure fled with wings of idle feare.

[1] *Forlore*, abandoned.

LIII. 9. — *As ye may elswhere.*] See the eleventh and twelfth cantos of this book.

CANTO VII.

The Witches Sonne loves Florimell:
  She flyes; he faines to dy.
Satyrane saves the Squyre of Dames
  From Gyaunts tyranny.

1 LIKE as an hynd forth singled from the heard,
That hath escaped from a ravenous beast,
Yet flyes away of her owne feete afeard;
And every leafe, that shaketh with the least
Murmure of winde, her terror hath encreast:
So fledd fayre Florimell from her vaine feare,
Long after she from perill was releast:
Each shade she saw, and each noyse she did heare,
Did seeme to be the same which she escapt whileare.

2 All that same evening she in flying spent,
And all that night her course continewed:
Ne did she let dull sleepe once to relent,
Nor wearinesse to slack her hast, but fled
Ever alike, as if her former dred
Were hard behind, her ready to arrest:
And her white palfrey, having conquered
The maistring [1] raines out of her weary wrest,[2]
Perforce her carried where ever he thought best.

[1] *Maistring*, mastering, or controlling. [2] *Wrest*, wrist.

3 So long as breath and hable puissaunce
Did native corage unto him supply,
His pace he freshly forward did advaunce,
And carried her beyond all ieopardy;
But nought that wanteth rest can long aby[1]:
He, having through incessant traveill spent
His force, at last perforce adowne did ly,
Ne foot could further move. The Lady gent
Thereat was suddein strook with great astonishment;

4 And, forst t' alight, on foot mote algates[2] fare,
A traveiler unwonted to such way;
Need teacheth her this lesson hard and rare,—
That Fortune all in equall launce[3] doth sway,
And mortall miseries doth make her play.
So long she traveild, till at length she came
To an hilles side, which did to her bewray
A litle valley subiect to[4] the same,
All coverd with thick woodes that quite it overcame.[5]

5 Through the tops of the high trees she did descry
A litle smoke, whose vapour thin and light
Reeking aloft uprolled to the sky:
Which chearefull signe did send unto her sight
That in the same did wonne[6] some living wight.
Eftsoones her steps she thereunto applyd,
And came at last, in weary wretched plight,
Unto the place, to which her hope did guyde
To finde some refuge there, and rest her wearie syde.

1 *Aby*, abide.
2 *Algates*, at all events.
3 *Launce*, balance.
4 *Subiect to*, lying beneath.
5 *Overcame*, came over, clothed.
6 *Wonne*, dwell.

6 There in a gloomy hollow glen she found
A little cottage, built of stickes and reedes
In homely wize, and wald with sods around,
In which a Witch did dwell, in loathly weedes
And wilfull want, all carelesse of her needes;
So choosing solitarie to abide,
Far from all neighbours, that her divelish deedes
And hellish arts from people she might hide,
And hurt far off unknowne whomever she envíde.

7 The Damzell there arriving entred in;
Where sitting on the flore the Hag she found,
Busie (as seem'd) about some wicked gin[1]:
Who, soone as she beheld that suddein stound,[2]
Lightly upstarted from the dustie ground,
And with fell looke and hollow deadly gaze
Stared on her awhile, as one astound,
Ne had one word to speake for great amaze;
But shewd by outward signes that dread her sence did daze.[3]

8 At last, turning her feare to foolish wrath,
She askt, what devill had her thether brought,
And who she was, and what unwonted path
Had guided her, unwelcomed, unsought.
To which the Damzell, full of doubtfull thought,
Her mildly answer'd: "Beldame,[4] be not wroth
With silly[5] virgin, by adventure brought

1 *Gin*, contrivance.
2 *Stound*, exigency.
3 *Daze*, dazzle, confound.
4 *Beldame*, good mother.
5 *Silly*, harmless.

Unto your dwelling, ignorant and loth,
That crave but rowme to rest while tempest overblo'th."

9 With that, adowne out of her christall eyne
Few trickling teares she softly forth let fall,
That like to * orient perles did purely shyne
Upon her snowy cheeke; and therewithall
She sighed soft, that none so bestiall
Nor salvage hart but ruth of her sad plight
Would make to melt, or pitteously appall;
And that vile Hag, all were her whole delight
In mischiefe, was much moved at so pitteous sight;

10 And gan recomfort her, in her rude wyse,
With womanish compassion of her plaint,
Wiping the teares from her suffused eyes,
And bidding her sit downe to rest her faint
And wearie limbs awhile: she nothing quaint[1]
Nor 'sdeignfull of so homely fashion,
Sith brought she was now to so hard constraint,
Sate downe upon the dusty ground anon;
As glad of that small rest, as bird of tempest gon.

11 Tho gan she gather up her garments rent,
And her loose lockes to dight in order dew
With golden wreath and gorgeous ornament;
Whom such whenas the wicked Hag did vew,
She was astonisht at her heavenly hew,
And doubted her to deeme an earthly wight,

1 *Quaint*, nice.

* All the old editions have *two*.

But or some goddesse, or of Dianes crew,
And thought her to adore with humble spright:
T' adore thing so divine as beauty were but right.

12 This wicked woman had a wicked sonne,
The comfort of her age and weary dayes,
A laesy loord,[1] for nothing good to donne,[2]
But stretched forth in ydlenesse alwayes,
Ne ever cast his mind to covet prayse,
Or ply himselfe to any honest trade;
But all the day before the sunny rayes
He us'd to slug,[3] or sleepe in slothfull shade:
Such laesinesse both lewd[4] and poore attonce him made.

13 He, comming home at undertime, there found
The fayrest creature that he ever saw
Sitting beside his mother on the ground;
The sight whereof did greatly him adaw,[5]
And his base thought with terrour and with aw
So inly smot, that, as one which hath gaz'd
On the bright sunne unwares, doth soone withdraw
His feeble eyne with too much brightnes daz'd,
So stared he on her, and stood long while amaz'd.

14 Softly at last he gan his mother aske,
What mister wight[6] that was, and whence deriv'd,

1 *Loord*, lubber.
2 *Donne*, do.
3 *Slug*, drone.
4 *Lewd*, ignorant.
5 *Adaw*, stupefy.
6 *Mister wight*, kind of creature.

XIII. 1. — *Undertime.*] *Undern* is properly nine o'clock in the morning, *undertime* the three hours from nine to twelve. Florimell had been riding *all night* (stanza 2). C.

That in so straunge disguizement there did maske,
And by what accident she there arriv'd?
But she, as one nigh of her wits depriv'd,
With nought but ghastly lookes him answered;
Like to a ghost, that lately is reviv'd
From Stygian shores where late it wandered:
So both at her, and each at other wondered.

15 But the fayre Virgin was so meeke and myld,
That she to them vouchsafed to embace[1]
Her goodly port, and to their senses vyld[2]
Her gentle speach applyde, that in short space
She grew familiare in that desert place.
During which time the Chorle, through her so kind
And courteise use, conceiv'd affection bace,
And cast to love her in his brutish mind;
No love, but brutish lust, that was so beastly tind.[3]

16 Closely[4] the wicked flame his bowels brent,[5]
And shortly grew into outrageous fire;
Yet had he not the hart, nor hardiment,
As unto her to utter his desire;
His caytive thought durst not so high aspire:
But with soft sighes and lovely semblaunces
He ween'd that his affection entire
She should aread[6]; many resemblaunces
To her he made, and many kinde remembraunces.

1 *Embace*, bring down.
2 *Vyld*, vile, low.
3 *Tind*, kindled.
4 *Closely*, secretly.
5 *Brent*, burned.
6 *Aread*, perceive.

XVI. 8. — *Resemblaunces.*] Imitations, exhibitions of affection; equivalent to "*lovely* (love-like) *semblaunces*," shows of love. C.

17 Oft from the forrest wildings[1] he did bring,
Whose sides empurpled were with smyling red;
And oft young birds, which he had taught to sing
His maistresse praises sweetly caroled:
Girlonds of flowres sometimes for her faire hed
He fine would dight; sometimes the squirrell wild
He brought to her in bands, as conquered
To be her thrall, his fellow-servant vild:
All which she of him tooke with countenance meeke and mild.

18 But, past a while, when she fit season saw
To leave that desert mansion, she cast[2]
In secret wize herselfe thence to withdraw,
For feare of mischiefe, which she did forecast
Might [be] by the witch or by her sonne compast.
Her wearie palfrey closely, as she might,
Now well recovered after long repast,
In his proud furnitures she freshly dight,
His late miswandred wayes now to remeasure right;

19 And earely, ere the dawning day appeard,
She forth issewed, and on her iourney went;
She went in perill, of each noyse affeard
And of each shade that did itselfe present;
For still she feared to be overhent[3]
Of that vile hag, or her uncivile sonne;
Who when, too late awaking, well they kent[4]
That their fayre guest was gone, they both begonne
To make exceeding mone as they had beene undonne.

1 *Wildings*, wild apples.
2 *Cast*, considered how.
3 *Overhent*, overtaken.
4 *Kent*, knew.

20 But that lewd lover did the most lament
For her depart, that ever man did heare;
He knockt his brest with desperate intent,
And scratcht his face, and with his teeth did teare
His rugged flesh, and rent his ragged heare:
That his sad mother, seeing his sore plight,
Was greatly woe-begon, and gan to feare
Least his fraile senses were emperisht quight,
And love to frenzy turnd; sith love is franticke hight.

21 All wayes shee sought him to restore to plight,[1]
With herbs, with charms, with counsel, and with teares;
But tears, nor charms, nor herbs, nor counsell, might
Asswage the fury which his entrails teares:
So strong is passion that no reason heares!
Tho, when all other helpes she saw to faile,
She turnd herselfe backe to her wicked leares[2]:
And by her divelish arts thought to prevaile
To bring her backe againe, or worke her finall bale.

22 Eftesoones out of her hidden cave she cald
An hideous beast of horrible aspéct,
That could the stoutest corage have appald;
Monstrous, mishapt,[3] and all his backe was spect
With thousand spots of colours queint elect[4];
Thereto so swifte that it all beasts did pas:
Like never yet did living eie detect;
But likest it to an Hyena was,
That feeds on wemens flesh, as others feede on gras.

[1] I. e. to his usual state.
[2] *Leares*, lessons, lore.
[3] *Mishapt*, misshaped.
[4] *Queint elect*, oddly chosen.

23 It forth she cald, and gave it streight in charge
Through thicke and thin her to poursew apace,
Ne once to stay to rest, or breath at large,
Till her hee had attaind and brought in place,[1]
Or quite devourd her beauties scornefull grace.
The monster, swifte as word that from her went,
Went forth in haste, and did her footing trace
So sure and swiftly, through his perfect sent
And passing speede, that shortly he her overhent.

24 Whom when the fearefull Damzell nigh espide,
No need to bid her fast away to flie;
That ugly shape so sore her terrifide,
That it she shund no lesse then dread to die;
And her flitt palfrey did so well apply
His nimble feet to her conceived feare,
That whilest his breath did strength to him supply,
From perill free he her away did beare;
But, when his force gan faile, his pace gan wex areare.[2]

25 Which whenas she perceiv'd, she was dismayd
At that same last extremity ful sore,
And of her safety greatly grew afrayd:
And now she gan approch to the sea shore,
As it befell, that she could flie no more,
But yield herselfe to spoile of greedinesse:
Lightly she leaped, as a wight forlore,
From her dull horse, in desperate distresse,
And to her feet betooke her doubtfull sickernesse.[3]

[1] I. e. to that place.
[2] I. e. fell behind, slackened.
[3] I. e. committed her safety.

26 Not halfe so fast the wicked Myrrha fled
From dread of her revenging fathers hond,
Nor halfe so fast to save her maydenhed
Fled fearfull Daphne on th' Ægæan strond,
As Florimell fled from that monster yond,[1]
To reach the sea ere she of him were raught:
For in the sea to drowne herselfe she fond,[2]
Rather then of the tyrant to be caught:
Thereto fear gave her wings, and need her corage taught.

27 It fortuned, (High God did so ordaine,)
As shee arrived on the roring shore,
In minde to leape into the mighty maine,
A little bote lay hoving[3] her before,
In which there slept a fisher old and pore,
The whiles his nets were drying on the sand:
Into the same shee lept, and with the ore
Did thrust the shallop from the floting strand:
So safety fownd at sea, which she fownd not at land.

28 The monster, ready on the pray to sease,
Was of his forward[4] hope deceived quight,
Ne durst assay to wade the perlous seas,
But, greedily long gaping at the sight,
At last in vaine was forst to turne his flight,
And tell the idle tidings to his dame:
Yet, to avenge his divelishe despight,

1 *Yond*, furious, outrageous (*outré*).
2 *Fond*, projected.
3 *Hoving*, hovering, resting on the water.
4 I. e. on the point of being gratified.

He sett upon her palfrey tired lame,
And slew him cruelly ere any reskew came:

29 And, after having him embowelled
To fill his hellish gorge, it chaunst a Knight
To passe that way, as forth he traveiled:
Yt was a goodly swaine, and of great might,
As ever man that bloody field did fight;
But in vain sheows, that wont yong knights bewitch,
And courtly services, tooke no delight,
But rather ioyd to bee than seemen sich[1];
For both to be and seeme to him was labor lich.[2]

30 It was to weete the good Sir Satyrane
That raungd abrode to seeke adventures wilde,
As was his wont, in forest and in plaine:
He was all armd in rugged steele unfilde,[3]
As in the smoky forge it was compilde,[4]
And in his scutchin[5] bore a satyres hedd:
He comming present, where the monster vilde
Upon that milke-white palfreyes carcas fedd,
Unto his reskew ran, and greedily him spedd.[6]

31 There well perceivd he that it was the horse
Whereon faire Florimell was wont to ride,
That of that feend was rent without remorse:

1 *Sich*, such.
2 *Lich*, like.
3 *Unfilde*, unpolished.
4 *Compilde*, put together.
5 *Scutchin*, shield.
6 I. e. hastened eagerly.

XXX. 1.—*Sir Satyrane.*] Sir Satyrane reappears from the sixth canto of the first book, where we left him fighting with Sansloy. H.

Much feared he least ought did ill betide
To that faire maide, the flowre of wemens pride;
For her he dearely loved, and in all
His famous conquests highly magnifide:
Besides, her golden girdle, which did fall
From her in flight, he fownd, that did him sore apall.

32 Full of sad feare and doubtfull agony,
Fiercely he flew upon that wicked feend;
And with huge strokes and cruell battery
Him forst to leave his pray, for to attend
Himselfe from deadly daunger to defend:
Full many wounds in his corrupted flesh
He did engrave,[1] and muchell[2] blood did spend,
Yet might not doe him die; but aie more fresh
And fierce he still appeard, the more he did him thresh.

33 He wist not how him to despoile of life,
Ne how to win the wished victory,
Sith him he saw still stronger grow through strife,
And himselfe weaker through infirmity:
Greatly he grew enrag'd, and furiously
Hurling his sword away, he lightly lept
Upon the beast, that with great cruelty
Rored and raged to be underkept;
Yet he perforce him held, and strokes upon him hept.

34 As he that strives to stop a suddein flood,
And in strong bancks his violence enclose,

1 *Engrave*, cut into. 2 *Muchell*, much.

XXXIV. 2.—The rhyme requires some such word as *constraine*.

Forceth it swell above his wonted mood,
And largely overflow the fruitfull plaine,
That all the countrey seemes to be a maine,[1]
And the rich furrowes flote, all quite fordonne[2]:
The wofull husbandman doth lowd complaine
To see his whole yeares labor lost so soone,
For which to God he made so many an idle boone[3].

35 So him he held, and did through might amate[4]:
So long he held him, and him bett so long,
That at the last his fiercenes gan abate,
And meekely stoup unto the victor strong:
Who, to avenge the ímplacable wrong
Which he supposed donne to Florimell,
Sought by all meanes his dolor[5] to prolong,
Sith dint of steele his carcas could not quell,
His maker with her charmes had framed him so well.

36 The golden ribband, which that Virgin wore
About her sclender waste, he tooke in hand,
And with it bownd the beast that lowd did rore
For great despight of that unwonted band,
Yet dared not his victor to withstand,
But trembled like a lambe fled from the pray[6];
And all the way him followd on the strand,
As he had long bene learned to obay;
Yet never learned he such service till that day.

37 Thus as he led the beast along the way,
He spide far of a mighty Giauntesse

1 *Maine*, sea.
2 *Fordonne*, ruined.
3 *Boone*, prayer.
4 *Amate*, subdue.
5 *Dolor*, pain.
6 I. e. of some wild beast.

Fast flying, on a courser dapled gray,
From a bold Knight that with great hardinesse
Her hard pursewd, and sought for to suppresse:
She bore before her lap a dolefull Squire,
Lying athwart her horse in great distresse,
Fast bounden hand and foote with cords of wire,
Whome she did meane to make the thrall of her desire.

38 Which whenas Satyrane beheld, in haste
He lefte his captive beast at liberty,
And crost the nearest way, by which he cast[1]
Her to encounter ere she passed by;
But she the way shund nathëmore forthy,[2]
But forward gallopt fast; which when he spyde,
His mighty speare he couched warily,
And at her ran; she, having him descryde,
Herselfe to fight addrest, and threw her lode aside.

39 Like as a goshauke, that in foote doth beare
A trembling culver,[3] having spide on hight
An eagle that with plumy wings doth sheare
The subtile ayre stouping with all his might,
The quarrey throwes to ground with fell despight,
And to the batteill doth herselfe prepare:
So ran the Geauntesse unto the fight;
Her fyrie eyes with furious sparkes did stare,
And with blasphémous bannes[4] High God in peeces tare.

1 *Cast*, purposed.
2 *Forthy*, therefore.
3 *Culver*, dove.
4 *Bannes*, curses.

XXXIX. 9.—That is, she swore by all the parts of God's body, a kind of blasphemy once much in vogue, of which some relics are

40 She caught in hand an huge great yron mace,
Wherewith she many had of life depriv'd;
But, ere the stroke could seize his aymed place,
His speare amids her sun-brode shield arriv'd;
Yet nathëmore the steele asonder riv'd,
All were the beame in bignes like a mast,
Ne her out of the stedfast sadle driv'd;
But, glauncing on the tempred metall, brast[1]
In thousand shivers, and so forth beside her past.

41 Her steed did stagger with that puissaunt strooke;
But she no more was moved with that might
Then it had lighted on an aged oke,
Or on the marble pillour that is pight[2]
Upon the top of Mount Olympus hight,
For the brave youthly champions to assay
With burning charet wheeles it nigh to smite;
But who that smites it mars his ioyous play,
And is the spectacle of ruinous decay.[3]

42 Yet, therewith sore enrag'd, with sterne regard
Her dreadfull weapon she to him addrest,
Which on his helmet martelled[4] so hard

1 *Brast*, burst.
2 *Pight*, placed.
3 *Decay*, destruction.
4 *Martelled*, hammered.

still preserved, such as 'zounds, 'sblood, &c., not to mention Bob Acres's "genteel" method, which, as he truly says, he did not invent. C.

XLI. 4, 5. — These lines may have been transposed by the printers. But Spenser's classical learning is not very accurate, and the writers of his time often represent the Olympic games as taking place on Mount Olympus. C.

That made him low incline his lofty crest,
And bowd his battred visour to his brest:
Wherewith he was so stund that he n'ote[1] ryde,
But reeled to and fro from east to west:
Which when his cruell enimy espyde,
She lightly unto him adioyned syde to syde;

43 And, on his collar laying puissaunt hand,
Out of his wavering seat him pluckt perforse,
Perforse him pluckt, unable to withstand
Or helpe himselfe; and laying thwart her horse,
In loathly wise like to a carrion corse,
She bore him fast away: which when the knight
That her pursewed saw, with great remorse[2]
He nere was touched in his noble spright,
And gan encrease his speed as she encreast her flight.

44 Whom whenas nigh approching she espyde,
She threw away her burden angrily;
For she list not the batteill to abide,
But made herselfe more light away to fly:
Yet her the hardy Knight pursewd so nye
That almost in the backe he oft her strake:
But still, when him at hand she did espy,
She turnd, and semblaunce of faire fight did make;
But, when he stayd, to flight againe she did her take.

45 By this the good Sir Satyrane gan wake
Out of his dreame that did him long entraunce,
And, seeing none in place, he gan to make
Exceeding mone, and curst that cruell chaunce

[1] *N'ote*, could not. [2] *Remorse*, pity.

Which reft from him so faire a chevisaunce[1]:
At length he spyde whereas that wofull Squyre,
Whom he had reskewed from captivaunce
Of his strong foe, lay tombled in the myre,
Unable to arise, or foot or hand to styre.[2]

46 To whom approching, well he mote perceive
In that fowle plight a comely personage
And lovely face, made fit for to deceive
Fraile ladies hart with loves consuming rage,
Now in the blossome of his freshest age:
He reard him up, and loosd his yron bands,
And after gan inquire his parentage,
And how he fell into the gyaunts hands,
And who that was which chaced her along the lands.

47 Then trembling yet through feare the Squire bespake:
"That geauntesse Argantè is behight,[3]
A daughter of the Titans which did make
Warre against heven, and heaped hils on hight
To scale the skyes and put Iove from his right:
Her syre Typhoeus was; who, mad through merth,
And dronke with blood of men slaine by his might,
Through incest her of his owne mother Earth
Whylome begot, being but halfe twin of that berth:

48 "For at that berth another babe she bore;
To weet, the mightie Ollyphant, that wrought
Great wreake[4] to many errant knights of yore,

[1] *Chevisaunce*, achievement.
[2] *Styre*, stir.
[3] *Behight*, called.
[4] *Wreake*, vengeance, spite.

And many hath to foule confusion brought.
These twinnes, men say, (a thing far passing thought,)
Whiles in their mothers wombe enclosd they were,
Ere they into the lightsom world were brought,
In fleshly lust were mingled both yfere,[1]
And in that monstrous wise did to the world appere.

49 "So liv'd they ever after in like sin,
Gainst natures law and good behaveoure:
But greatest shame was to that maiden twin;
Who, not content so fowly to devoure
Her native flesh and staine her brothers bowre,[2]
Did wallow in all other fleshly myre,
And suffred beastes her body to deflowre,
So whot she burned in that lustfull fyre:
Yet all that might not slake her sensuall desyre:

50 "But over all the countrie she did raunge,
To seeke young men to quench her flaming thrust,[3]
And feed her fancy with delightfull chaunge:
Whom so she fittest findes to serve her lust,
Through her maine strength, in which she most doth trust,
She with her bringes into a secret ile,
Where in eternall bondage dye he must,
Or be the vassall of her pleasures vile,
And in all shamefull sort himselfe with her defile.

51 "Me seely[4] wretch she so at vauntage caught,
After she long in waite for me did lye,

1 *Yfere*, together.
2 *Bowre*, chamber.
3 *Thrust*, thirst.
4 *Seely*, simple.

And meant unto her prison to have brought,
Her lothsom pleasure there to satisfye;
That thousand deathes me lever[1] were to dye
Then breake the vow that to faire Columbell
I plighted have, and yet keepe stedfastly:
As for my name, it mistreth[2] not to tell;
Call me the Squyre of Dames; that me beseemeth well.

52 "But that bold knight, whom ye pursuing saw
That geauntesse, is not such as she seemd,
But a faire virgin that in martiall law
And deedes of armes above all dames is deemd,
And above many knightes is eke esteemd
For her great worth; she Palladine is hight:
She you from death, you me from dread, redeemd.
Ne any may that monster match in fight,
But she, or such as she, that is so chaste a wight."

53 "Her well beseemes that quest," quoth Satyrane
"But read,[3] thou Squyre of Dames, what vow is this,
Which thou upon thyselfe hast lately ta'ne?"
"That shall I you recount," quoth he, "ywis,[4]
So be ye pleasd to pardon all amis.
That gentle lady whom I love and serve,

[1] *Me lever*, I would rather.
[2] *Mistreth*, signifieth.
[3] *Read*, explain.
[4] *Ywis*, certainly.

LIII. 4.—"*That shall I you recount*," *quoth he.*] The tale of the Squire of Dames is a copy of the Host's tale in Ariosto, Canto XXVIII.—WARTON.

After long suit and wearie servicis,
Did aske me how I could her love deserve,
And how she might be sure that I would never swerve.

54 "I, glad by any meanes her grace to gaine,
Badd her commaund my life to save or spill[1]:
Eftsoones she badd me with incessaunt paine
To wander through the world abroad at will,
And every where, where with my power or skill
I might doe service unto gentle dames,
That I the same should faithfully fulfill;
And at the twelve monethes end should bring their names
And pledges, as the spoiles of my victorious games

55 "So well I to faire ladies service did,
And found such favour in their loving hartes,
That, ere the yeare his course had compassid,
Thre hundred pledges for my good desartes,
And thrice three hundred thanks for my good partes,
I with me brought and did to her present:
Which when she saw, more bent to eke[2] my smartes
Then to reward my trusty true intent,
She gan for me devise a grievous punishment;

56 "To weet, that I my traveill should resume,
And with like labour walke the world arownd,
Ne ever to her presence should presume,
Till I so many other dames had fownd,

[1] *Spill*, spoil, destroy. [2] *Eke*, increase.

The which, for all the suit I could propownd,
Would me refuse their pledges to afford,
But did abide for ever chaste and sownd."
"Ah! gentle Squyre," quoth he, "tell at one word,
How many fowndst thou such to put in thy record?"

57 "Indeed, Sir Knight," said he, "one word may tell
All that I ever fownd so wisely stayd[1];
For onely three they were, disposd so well,
And yet three yeares I now abrode have strayd,
To fynd them out." "Mote I," then laughing sayd
The Knight, "inquire of thee what were those three,
The which thy proffred curtesie denayd[2]?
Or ill they seemed sure avizd to bee,
Or brutishly brought up, that nev'r did fashions see."

58 "The first which then refused me," said hee,
"Certes was but a common courtisane;
Yet flat refusd to have adoe with mee,
Because I could not give her many a iane."
(Thereat full hartely laughed Satyrane.)
"The second was an holy nunne to chose,
Which would not let me be her chappellane,
Because she knew, she sayd, I would disclose
Her counsell, if she should her trust in me repose.

[1] *Stayd*, staid, or discreet. [2] *Denayd*, denied.

LVIII. 4. — *Many a iane.*] Much money. — A Jane was a small coin of Genoa, or Janua.

59 "The third a damzell was of low degree,
Whom I in countrey cottage fownd by chaunce:
Full litle weened I that chastitee
Had lodging in so meane a maintenaunce[1];
Yet was she fayre, and in her countenaunce
Dwelt simple truth in seemely fashion:
Long thus I woo'd her with due óbservaunce,
In hope unto my pleasure to have won;
But was as far at last, as when I first begon.

60 "Safe her, I never any woman found
That chastity did for itselfe embrace,
But were for other causes firme and sound;
Either for want of handsome time and place,
Or else for feare of shame and fowle disgrace.
Thus am I hopelesse ever to attaine
My Ladies love, in such a desperate case,
But all my dayes am like to waste in vaine,
Seeking to match the chaste with th' unchaste ladies traine."

61 "Perdy," sayd Satyrane, "thou Squyre of Dames,
Great labour fondly[2] hast thou hent[3] in hand,
To get small thankes, and therewith many blames;
That may emongst Alcides labours stand." —

1 *Maintenaunce*, condition.
2 *Fondly*, foolishly.
3 *Hent*, taken.

LX. 1.— *Safe her*, &c.] Let it be remembered that these sentiments are put into the mouth of a light and vain profligate. No poet ever had a truer respect for woman than Spenser. H.

Thence backe returning to the former land,[1]
Where late he left the beast he overcame,
He found him not; for he had broke his band,
And was returnd againe unto his dame,
To tell what tydings of fayre Florimell became.

1 *Land*, place.

CANTO VIII.

The Witch creates a snowy La-
dy like to Florimell:
Who wronged by carle, by Proteus sav'd,
Is sought by Paridell.

1 So oft as I this history record,
My hart doth melt with meere compassion,
To thinke how causelesse of her owne accord
This gentle Damzell, whom I write upon,
Should plonged be in such affliction,
Without all hope of comfort or reliefe;
That sure I weene the hardest hart of stone
Would hardly finde[1] to aggravate her griefe:
For misery craves rather mercy then repriefe.[2]

2 But that accursed Hag, her hostesse late,
Had so enranckled her malitious hart,
That she desyrd th' abridgement of her fate,
Or long enlargement of her painefull smart.
Now when the beast, which by her wicked art
Late foorth she sent, she backe retourning spyde
Tyde with her golden girdle; it a part

1 *Finde*, find itself disposed. 2 *Repriefe*, reproof.

I. 3. — *Causelesse of her owne accord.*] Without having been a voluntary party to anything that caused her misfortunes. C.

Of her rich spoyles whom he had earst destroyd
She weend, and wondrous gladnes to her hart applyde:

3 And, with it ronning hast'ly to her sonne,
Thought with that sight him much to have reliv'd[1];
Who, thereby deeming sure the thing as donne,
His former griefe with furie fresh reviv'd
Much more then earst, and would have algates[2] riv'd
The hart out of his brest: for sith her dedd
He surely dempt,[3] himselfe he thought depriv'd
Quite of all hope wherewith he long had fedd
His foolish malady, and long time had misledd.

4 With thought whereof exceeding mad he grew,
And in his rage his mother would have slaine,
Had she not fled into a secret mew,[4]
Where she was wont her sprightes to entertaine,
The maisters of her art: there was she faine
To call them all in order to her ayde,
And them coniure, upon eternall paine,
To counsell her so carefully[5] dismayd
How she might heale her sonne whose senses were decayd.[6]

5 By their advice, and her owne wicked wit,
She there deviz'd a wondrous worke to frame,
Whose like on earth was never framed yit;
That even Nature selfe envide the same,

1 *Reliv'd*, reanimated.
2 *Algates*, by all means.
3 *Dempt*, deemed.
4 *Mew*, hiding place.
5 *Carefully*, sorrowfully.
6 *Decayd*, impaired.

And grudg'd to see the counterfet should shame
The thing itselfe. In hand she boldly tooke
To make another like the former dame,
Another Florimell, in shape and looke
So lively,[1] and so like, that many it mistooke.

6 The substance, whereof she the body made,
Was purest snow in massy mould congeald,
Which she had gathered in a shady glade
Of the Riphœan hils, to her reveald
By errant[2] sprights, but from all men conceald:
The same she tempred with fine mercury
And virgin wex[3] that never yet was seald,
And mingled them with perfect vermily[4];
That like a lively sanguine it seemd to the eye.

7 In stead of eyes, two burning lampes she set
In silver sockets, shyning like the skyes,
And a quicke moving spirit did arret[5]
To stirre and roll them like to womens eyes:
In stead of yellow lockes, she did devyse
With golden wyre to weave her curled head;
Yet golden wyre was not so yellow thryse[6]
As Florimells fayre heare: and, in the stead
Of life, she put a spright to rule the carcas dead;—

1 *Lively*, life-like.
2 *Errant*, wandering.
3 *Wex*, wax.
4 *Vermily*, vermilion.
5 *Arret*, appoint.
6 I. e. a third part.

VI. 4.—*Riphœan hils.*] These were mountains (probably im aginary) in the north of Scythia. H.

8 A wicked spright, yfraught with fawning guyle
And fayre resemblance above all the rest,
Which with the Prince of Darkenes fell somewhyle[1]
From heavens blis and everlasting rest:
Him needed not instruct which way were best
Himselfe to fashiōn likest Florimell,
Ne how to speake, ne how to use his gest[2];
For he in counterfesaunce[3] did excell,
And all the wyles of wemens wits knew passing well.

9 Him shaped thus she deckt in garments gay,
Which Florimell had left behind her late;
That whoso then her saw would surely say
It was herselfe whom it did imitate,
Or fayrer then herselfe, if ought algate[4]
Might fayrer be. And then she forth her brought
Unto her sonne that lay in feeble state;
Who, seeing her, gan streight upstart, and thought
She was the Lady selfe whom he so long had sought.

10 Tho, fast her clipping[5] twixt his armës twayne,
Extremely ioyed in so happy sight,
And soone forgot his former sickely payne:
But she, the more to seeme such as she hight,
Coyly rebutted his embracement light;
Yet still, with gentle countenaunce, retain'd
Enough to hold a foole in vaine delight:
Him long she so with shadowes entertain'd,
As her creatresse had in charge to her ordain'd:

1 *Somewhyle*, once on a time.
2 *Gest*, bearing.
3 *Counterfesaunce*, counterfeiting.
4 *Algate*, by any means.
5 *Clipping*, embracing.

11 Till on a day, as he disposed was
To walke the woodes with that his idole[1] faire,
Her to disport and idle time to pas
In th' open freshnes of the gentle aire,
A Knight that way there chaunced to repaire;
Yet knight he was not, but a boastfull swaine
That deedes of armes had ever in despaire,
Proud Braggadocchio, that in vaunting vaine
His glory did repose and credit did maintaine.

12 He, seeing with that chorle[2] so faire a wight
Decked with many a costly ornament,
Much merveiled thereat, as well he might,
And thought that match a fowle disparagement:
His bloody speare eftesoones he boldly bent
Against the silly clowne, who dead through feare
Fell streight to ground in great astonishment:
"Villein," sayd he, "this lady is my deare;
Dy, if thou it gainesay: I will away her beare."

13 The fearefull chorle[2] durst not gainesay nor dooe,
But trembling stood, and yielded him the pray;
Who, finding litle leasure her to wooe,
On Tromparts steed her mounted without stay,
And without reskew led her quite away.
Proud man himselfe then Braggadochio deem'd,
And next[3] to none, after that happy day,

1 *Idole*, image.
2 *Chorle*, churl.
3 *Next*, second.

XI. 8. — *Proud Braggadocchio.*] Braggadochio reappears from the third canto of the second book.

Being possessed of that spoyle, which seem'd
The fairest wight on ground and most of men esteem'd.

14 But, when hee saw himselfe free from poursute,
He gan make gentle purpose[1] to his dame
With termes of love and lewdnesse dissolute;
For he could well his glozing speaches frame
To such vaine uses that him best became:
But she thereto would lend but light regard,
As seeming sory that she ever came
Into his powre, that used her so hard
To reave[2] her honor which she more then life prefard.

15 Thus as they two of kindnes treated long,
There them by chaunce encountred on the way
An armed Knight upon a courser strong,
Whose trampling feete upon the hollow lay[3]
Seemed to thunder, and did nigh affray
That capons corage; yet he looked grim,
And faynd to cheare his lady in dismay,
Who seemd for feare to quake in every lim,
And her to save from outrage meekely prayed him.

16 Fiercely that straunger forward came; and, nigh
Approching, with bold words and bitter threat
Bad that same boaster, as he mote on high,[4]

1 *Purpose*, conversation.
2 *Reave*, take away.
3 *Lay*, lea.
4 I. e. As loudly as he could.

XV. 3. — *An armed Knight.*] Sir Ferraugh, as we learn in the second canto of the fourth book.

To leave to him that lady for excheat,
Or bide[1] him batteill without further treat.[2]
That challenge did too peremptory seeme,
And fild his senses with abashment great;
Yet, seeing nigh him ieopardy extreme,
He it dissembled well, and light seemd to esteeme;

17 Saying, "Thou foolish Knight! that weenst with words
To steale away that I with blowes have wonne,
And brought through points of many perilous swords.
But if thee list to see thy courser ronne,
Or prove thyselfe, — this sad encounter shonne,
And seeke els[3] without hazard of thy hedd."
At those prowd words that other knight begonne
To wex exceeding wroth, and him aredd[4]
To turne his steede about, or sure he should be dedd.

18 "Sith then," said Braggadochio, "needes thou wilt
Thy daies abridge, through proofe of puissaunce;
Turne we our steeds; that both in equall tilt
May meete againe, and each take happy chaunce."
This said, they both a furlongs mountenaunce[5]
Retird their steeds, to ronne in even race:
But Braggadochio with his bloody launce,

1 *Bide*, bid, offer.
2 *Treat*, parley.
3 *Els*, some other.
4 *Aredd*, advised.
5 *Mountenaunce*, amount.

XVI. 4. — *Excheat.*] *Escheat.* — Lands which are forfeited, or to which there is no heir, *escheat*, or revert to the lord of whom they are held. H.

Once having turnd, no more returnd his face,
But lefte his Love to losse, and fled himselfe apace.

19 The Knight, him seeing flie, had no regard
Him to poursew, but to the Lady rode;
And, having her from Trompart lightly reard,[1]
Upon his courser sett the lovely lode,
And with her fled away without abode[2]:
Well weened he, that fairest Florimell
It was with whom in company he yode,[3]
And so herselfe did alwaies to him tell;
So made him thinke himselfe in heven that was in hell.

20 But Florimell herselfe was far away,
Driven to great distresse by fortune straunge,
And taught the carefull mariner to play,
Sith late mischaunce had her compeld to chaunge
The land for sea, at randon there to raunge:
Yett there that cruell Queene Avengeresse,[4]
Not satisfyde so far her to estraunge
From courtly blis and wonted happinesse,
Did heape on her new waves of weary wretchednesse.

21 For, being fled into the fishers bote
For refuge from the monsters cruelty,
Long so she on the mighty maine did flote,
And with the tide drove forward carelesly;
For th' ayre was milde and cleared was the skie,
And all his windes Dan Aeolus did keepe

1 *Reard*, taken.
2 *Abode*, delay.
3 *Yode*, went.
4 I. e. Fortune.

From stirring up their stormy enmity,
As pittying to see her waile and weepe;
But all the while the fisher did securely sleepe.

22 At last when droncke with drowsinesse he woke,
And saw his drover[1] drive along the streame,
He was dismayd; and thrise his brest he stroke,
For marveill of that accident extreame:
But when he saw that blazing beauties beame,
Which with rare light his bote did beautifye,
He marveild more, and thought he yet did dreame,
Not well awakte; or that some extasye
Assotted had his sence, or dazed was his eye.

23 But, when her well avizing[2] hee perceiv'd
To be no vision nor fantasticke sight,
Great comfort of her presence he conceiv'd,
And felt in his old corage[3] new delight
To gin awake, and stir his frosen spright:
Tho rudely askte her, how she thether came?
"Ah!" sayd she, "father, I note read[4] aright
What hard misfortune brought me to this same;
Yet am I glad that here I now in safety ame.

24 "But thou, good man, sith far in sea we bee,
And the great waters gin apace to swell,
That now no more we can the mayn-land see,
Have care, I pray, to guide the cock-bote well,
Least worse on sea then us on land befell."

1 *Drover*, boat (?).
2 *Avizing*, looking at.
3 *Corage*, heart.
4 *Note read*, cannot explain.

Thereat th' old man did nought but fondly grin,
And saide, his boat the way could wisely tell:
But his deceiptfull eyes did never lin[1]
To looke on her faire face and marke her snowy skin.

25 The sight whereof in his congealed flesh
Infixt such secrete sting of greedy lust,
That the drie withered stocke it gan refresh,
And kindled heat, that soone in flame forth brust:
The driest wood is soonest burnt to dust.
Rudely to her he lept, and his rough hand,
Where ill became him, rashly would have thrust;
But she with angry scorne him did withstond,
And shamefully reproved for his rudenes fond.[2]

26 But he, that never good nor maners knew,
Her sharpe rebuke full litle did esteeme;
Hard is to teach an old horse amble trew:
The inward smoke, that did before but steeme,
Broke into open fire and rage extreme;
And now he strength gan adde unto his will,
Forcyng[3] to doe that did him fowle misseeme:
Beastly he threwe her downe, ne car'd to spill[4]
Her garments gay with scales of fish, that all did fill.

27 The silly[5] Virgin strove him to withstand
All that she might, and him in vaine revild;
Shee strugled strongly both with foote and hand
To save her honor from that villaine vilde,

1 *Lin*, cease.
2 *Fond*, foolish, doting.
3 *Forcyng*, using force.
4 *Spill*, spoil.
5 *Silly*, innocent.

And cride to heven, from humane helpe exild.
O ye brave knights, that boast this Ladies love,
Where be ye now, when she is nigh defild
Of filthy wretch? Well may she you reprove
Of falsehood or of slouth, when most it may behove!

28 But if that thou, Sir Satyran, didst weete,
Or thou, Sir Peridure, her sory state,
How soone would yee assemble many a fleete,
To fetch from sea that ye at land lost late!
Towres, citties, kingdomes, ye would ruinate
In your avengement and dispiteous rage,
Ne ought your burning fury mote abate:
But, if Sir Calidore could it presage,
No living creature could his cruelty asswage.

29 But, sith that none of all her knights is nye,
See how the heavens, of voluntary grace
And soveraine favor towards chastity,
Doe succor send to her distressed cace:
So much High God doth innocence embrace[1]!
It fortuned, whilest thus she stifly strove,
And the wide sea impórtuned long space
With shrilling shriekes, Proteus abrode did rove,
Along the fomy waves driving his finny drove.

30 Proteus is shepheard of the seas of yore,
And hath the charge of Neptunes mighty heard;

1 *Embrace*, protect.

XXVIII. 2, 8. — Sir Calidore we meet hereafter; but of Sir Peridure we hear no more. H.

An aged sire with head all frowy[1] hore,
And sprinckled frost upon his deawy beard:
Who when those pittifull outcries he heard
Through all the seas so ruefully resownd,
His charett swifte in hast he thether steard,
Which, with a teeme of scaly phocas[2] bownd,
Was drawne upon the waves, that fomed him arownd.

31 And comming to that fishers wandring bote,
That went at will withouten card or sayle,
He therein saw that yrkesome sight, which smote
Deepe indignation and compassion frayle[3]
Into his hart attonce: streight did he hayle
The greedy villein from his hoped pray,
Of which he now did very litle fayle;
And with his staffe, that drives his heard astray,
Him bett so sore, that life and sence did much dismay.

32 The whiles the pitteous lady up did ryse,
Ruffled and fowly raid[4] with filthy soyle,
And blubbred face with teares of her faire eyes;
Her heart nigh broken was with weary toyle,
To save herselfe from that outrageous spoyle:
But when she looked up, to weet what wight
Had her from so infâmous fact assoyld,[5]
For shame, but more for feare of his grim sight,
Downe in her lap she hid her face, and lowdly shright.[6]

1 *Frowy*, musty, mossy. But Qu. *frory?* frosty.
2 *Phocas*, seals.
3 *Frayle*, soft.
4 *Raid*, defiled.
5 *Assoyld*, delivered.
6 *Shright*, shrieked.

33 Herselfe not saved yet from daunger dredd
She thought, but chaung'd from one to other feare.
Like as a fearefull partridge, that is fledd
From the sharpe hauke which her attached[1] neare,
And fals to ground to seeke for succor theare,
Whereas[2] the hungry spaniells she does spye
With greedy iawes her ready for to teare:
In such distresse and sad perplexity
Was Florimell, when Proteus she did see her by.

34 But he endevored with speaches milde
Her to recomfort, and accourage bold,
Bidding her feare no more her foeman vilde,
Nor doubt himselfe; and who he was her told:
Yet all that could not from affright her hold,
Ne to recomfort her at all prevayld;
For her faint hart was with the frosen cold
Benumbd so inly, that her wits nigh fayld,
And all her sences with abashment quite were quayld.

35 Her up betwixt his rugged hands he reard,
And with his frory[3] lips full softly kist,
Whiles the cold ysickles from his rough beard
Dropped adowne upon her yvory brest:
Yet he himselfe so busily addrest,[4]
That her out of astonishment he wrought;
And, out of that same fishers filthy nest
Removing her, into his charet brought,
And there with many gentle termes her faire besought.

1 *Attached*, attacked.
2 *Whereas*, where.
3 *Frory*, frosty.
4 *Addrest*, applied.

36 But that old leachour, which with bold assault
That beautie durst presume to violate,
He cast[1] to punish for his hainous fault:
Then tooke he him, yet trembling sith of late,[2]
And tyde behind his charet, to aggrate[3]
The Virgin whom he had abusde so sore;
So drag'd him through the waves in scornfull state,
And after cast him up upon the shore;
But Florimell with him unto his bowre[4] he bore.

37 His bowre is in the bottom of the maine,
Under a mightie rocke gainst which doe rave
The roring billowes in their proud disdaine,
That with the angry working of the wave
Therein is eaten out an hollow cave,
That seemes rough masons hand with engines keene
Had long while laboured it to engrave[5]:
There was his wonne[6]; ne living wight was seene
Save one old nymph, hight Panopè, to keepe it cleane.

38 Thether he brought the sory[7] Florimell,
And entertained her the best he might,
And Panopè her entertaind eke well,
As an immortall mote a mortall wight,
To winne her liking unto his delight:
With flattering wordes he sweetly wooed her,
And offered faire guiftes t' allure her sight;

1 *Cast*, considered how.
2 I. e. since the late attack of Proteus.
3 *Aggrate*, gratify.
4 *Bowre*, home.
5 *Engrave*, cut in.
6 *Wonne*, dwelling.
7 *Sory*, sad.

But she both offers and the offerer
Despysde, and all the fawning of the flatterer.

39 Dayly he tempted her with this or that,
And never suffred her to be at rest:
But evermore she him refused flat,
And all his fained kindnes did detest;
So firmely she had sealed up her brest.
Sometimes he boasted that a god he hight,
But she a mortall creature loved best:
Then he would make himselfe a mortall wight;
But then she said she lov'd none but a Faery Knight.

40 Then like a Faerie Knight himselfe he drest;
For every shape on him he could endew:
Then like a king he was to her exprest,
And offred kingdoms unto her in vew
To be his leman and his lady trew:
But when all this he nothing saw prevaile,
With harder meanes he cast her to subdew,
And with sharpe threates her often did assayle;
So thinking for to make her stubborne corage quayle.

41 To dreadfull shapes he did himselfe transforme:
Now like a gyaunt; now like to a feend;
Then like a centaure; then like to a storme
Raging within the waves. Thereby he weend
Her will to win unto his wished eend:
But when with feare, nor favour, nor with all
He els could doe, he saw himselfe esteemd,
Downe in a dongeon deepe he let her fall,
And threatned there to make her his eternall thrall.

42 Eternall thraldome was to her more liefe[1]
Then losse of chastitie, or chaunge of love:
Dye had she rather in tormenting griefe
Then any should of falsenesse her reprove,
Or loosenes, that she lightly did remove.[2]
Most vertuous Virgin! glory be thy meed,
And crowne of heavenly prayse with saintes above,
Where most sweet hymmes of this thy famous deed
Are still emongst them song, that far my rymes exceed.

43 Fit song of angels caroled to bee!
But yet whatso my feeble Muse can frame,
Shal be t' advance[3] thy goodly chastitee,
And to enroll thy memorable name
In th' heart of every honourable dame,
That they thy vertuous deedes may imitate,
And be partakers of thy endlesse fame.
Yt yrkes me leave thee in this wofull state,
To tell of Satyrane where I him left of late:

44 Who having ended with that Squyre of Dames
A long discourse of his adventures vayne,
The which himselfe then ladies more defames,
And finding not th' Hyena to be slayne,
With that same Squyre retourned back agayne
To his first way: and, as they forward went,
They spyde a Knight fayre pricking on the playne,
As if he were on some adventure bent,
And in his port appeared manly hardiment.

[1] *Liefe*, dear. [2] *Remove*, change. [3] *Advance*, extol.

45 Sir Satyrane him towardes did addresse,
To weet what wight he was, and what his quest:
And, comming nigh, eftsoones he gan to gesse
Both by the burning hart which on his brest
He bare, and by the colours in his crest,
That Paridell it was: tho to him yode,
And, him saluting as beseemed best,
Gan first inquire of tydinges farre abrode;
And afterwardes on what adventure now he rode.

46 Who thereto answering said: "The tydinges bad,
Which now in Faery Court all men doe tell,
Which turned hath great mirth to mourning sad,
Is the late ruine of proud Marinell,
And suddein parture of faire Florimell
To find him forth: and after her are gone
All the brave knightes, that doen in armes excell,
To savegard her ywandred all alone;
Emongst the rest my lott (unworthy') is to be one."

47 "Ah! gentle Knight," said then Sir Satyrane,
"Thy labour all is lost, I greatly dread,
That hast a thanklesse service on thee ta'ne,
And offrest sacrifice unto the dead:
For dead, I surely * doubt,[1] thou maist aread[2]

[1] *Doubt*, fear. [2] *Aread*, conceive.

XLV. 6. — *That Paridell it was.*] Paridell is an agreeable and accomplished libertine. The burning heart is also a part of the description of Lechery in the fourth canto of the first book. Paridell, according to Upton, represents the Earl of Westmoreland. H.

* Qu. *sorely?*

Henceforth for ever Florimell to bee ;
That all the noble Knights of Maydenhead,
Which her ador'd, may sore repent with mee,
And all faire ladies may for ever sory bee."

48 Which wordes when Paridell had heard, his hew
Gan greatly chaung, and seemd dismaid to bee;
Then said: "Fayre Sir, how may I weene it trew,
That ye doe tell in such uncerteintee?
Or speake ye of report, or did ye see
Iust cause of dread, that makes ye doubt so sore?
For, perdie, elles how mote it ever bee,
That ever hand should dare for to engore[1]
Her noble blood! The hevens such crueltie abhore."

49 "These eyes did see that they will ever rew
To have seene," quoth he, "whenas a monstrous beast
The palfrey whereon she did travell slew,
And of his bowels made his bloody feast:
Which speaking token sheweth at the least
Her certeine losse, if not her sure decay[2]:
Besides, that more suspicion encreast,
I found her golden girdle cast astray,
Distaynd with durt and blood, as relique of the pray."

[1] *Engore*, pierce, shed. [2] *Decay*, destruction.

XLIX. 8. — *I found her golden girdle cast astray.*] In the second stanza of this book, we are told that the beast went back with the girdle to the witch. H.

50 "Ay me!" said Paridell, "the signes be sadd;
And, but God turne the same to good soothsay,[1]
That ladies safetie is sore to be dradd:
Yet will I not forsake my forward way,
Till triall doe more certeine truth bewray."
"Faire Sir," quoth he, "well may it you succeed!
Ne long shall Satyrane behind you stay;
But to the rest, which in this quest proceed,
My labour adde, and be partaker of their speed."

51 "Ye noble Knights," said then the Squyre of Dames,
"Well may yee speede in so praiseworthy payne!
But sith the sunne now ginnes to slake his beames
In deawy vapours of the westerne mayne,
And lose the teme out of his weary wayne,
Mote not mislike you also to abate
Your zealous hast, till morrow next againe
Both light of heven and strength of men relate[2]:
Which if ye please, to yonder Castle turne your gate."

52 That counsell pleased well; so all yfere[3]
Forth marched to a castle them before;
Where soone arryving they restrained were
Of ready entraunce, which ought evermore
To errant knights be commune. Wondrous sore
Thereat displeasd they were, till that young Squyre
Gan them informe the cause why that same dore
Was shut to all which lodging did desyre:
The which to let you weet will further time requyre.

1 *Soothsay*, omen.
2 *Relate*, bring back.
3 *Yfere*, together.

CANTO IX.

Malbecco will no straunge knights host,[1]
For peevish gealosy:
Paridell giusts with Britomart:
Both shew their auncestry.

1 Redoubted Knights, and honorable Dames,
To whom I levell all my labours end,
Right sore I feare least with unworthie blames
This odious argument my rymes should shend,[2]
Or ought your goodly patience offend,
Whiles of a wanton lady I doe write,
Which with her loose incontinence doth blend[3]
The shyning glory of your soveraine light;
And knighthood fowle defaced by a faithlesse knight.

2 But never let th' ensample of the bad
Offend the good: for good, by paragone[4]
Of evill, may more notably be rad[5];
As white seemes fayrer macht with blacke attone[6]:
Ne all are shamed by the fault of one:
For lo! in heven, whereas all goodnes is,
Emongst the angels, a whole legione

[1] *Host*, entertain.
[2] *Shend*, disgrace.
[3] *Blend*, blind, dim.
[4] *Paragone*, contrast.
[5] *Rad*, discerned.
[6] *Attone*, at one, together.

Of wicked sprightes did fall from happy blis;
What wonder then if one, of women all, did mis[1]?

3 Then listen, Lordings, if ye list to weet
The cause why Satyrane and Paridell
Mote not be entertaynd,[2] as seemed meet,
Into that castle, as that squyre does tell.
"Therein a cancred crabbed carle[3] does dwell,
That has no skill of court nor courtesie,
Ne cares what men say of him ill or well:
For all his dayes he drownes in privitie,
Yet has full large to live and spend at libertie.

4 "But all his mind is set on mucky pelfe,
To hoord up heapes of evill-gotten masse,
For which he others wrongs, and wreckes himselfe.
Yet is he lincked to a lovely lasse,
Whose beauty doth her bounty[4] far surpasse.
The which to him both far unequall yeares
And also far unlike conditions[5] has;
For she does ioy to play emongst her peares,
And to be free from hard restraynt and gealous feares.

5 "But he is old, and withered like hay,
Unfit faire ladies service to supply;
The privie guilt whereof makes him alway
Suspect her truth, and keepe continuall spy
Upon her with his other blincked eye;

1 *Mis*, go astray.
2 *Entertaynd*, received.
3 *Carle*, churl.
4 *Bounty*, virtue.
5 *Conditions*, qualities.

V. 5. — *His other blincked eye.*] *Other*, as before, in the sense

Ne suffreth he resort of living wight
Approch to her, ne keepe her company,
But in close bowre[1] her mewes from all mens sight,
Depriv'd of kindly ioy and naturall delight.

6 "Malbecco he, and Hellenore she hight;
Unfitly yokt together in one teeme.
That is the cause why never any knight
Is suffred here to enter, but he seeme
Such as no doubt of him he neede misdeeme."
Thereat Sir Satyrane gan smyle, and say:
"Extremely mad the man I surely deeme
That weenes, with watch and hard restraynt, to stay
A womans will which is disposd to go astray.

7 "In vaine he feares that which he cannot shonne:
For who wotes not, that womans subtiltyes
Can guylen[2] Argus, when she list misdonne?
It is not yron bandes, nor hundred eyes,
Nor brasen walls, nor many wakefull spyes,
That can withhold her wilfull-wandring feet;
But fast goodwill, with gentle courtesyes,
And timely service to her pleasures meet,
May her perhaps containe[3] that else would algates[4] fleet.[5]"

1 *Bowre*, chamber.
2 *Guylen*, deceive.
3 *Containe*, hold in.
4 *Algates*, at all events.
5 *Fleet*, flee.

---

of *one of two*. Malbecco was quite blind of one eye, and the other was "blincked" or dimmed. C.

VI. 1. — *Malbecco* means cuckold. *Hellenore* is derived from the Grecian Helen.

8 "Then is he not more mad," sayd Paridell,
"That hath himselfe unto such service sold,[1]
In dolefull thraldome all his dayes to dwell?
For sure a foole I doe him firmely hold,
That loves his fetters, though they were of gold.
But why doe wee devise of others ill,[2]
Whyles thus we suffer this same dotard old
To keepe us out in scorne, of his owne will,
And rather do not ransack all, and himselfe kill?"

9 "Nay, let us first," sayd Satyrane, "entreat
The man, by gentle meanes, to let us in;
And afterwardes affray with cruell threat,
Ere that we to efforce it doe begin:
Then, if all fayle, we will by force it win,
And eke reward the wretch for his mesprise,[3]
As may be worthy of his haynous sin."
That counsell pleasd: then Paridell did rise,
And to the castle-gate approcht in quiet wise:

10 Whereat soft knocking, entrance he desyrd.
The good man selfe, which then the porter playd,
Him answered, that all were now retyrd
Unto their rest, and all the keyes convayd
Unto their maister who in bed was layd,
That none him durst awake out of his dreme;
And therefore them of patience gently prayd.
Then Paridell began to chaunge his theme,
And threatned him with force and punishment extreme.

1 I. e. who has married at all.
2 I. e. talk of other's misfortunes.
3 *Mesprise*, contempt.

11 But all in vaine; for nought mote him relent:
And now so long before the wicket fast
They wayted, that the night was forward spent,
And the faire welkin [1] fowly overcast
Gan blowen up a bitter stormy blast,
With showre and hayle so horrible and dred,
That this faire many [2] were compeld at last
To fly for succour to a little shed,
The which beside the gate for swyne was ordered.

12 It fortuned, soone after they were gone,
Another Knight, whom tempest thether brought,
Came to that castle, and with earnest mone,
Like as the rest, late entrance deare [3] besought;
But, like so as the rest, he prayd for nought;
For flatly he of entrance was refusd:
Sorely thereat he was displeasd, and thought
How to avenge himselfe so sore abusd,
And evermore the carle of courtesie accusd.[4]

13 But, to avoyde th' intollerable stowre,[5]
He was compeld to seeke some refuge neare,
And to that shed, to shrowd him from the showre,
He came, which full of guests he found whyl-
eare,[6]
So as he was not let to enter there:
Whereat he gan to wex exceeding wroth,
And swore that he would lodge with them yfere,[7]

1 *Welkin*, sky
2 *Many*, company.
3 *Deare*, earnestly.
4 I. e. of lack of courtesy.
5 *Stowre*, storm.
6 *Whyleare*, before (him).
7 *Yfere*, together.

Or them dislodg, all were they liefe[1] or loth;
And so defyde them each, and so defyde them both.

14 Both were full loth to leave that needful tent,[2]
And both full loth in darkenesse to debate[3];
Yet both full liefe him lodging to have lent,[4]
And both full liefe his boasting to abate:
But chiefely Paridell his hart did grate
To heare him threaten so despightfully,
As if he did a dogge in kenell rate
That durst not barke; and rather had he dy
Then, when he was defyde, in coward corner ly.

15 Tho, hastily remounting to his steed,
He forth issew'd; like as a boystrous winde,
Which in th' earthes hollow caves hath long ben hid
And shut up fast within her prisons blind,
Makes the huge element, against her kinde,[5]
To move and tremble as it were aghast,
Untill that it an issew forth may finde;
Then forth it breakes, and with his furious blast
Confounds both land and seas, and skyes doth overcast.

16 Their steel-hed speares they strongly coucht, and met
Together with impetuous rage and forse,
That with the terrour of their fierce affret[6]
They rudely drove to ground both man and horse,
That each awhile lay like a sencelesse corse.
But Paridell, sore brused with the blow,

1 *Liefe*, willing.
2 *Tent*, shelter.
3 *Debate*, quarrel.
4 I. e. if there had been room.
5 *Kinde*, nature.
6 *Affret*, encounter.

Could not arise, the counterchaunge to scorse[1];
Till that young Squyre him reared from below;
Then drew he his bright sword, and gan about him
throw.

7 But Satyrane, forth stepping, did them stay,
And with faire treaty pacifide their yre:
Then, when they were accorded[2] from the fray,
Against that Castles lord they gan conspire,
To heape on him dew vengeaunce for his hire.
They beene agreed, and to the gates they goe
To burne the same with únquenchable fire,
And that uncurteous carle, their commune foe,
To doe fowle death to die, or wrap in grievous woe.

18 Malbecco seeing them resolvd in deed
To flame the gates, and hearing them to call
For fire in earnest, ran with fearfull speed,
And, to them calling from the castle wall,
Besought them humbly him to beare with all,
As ignorant of servants bad abuse
And slacke attendaunce unto straungers call.
The knights were willing all things to excuse,
Though nought belev'd, and entraunce late did not
refuse.

19 They beene ybrought into a comely bowre,
And servd of all things that mote needfull bee;
Yet secretly their hoste did on them lowre,
And welcomde more for feare then charitee;

1 *Scorse*, exchange, give back. 2 *Accorded*, made to agree.

But they dissembled what they did not see,[1]
And welcomed themselves. Each gan undight
Their garments wett, and weary armour free,
To dry themselves by Vulcanes flaming light,
And eke their lately bruzed parts to bring in plight.[2]

20 And eke that straunger knight emongst the rest
Was for like need enforst to disaray:
Thò, whenas vailed was her lofty crest,[3]
Her golden locks, that were in tramells[4] gay
Upbounden, did themselves adowne display,
And raught unto her heeles; like sunny beames,
That in a cloud their light did long time stay,
Their vapour vaded,[5] shewe their golden gleames,
And through the persant[6] aire shoote forth their azure streames.

21 Shee also dofte her heavy haberieon,[7]
Which the faire feature of her limbs did hyde;
And her well-plighted[8] frock, which she did won[9]
To tucke about her short when she did ryde,
Shee low let fall, that flowd from her lanck[10] syde
Downe to her foot with carelesse modestee.
Then of them all she plainly was espyde
To be a woman wight, unwist to bee,
The fairest woman wight that ever eie did see.

1 I. e. to be hospitably received.
2 *Plight*, order.
3 I. e. when she had doffed her helmet.
4 *Tramells*, braids.
5 *Vaded*, dissipated.
6 *Persant*, sharp, clear.
7 *Haberieon*, coat of mail.
8 *Well-plighted*, well-folded.
9 *Won*, use.
10 *Lanck*, slender.

22 Like as Bellona, being late returnd
From slaughter of the giaunts conquered, —
Where proud Encelade, whose wide nosethrils burnd
With breathed flames like to a furnace redd,
Transfixed with her speare, downe tombled dedd
From top of Hemus by him heaped hye, —
Hath loosd her helmet from her lofty hedd,
And her Gorgonian shield gins to untye
From her lefte arme, to rest in glorious victorye.

23 Which whenas they beheld, they smitten were
With great amazement of so wondrous sight;
And each on other, and they all on her,
Stood gazing; as if suddein great affright
Had them surprizd. At last avizing[1] right
Her goodly personage and glorious hew,
Which they so much mistooke, they tooke delight
In their first error, and yett still anew
With wonder of her beauty fed their hongry vew.

24 Yet note[2] their hongry vew be satisfide,
But, seeing, still the more desir'd to see,
And ever firmely fixed did abide
In contemplation of divinitee:
But most they mervaild at her chevalree
And noble prowesse which they had approv'd,

1 *Avizing*, contemplating. 2 *Note*, could not.

XXII. 1. — Bellona here is meant for Minerva, which is indeed the reading of all the later editions. C.

That much they faynd to know who she mote bee;
Yet none of all them her thereof amov'd[1];
Yet every one her likte, and every one her lov'd.

25 And Paridell, though partly discontent
With his late fall and fowle indignity,
Yet was soone wonne his malice to relent,
Through gratious regard of her faire eye,
And knightly worth which he too late did try,
Yet tried did adore. Supper was dight;
Then they Malbecco prayd of courtesy,
That of his lady they might have the sight
And company at meat, to doe them more delight.

26 But he, to shifte[2] their curious request,
Gan causen[3] why she could not come in place,
Her crased[4] helth, her late recourse to rest,
And humid evening, ill for sicke folkes cace:
But none of those excuses could take place;
Ne would they eate, till she in presence came:
Shee came in presence with right comely grace,
And fairely them saluted, as became,
And shewd herselfe in all a gentle, courteous dame.

27 They sate to meat; and Satyrane his chaunce
Was her before, and Paridell beside;
But he himselfe[5] sate looking still askaunce
Gainst Britomart, and ever closely eide
Sir Satyrane, that glaunces might not glide:

1 I. e. questioned.
2 *Shifte*, evade.
3 *Causen*, assign reasons.
4 *Crased*, impaired.
5 I. e. Malbecco.

But his blinde eie, that sided[1] Paridell,
All his demeasnure[2] from his sight did hide:
On her faire face so did he feede his fill,
And sent close[3] messages of love to her at will.

28 And ever and anone, when none was ware,
With speaking lookes, that close embassage bore,
He rov'd[4] at her, and told his secret care;
For all that art he learned had of yore:
Ne was she ignoraunt of that leud lore,
But in his eye his meaning wisely redd,
And with the like him aunswerd evermore:
Shee sent at him one fyrie dart, whose hedd
Empoisned was with privy lust and gealous dredd.

29 He from that deadly throw made no defence,
But to the wound his weake heart opened wyde:
The wicked engine through false influence
Past through his eies, and secretly did glyde
Into his heart, which it did sorely gryde.[5]
But nothing new to him was that same paine,
Ne paine at all; for he so ofte had tryde
The powre thereof, and lov'd so oft in vaine,
That thing of course he counted, love to entertaine.

30 Thenceforth to her he sought to intimate
His inward griefe, by meanes to him well knowne:
Now Bacchus fruit out of the silver plate

1 *Sided*, was on the side towards.
2 *Demeasnure*, demeanor.
3 *Close*, secret.
4 *Rov'd*, shot.
5 *Gryde*, pierce.

XXX. 3.— So Paris (after whom Paridell is named) makes love

He on the table dasht, as overthrowne,
Or of the fruitfull liquor overflowne;
And by the dauncing bubbles did divine,
Or therein write to lett his love be showne;
Which well she redd out of the learned line:
A sacrament prophane in mistery of wine.[1]

31 And, whenso of his hand the pledge she raught,[2]
The guilty cup she fained to mistake,
And in her lap did shed her idle draught,
Shewing desire her inward flame to slake.
By such close signes they secret way did make
Unto their wils, and One-eies watch escape:
Two eies him needeth, for to watch and wake,
Who lovers will deceive. Thus was the ape,
By their faire handling,[3] put into Malbeccoes cape.

32 Now, when of meats and drinks they had their fill,
Purpose was moved[4] by that gentle dame
Unto those knights adventurous, to tell
Of deeds of armes which unto them became,[5]
And every one his kindred and his name.
Then Paridell, in whom a kindly[6] pride
Of gratious speach and skill his words to frame

[1] I. e. wine being profanely used to symbolize unlawful love.
[2] *Raught*, reached.
[3] *Handling*, management.
[4] I. e. a proposition was made.
[5] *Became*, happened.
[6] *Kindly*, natural.

---

to Helen, Hellenore's prototype. Ovid. Epist. XVII. 75, cited by Upton. C.

XXXI. 8. — *Thus was the ape*, &c.] To put an ape into one's hood or cap, is a proverbial expression for making a fool of him.

Abounded, being yglad of so fitte tide[1]
Him to commend to her, thus spake, of al well eide:

33 "Troy, that art now nought but an idle name,
And in thine ashes buried low dost lie,
Though whilome far much greater then thy fame,
Before that angry gods and cruell skie
Upon thee heapt a direfull destinie;
What boots it boast thy glorious descent,
And fetch from heven thy great genealogie,
Sith all thy worthie prayses being blent,
Their ofspring hath embaste, and later glory shent!

34 "Most famous worthy of the world, by whome
That warre was kindled which did Troy inflame,
And stately towres of Ilion whilóme
Brought unto balefull ruine, was by name
Sir Paris far renowmd through noble fame;
Who, through great prowesse and bold hardinesse,
From Lacedæmon fetcht the fayrest dame
That ever Greece did boast, or knight possesse,
Whom Venus to him gave for meed of worthinesse:

35 "Fayre Helene, flowre of beautie excellent,
And girlond of the mighty conquerours,
That madest many ladies deare[2] lament

1 *Tide*, time. 2 *Deare*, dearly.

XXXIII. 8, 9.—"Since the stain which has come upon thine ancient renown has disgraced the offspring of thy great ancestors, and sullied thy glory in later times." C.

The heavie losse of their brave paramours,
Which they far off beheld from Troian toures,
And saw the fieldes of faire Scamander strowne
With carcases of noble warrioures,
Whose fruitlesse lives were under furrow sowne,
And Xanthus sandy bankes with blood all overflowne!

36 "From him my linage I derive aright,
Who long before the ten yeares siege of Troy,
Whiles yet on Ida he a shepeheard hight,
On faire Oenone got a lovely boy,
Whom, for remembrance of her passed ioy,
She, of his father, Parius did name;
Who, after Greekes did Priams realme destroy,
Gathred the Troian reliques sav'd from flame,
And, with them sayling thence, to th' isle of Paros came.

37 "That was by him cald Paros, which before
Hight Nausa; there he many yeares did raine,
And built Nausicle by the Pontick shore;
The which he dying lefte next in remaine
To Paridas his sonne,
From whom I, Paridell, by kin descend:
But, for faire ladies love and glories gaine,

XXXV. 9. — *Xanthus.*] Scamander and Xanthus are different names of the same river. He should have said Scamander and Simois.

XXXVI. 4. — *On faire Oenone*, &c.] Paris had a son by Oenone, a nymph of Mount Ida, before he went to Sparta. The rest of this narrative is the poet's own invention. H.

My native soile have lefte, my dayes to spend
In seewing[1] deeds of armes, my lives and labors end."

38 Whenas the noble Britomart heard tell
Of Troian warres and Priams citie sackt,
(The ruefull story of Sir Paridell,)
She was empassiond[2] at that piteous act,
With zelous envy[3] of Greekes cruell fact[4]
Against that nation, from whose race of old
She heard that she was lineally extract:
For noble Britons sprong from Troians bold,
And Troynovant[5] was built of old Troyes ashes cold

39 Then, sighing soft awhile, at last she thus:
"O lamentable fall of famous towne,
Which raignd so many yeares victorious,
And of all Asie bore the soveraine crowne,
In one sad night consumd and throwen downe!
What stony hart, that heares thy haplesse fate,
Is not empierst with deepe compassiowne,
And makes ensample of mans wretched state,
That floures so fresh at morne, and fades at evening late!

40 "Behold, Sir, how your pitifull complaint
Hath fownd another partner of your payne:
For nothing may impresse so deare constraint
As countries cause, and commune foes disdayne.

1 *Seewing*, pursuing.
2 *Empassiond*, moved.
3 *Envy*, indignation.
4 *Fact*, deed.
5 *Troynovant*, London.

But, if it should not grieve you backe agayne
To turne your course, I would to heare desyre
What to Aeneas fell; sith that men sayne[1]
He was not in the cities wofull fyre
Consum'd, but did himselfe to safëty retyre."

41 "Anchyses sonne, begott of Venus fayre,"
Said he, "out of the flames for safegard fled,
And with a remnant did to sea repayre;
Where he, through fatall errour,[2] long was led
Full many yeares, and weetlesse[3] wandered
From shore to shore emongst the Lybick sandes,
Ere rest he fownd. Much there he suffered,
And many perilles past in forreine landes,
To save his people sad from victours vengefull handes.

42 "At last in Latium he did arryve,
Where he with cruell warre was entertaind[4]
Of th' inland folke which sought him backe to drive,
Till he with old Latinus was constraind
To contract wedlock, so the Fates ordaind;
Wedlocke contract in blood, and eke in blood
Accomplished, that many deare complaind:
The rivall slaine, the victour (through the flood
Escaped hardly) hardly praisd his wedlock good.

43 "Yet, after all, he victour did survive,
And with Latinus did the kingdom part:
But after, when both nations gan to strive

1 *Sayne*, say.
2 *Fatall errour*, predestined wandering.
3 *Weetlesse*, unknowing.
4 *Entertaind*, received.

Into their names the title to convart,
His sonne Iülus did from thence depart
With all the warlike youth of Troians bloud,
And in Long Alba plast his throne apart;
Where faire it florished and long time stoud,
Till Romulus, renewing it, to Rome remoud."[1]

44 "There, there," said Britomart, "afresh appeard
The glory of the later world to spring,
And Troy againe out of her dust was reard
To sitt in second seat of soveraine king
Of all the world, under her governing.
But a third kingdom yet is to arise
Out of the Troians scattered ofspríng,
That, in all glory and great enterprise,
Both first and second Troy shall dare to equalise.

45 "It Troynovant is hight, that with the waves
Of wealthy Thamis washed is along,
Upon whose stubborne neck (whereat he raves
With roring rage, and sore himselfe does throng,
That all men feare to tempt his billowes strong)
She fastned hath her foot; which standes so hy,
That it a wonder of the world is song
In forreine landes; and all which passen by,
Beholding it from farre, doe thinke it threates the skye.

46 "The Troian Brute did first that citie fownd,
And Hygate made the meare[2] thereof by west,
And Overt-gate by north: that is the bownd

[1] *Remoud*, removed. [2] *Meare*, boundary.

Toward the land; two rivers bownd the rest.
So huge a scope at first him seemed best,
To be the compasse of his kingdomes seat:
So huge a mind could not in lesser rest,
Ne in small meares containe his glory great,
That Albion had conquered first by warlike feat."

47 "Ah! fairest Lady-Knight," said Paridell,
"Pardon I pray my heedlesse oversight,
Who had forgot that whylome I hard tell
From aged Mnemon; for my wits beene light.
Indeed he said, if I remember right,
That of the antique Troian stocke there grew
Another plant, that raught to wondrous hight,
And far abroad his mightie braunches threw
Into the utmost angle of the world he knew.

48 "For that same Brute, whom much he did advaunce
In all his speach, was Sylvius his sonne,
Whom having slain through luckles arrowes glaunce,
He fled for feare of that he had misdonne,
Or els for shame, so fowle reproch to shonne,
And with him ledd to sea an youthly trayne;
Where wearie wandring they long time did wonne,[1]
And many fortunes prov'd in th' ocean mayne,
And great adventures found, that now were long to
sayne.

49 "At last by fatall course they driven were
Into an island spatious and brode,

[1] *Wonne*, continue.

The furthest north that did to them appeare :
Which, after rest, they, seeking farre abrode,
Found it the fittest soyle for their abode,
Fruitfull of all thinges fitt for living foode,
But wholy waste and void of peoples trode,[1]
Save an huge nation of the geaunts broode
That fed on living flesh, and dronck mens vitall blood.

50 " Whom he, through wearie wars and labours long,
Subdewd with losse of many Britons bold :
In which the great Goëmagot of strong
Corineus, and Coulín of Debon old,
Were overthrowne and laide on th' earth full cold,
Which quaked under their so hideous masse :
A famous history to bee enrold
In everlasting moniments of brasse,
That all the ántique worthies merits far did passe.

51 " His worke great Troynovant, his worke is eke
Faire Lincolne, both renowmed far away ;
That who from east to west will endlong seeke,
Cannot two fairer cities find this day,
Except Cleopolis ; so heard I say
Old Mnemon ! — Therefore, Sir,[2] I greet you well
Your countrey kin[3] ; and you entyrely[4] pray
Of pardon for the strife which late befell
Betwixt us both unknowne." So ended Paridell.

52 But all the while that he these speeches spent,
Upon his lips hong faire Dame Hellenore,

1 *Trode*, tread, footstep.
2 He addresses her as a knight.
3 I. e. I welcome you for a countryman.
4 *Entyrely*, sincerely.

With vigilant regard and dew attent,[1]
Fashioning worldes of fancies evermore
In her fraile witt, that now her quite forlore[2]:
The whiles unwares away her wondring eye
And greedy eares her weake hart from her bore:
Which he perceiving, ever privily,
In speaking, many false belgardes[3] at her let fly.

53 So long these knightes discoursed diversly
Of straunge affaires, and noble hardiment,
Which they had past with mickle ieopardy,
That now the humid night was farforth spent,
And hevenly lampes were halfendeale[4] ybrent[5]:
Which th' old man seeing wel, who too long thought
Every discourse, and every argument,
Which by the houres he measured, besought
Them go to rest. So all unto their bowres[6] were brought.

1 *Attent*, attention.
2 *Forlore*, deserted.
3 *Belgardes*, sweet glances.
4 *Halfendeale*, the half part
5 *Ybrent*, burned.
6 *Bowres*, chambers.

CANTO X.

Paridell rapeth Hellenore;
  Malbecco her poursewes;
Fynds emongst Satyres, whence with him
  To turne she doth refuse.

1 THE morow next, so soone as Phœbus lamp
  Bewrayed had the world with early light,
  And fresh Aurora had the shady damp
  Out of the goodly heven amoved quight,
  Faire Britomart and that same Faery Knight
  Uprose, forth on their iourney for to wend:
  But Paridell complaynd, that his late fight
  With Britomart so sore did him offend,
That ryde he could not till his hurts he did amend.

2 So foorth they far'd; but he behind them stayd,
  Maulgre his host, who grudged grivously
  To house a guest that would be needes obayd,
  And of his owne him left not liberty:
  Might wanting measure moveth surquedry.
  Two things he feared, but the third was death;
  That fiers young mans unruly maystery;
  His money, which he lov'd as living breath;
And his faire wife, whom honest long he kept uneath.[1]

[1] *Uneath*, with difficulty.

II. 5.—*Might wanting measure*, &c.] Power unrestrained leads to insolence.

3 But patience perforce; he must abie[1]
What fortune and his fate on him will lay:
Fond is the feare that findes no remedie.
Yet warily he watcheth every way,
By which he feareth evill happen may;
So th' evill thinkes by watching to prevent:
Ne doth he suffer her, nor night nor day,
Out of his sight herselfe once to absent:
So doth he punish her, and eke himselfe torment.

4 But Paridell kept better watch then hee,
A fit occasion for his turne to finde.
False Love! why do men say thou canst not see,
And in their foolish fancy feigne thee blinde,
That with thy charmes the sharpest sight doest binde,
And to thy will abuse? Thou walkest free,
And seest every secret of the minde;
Thou seest all, yet none at all sees thee:
All that is by the working of thy deitee.

5 So perfect in that art was Paridell,
That he Malbeccoes halfen eye[2] did wyle;
His halfen eye he wiled wondrous well,
And Hellenors both eyes did eke beguyle,
Both eyes and hart attonce, during the whyle
That he there soiourned his woundes to heale;
That Cupid selfe, it seeing, close[3] did smyle

1 *Abie*, abide.
2 *Halfen eye*, his one "blincked" or imperfect eye.
3 *Close*, secretly.

III. 1.—*But patience perforce.*] A proverb equivalent to "What can't be cured must be endured."

To weet how he her love away did steale,
And bad that none their ioyous treason should reveale.

6 The learned[1] lover lost no time nor tyde
That least avantage mote to him afford,
Yet bore so faire a sayle, that none espyde
His secret drift till he her layd abord.
Whenso in open place and commune bord[2]
He fortùn'd her to meet, with commune speach
He courted her; yet bayted every word,
That his ungentle hoste n'ote[3] him appeach
Of vile ungentlenesse or hospitages breach.

7 But when apart, (if ever her apart
He found,) then his false engins fast he plyde,
And all the sleights unbosomd in his hart:
He sigh'd, he sobd, he swownd, he perdy dyde,
And cast himselfe on ground her fast besyde:
Tho, when againe he him bethought to live,
He wept, and wayld, and false laments belyde,[4]
Saying, but if she mercie would him give,
That he mote algates[5] dye, yet did his death forgive.

8 And otherwhyles with amorous delights
And pleasing toyes he would her entertaine;
Now singing sweetly to surprize her sprights,
Now making layes of love and lovers paine,
Bransles,[6] ballads, virelayes,[7] and verses vaine;

1 *Learned*, i. e. skilful.
2 *Bord*, table.
3 *N'ote*, might not.
4 *Belyde*, counterfeited.
5 *Algates*, at all events.
6 *Bransles*, brawls, dancing-tunes.
7 *Virelayes*, a sort of rondeau.

Oft purposes, oft riddles, he devysd,
And thousands like which flowed in his braine,
With which he fed her fancy, and entysd
To take to his new love, and leave her old despysd.

9 And every where he might and everie while
He did her service dewtifull, and sewd
At hand with humble pride and pleasing guile;
So closely yet, that none but she it vewd,
Who well perceived all, and all indewd.[1]
Thus finely did he his false nets dispred,
With which he many weake harts had subdewd
Of yore, and many had ylike misled:
What wonder then if she were likewise carried?

10 No fort so fensible, no wals so strong,
But that continuall battery will rive,
Or daily siege, through dispurvayaunce [2] long
And lacke of reskewes, will to parley drive;
And peece[3] that unto parley eare will give,
Will shortly yield itselfe, and will be made
The vassall of the victors will bylive[4]:
That stratageme had oftentimes assayd
This crafty paramoure, and now it plaine displayd:

1 I. e. took, or applied to herself.
2 *Dispurvayaunce*, want of provisions.
3 *Peece*, castle.
4 *Bylive*, quickly.

VIII. 6. — *Purposes* means the game of cross-purposes, or questions and answers. A knowledge of riddles seems to have been an accomplishment so necessary to the character of a lover, that Slender, in the Merry Wives of Windsor, is greatly distressed on finding, when he is introduced to Anne Page, that his man had not his *Book of Riddles* about him. — TODD.

11 For through his traines [1] he her intrapped hath,
That she her love and hart hath wholy sold
To him without regard of gaine, or scath,[2]
Or care of credite, or of husband old,
Whom she hath vow'd to dub a fayre cucquóld.
Nought wants but time and place, which shortly shee
Devized hath, and to her lover told.
It pleased well: so well they both agree;
So readie rype to ill, ill wemens counsels bee!

12 Darke was the evening, fit for lovers stealth;
When chaunst Malbecco busie be elsewhere,
She to his closet went, where all his wealth
Lay hid; thereof she countlesse summes did reare,[3]
The which she meant away with her to beare;
The rest she fyr'd, for sport or for despight:
As Hellene, when she saw aloft appeare
The Troiane flames and reach to hevens hight,
Did clap her hands, and ioyed at that dolefull sight.

13 This second Helene, fayre Dame Hellenore,
The whiles her husband ran with sory haste
To quench the flames which she had tyn'd[4] before,
Laught at his foolish labour spent in waste,
And ran into her lovers armes right fast;
Where streight embraced she to him did cry
And call alowd for helpe, ere helpe were past;
For lo! that guest did beare her forcibly,
And meant to ravish her, that rather had to dy!

[1] *Traines*, stratagems.
[2] *Scath*, injury.
[3] *Reare*, take away.
[4] *Tyn'd*, kindled.

14 The wretched man, hearing her call for ayd,
And ready seeing him with her to fly,
In his disquiet mind was much dismayd:
But when againe he backeward cast his eye,
And saw the wicked fire so furiously
Consume his hart, and scorch his idoles face,
He was therewith distressed diversely,
Ne wist he how to turne, nor to what place:
Was never wretched man in such a wofull cace.

15 Ay when to him she cryde, to her he turnd,
And left the fire; love, money overcame:
But when he marked how his money burnd,
He left his wife; money did love disclame:
Both was he loth to loose his loved dame,
And loth to leave his liefest[1] pelfe behinde;
Yet, sith he n'ote[2] save both, he sav'd that same
Which was the dearest to his dounghill minde,
The god of his desire, the ioy of misers blinde.

16 Thus whilest all things in troublous uprore were,
And all men busie to suppresse the flame,
The loving couple neede no reskew feare,
But leasure had and liberty to frame
Their purpost flight, free from all mens reclame;
And Night, the patronesse of love-stealth fayre,
Gave them safe conduct till to end they came:
So beene they gone yfere,[3] a wanton payre
Of lovers loosely knit, where list them to repayre.

1 *Liefest*, dearest.
2 *No'te*, could not.
3 *Yfere*, together.

17 Soone as the cruell flames yslaked were,
Malbecco, seeing how his losse did lye,
Out of the flames which he had quencht whylere,[1]
Into huge waves of griefe and gealosye
Full deepe emplonged was, and drowned nye
Twixt inward doole[2] and felonous despight:
He rav'd, he wept, he stampt, he lowd did cry;
And all the passions, that in man may light,
Did him attonce oppresse, and vex his caytive spright.

18 Long thus he chawd the cud of inward griefe,
And did consume his gall with anguish sore:
Still when he mused on his late mischíefe,
Then still the smart thereof increased more,
And seemd more grievous then it was before:
At last, when sorrow he saw booted nought,
Ne griefe might not his Love to him restore,
He gan devise how her he reskew mought;
Ten thousand wayes he cast in his confused thought.

19 At last resolving, like a pilgrim pore,
To search her forth whereso she might be fond,
And bearing him with treasure in close store,
The rest he leaves in ground. So takes in hond[3]
To seeke her endlong[4] both by sea and lond.
Long he her sought, he sought her far and nere,
And every where that he mote understond
Of knights and ladies any meetings were;
And of each one he mett he tidings did inquere.

1 *Whylere*, before.
2 *Doole*, grief.
3 *Takes in hond*, undertakes.
4 *Endlong*, in a continued course.

20 But all in vaine ; his woman was too wise
Ever to come into his clouch againe,
And hee too simple ever to surprise
The iolly Paridell, for all his paine.
One day, as hee forpassed[1] by the plaine
With weary pace, he far away espide
A couple, seeming well to be his twaine,
Which hoved[2] close under a forest side,
As if they lay in wait, or els themselves did hide.

21 Well weened hee that those the same mote bee;
And, as he better did their shape avize,[3]
Him seemed more their maner did agree ;
For th' one was armed all in warlike wize,
Whom to be Paridell he did devize ;
And th' other, al yclad in garments light
Discolourd[4] like to womanish disguise,
He did resemble[5] to his lady bright ;
And ever his faint hart much earned[6] at the sight.

22 Aed ever faine he towards them would goe,
But yet durst not for dread approchen nie,
But stood aloofe, unweeting what to doe ;
Till that prickt forth with loves extremity,
That is the father of fowle gealosy,
He closely nearer crept the truth to weet:
But, as he nigher drew, he easily
Might scerne that it was not his sweetest sweet,
Ne yet her belamour,[7] the partner of his sheet :

1 *Forpassed*, passed along.
2 *Hoved*, hovered, lurked.
3 *Avize*, discern.
4 *Discolourd*, variously colored.
5 *Resemble*, liken, compare.
6 *Earned*, yearned.
7 *Belamour*, lover.

23 But it was scornefull Braggadochio,
That with his servant Trompart hoverd there,
Sith late he fled from his too earnest foe:
Whom such whenas Malbecco spyed clere,
He turned backe, and would have fled arere[1];
Till Trompart, ronning hastely, him did stay,
And bad before his soveraine lord appere:
That was him loth, yet durst he not gainesay,
And, comming him before, low louted[2] on the lay.[3]

24 The Boaster at him sternely bent his browe,
As if he could have kild him with his looke,
That to the ground him meekely made to bowe,
And awfull terror deepe into him strooke,
That every member of his body quooke.
Said he, "Thou man of nought! what doest thou here,
Unfitly furnisht with thy bag and booke,
Where I expected one with shield and spere
To prove some deeds of armes upon an equall pere?"

25 The wretched man at his imperious speach
Was all abasht, and low prostrâting said:
"Good Sir, let not my rudenes[4] be no breach
Unto your patience, ne be ill ypaid[5];
For I unwares this way by fortune straid,
A silly[6] pilgrim driven to distresse,
That seeke a Lady —" There he suddein staid,

1 *Arere*, backward.
2 *Louted*, bent.
3 *Lay*, lea, plain.
4 I. e. rusticity.
5 *Ill ypaid*, ill apaid, dissatisfied.
6 *Silly*, simple, humble.

And did the rest with grievous sighes suppresse,
While teares stood in his eies, few drops of bitternesse.

26 "What lady, man?" said Trompart. "Take good hart,
And tell thy griefe, if any hidden lye:
Was never better time to shew thy smart
Then now, that noble succor is thee by,
That is the whole worlds commune remedy."
That chearful word his weak heart much did cheare,
And with vaine hope his spirits faint supply,
That bold he sayd: "O most redoubted Pere,
Vouchsafe with mild regard a wretches cace to heare."

27 Then sighing sore, "It is not long," saide hee,
"Sith I enioyd the gentlest dame alive;
Of whom a knight, (no knight at all perdee,
But shame of all that doe for honor strive,)
By treacherous deceipt did me deprive;
Through open outrage he her bore away,
And with fowle force unto his will did drive;
Which al good knights, that armes do bear this day,
Are bownd for to revenge and punish if they may.

28 "And you, most noble Lord, that can and dare
Redresse the wrong of miserable wight,
Cannot employ your most victorious speare
In better quarrell then defence of right,
And for a lady gainst a faithlesse knight:
So shall your glory bee advaunced much,
And all faire ladies magnify your might,

And eke myselfe, al bee I simple such,[1]
Your worthy paine shall wel reward with guerdon
rich."

29 With that, out of his bouget[2] forth he drew
Great store of treasure, therewith him to tempt;
But he on it lookt scornefully askew,
As much disdeigning to be so misdempt,[3]
Or a war-monger[4] to be basely nempt,[5]
And sayd: "Thy offers base I greatly loth,
And eke thy words uncourteous and unkempt[6]:
I tread in dust thee and thy money both;
That, were it not for shame —" So turned from him
wroth.

30 But Trompart, that his maistres humor knew
In lofty looks to hide an humble minde,
Was inly tickled with that golden vew,
And in his eare him rownded[7] close behinde:
Yet stoupt he not, but lay still in the winde,
Waiting advauntage on the pray to sease;
Till Trompart, lowly to the grownd inclinde,
Besought him his great corage[8] to appease,
And pardon simple man that rash did him displease.

1 I. e. although I am so humble.
2 *Bouget*, budget, pouch.
3 *Misdempt*, misconceived.
4 *War-monger*, mercenary soldier.
5 *Nempt*, named.
6 *Unkempt*, uncombed, rude.
7 *Rownded*, whispered.
8 *Corage*, heart.

XXX. 5. — *Yet stoupt he not*, &c.] Braggadochio did not stoop to seize his prey, but remained quiet in the air, — an image derived from falconry.

31 Big looking like a doughty doucëpere,[1]
At last he thus: "Thou clod of vilest clay,
I pardon yield, and with thy rudenes beare;
But weete henceforth, that all that golden pray,
And all that els the vaine world vaunten may,
I loath as doung, ne deeme my dew reward:
Fame is my meed, and glory vertues pay:
But minds of mortal men are muchell mard
And mov'd amisse with massy mucks unmeet regard.

32 "And more; I graunt to thy great misery
Gratious respect; thy wife shall backe be sent:
And that vile knight, whoever that he bee,
Which hath thy lady reft and knighthood shent,[2]
By Sanglamort,[3] my sword, whose deadly dent[4]
The blood hath of so many thousands shedd,
I sweare ere long shall dearly it repent;
Ne he twixt heven and earth shall hide his hedd,
But soone he shal be fownd, and shortly doen be dedd.[5]"

33 The foolish man thereat woxe wondrous blith,
As if the word so spoken were halfe donne,
And humbly thanked him a thousand sith,[6]
That had from death to life him newly wonne.
Tho forth the Boaster marching brave begonne
His stolen steed to thunder furiously,
As if he heaven and hell would overonne,

1 I. e. like one of the twelve peers of France.
2 *Shent*, disgraced.
3 I. e. Blood and Death.
4 *Dent*, stroke.
5 *Doen be dedd*, put to death.
6 *Sith*, times.

And all the world confound with cruelty;
That much Malbecco ioyed in his iollity.

34 Thus long they three together traveiled,
Through many a wood and many an uncouth way,
To seeke his wife that was far wandered:
But those two sought nought but the present pray,
To weete, the treasure which he did bewray,[1]
On which their eies and harts were wholly sett,
With purpose how they might it best betray;
For, sith the howre that first he did them lett
The same behold, therwith their keene desires were whett.

35 It fortuned, as they together far'd,
They spide where Paridell came pricking fast
Upon the plaine, the which himselfe prepar'd
To giust with that brave straunger knight a cast,
As on adventure by the way he past:
Alone he rode without his paragone[2];
For, having filcht her bells, her up he cast
To the wide world, and let her fly alone,—
He nould[3] be clogd: so had he served many one.

36 The gentle Lady, loose at randon lefte,
The greene-wood long did walke, and wander wide
At wilde adventure, like a forlorne wefte[4];
Till on a day the Satyres her espide
Straying alone withouten groome or guide:

[1] *Bewray*, discover.
[2] *Paragone*, companion.
[3] *Nould*, would not.
[4] *Wefte*, waif, wanderer.

Her up they tooke, and with them home her ledd,
With them as housewife ever to abide,
To milk their gotes, and make them cheese and bredd;
And every one as commune good her handeled:

37 That shortly she Malbecco has forgott,
And eke Sir Paridell, all[1] were he deare;
Who from her went to seeke another lott,
And now by fortune was arrived here,
Where those two guilers with Malbecco were.
Soone as the old man saw Sir Paridell,
He fainted, and was almost dead with feare,
Ne word he had to speake his griefe to tell,
But to him louted[2] low, and greeted goodly well;

38 And, after, asked him for Hellenore.
"I take no keepe[3] of her," sayd Paridell,
"She wonneth[4] in the forrest there before."
So forth he rode as his adventure fell;
The whiles the Boaster from his loftie sell[5]
Faynd to alight, something amisse to mend;
But the fresh swayne would not his leasure dwell,
But went his way; whom when he passed kend,[6]
He up remounted light, and after faind to wend.

39 "Perdy nay," said Malbecco, "shall ye not;
But let him passe as lightly as he came:
For litle good of him is to be got,

1 *All*, although.
2 *Louted*, bent.
3 I. e. I have no concern.
4 *Wonneth*, dwelleth.
5 *Sell*, saddle.
6 *Kend*, perceived.

And mickle perill to bee put to shame.
But let us goe to seeke my dearest dame,
Whom he hath left in yonder forest wyld:
For of her safety in great doubt I ame,
Least salvage beastes her person have despoyld:
Then all the world is lost, and we in vaine have toyld!"

40 They all agree, and forward them addresse:
"Ah! but," said crafty Trompart, "weete ye well,
That yonder in that wastefull wildernesse
Huge monsters haunt, and many dangers dwell;
Dragons, and minotaures, and feendes of hell,
And many wilde woodmen which robbe and rend
All traveilers; therefore advise ye well,
Before ye enterprise that way to wend:
One may his iourney bring too soone to evill end."

41 Malbecco stopt in great astonishment,
And, with pale eyes fast fixed on the rest,
Their counsell crav'd in daunger imminent.
Said Trompart: "You, that are the most opprest
With burdein of great treasure, I thinke best
Here for to stay in safëtie behynd:
My Lord and I will search the wide forést."
That counsell pleased not Malbeccoes mynd;
For he was much afraid himselfe alone to fynd.

42 "Then is it best," said he, "that ye doe leave
Your treasure here in some security,
Either fast closed in some hollow greave,[1]

[1] *Greave*, grove, tree.

Or buried in the ground from ieopardy,
Till we returne againe in safëty:
As for us two, least doubt of us ye have,
Hence farre away we will blyndfolded ly,
Ne privy bee unto your treasures grave."
It pleased: so he did: then they march forward brave.

43 Now when amid the thickest woodes they were,
They heard a noyse of many bagpipes shrill,
And shrieking hububs[1] them approching nere,
Which all the forest did with horrour fill:
That dreadfull sound the Bosters hart did thrill
With such amazment, that in hast he fledd,
Ne ever looked back for good or ill;
And after him eke fearefull Trompart spedd:
The old man could not fly, but fell to ground half dedd:

44 Yet afterwardes, close creeping as he might,
He in a bush did hyde his fearefull hedd.
The iolly Satyres full of fresh delight
Came dauncing forth, and with them nimbly ledd
Faire Helenore with girlonds all bespredd,
Whom their May-lady they had newly made:
She, proude of that new honour which they redd,[2]
And of their lovely fellowship full glade,
Daunst lively, and her face did with a lawrell shade.

45 The silly man that in the thickett lay
Saw all this goodly sport, and grieved sore;
Yet durst he not against it doe or say,

1 *Hububs*, hubbubs, confused cries.
2 *Redd*, declared, bestowed.

But did his hart with bitter thoughts engore,[1]
To see th' unkindnes of his Hellenore.
All day they daunced with great lustyhedd,[2]
And with their horned feet the greene gras wore;
The whiles their gotes upon the brouzes [3] fedd,
Till drouping Phœbus gan to hyde his golden hedd.

46 Tho up they gan their mery pypes to trusse,
And all their goodly heardes did gather rownd;
But every Satyre first did give a busse
To Hellenore; so busses did abound.
Now gan the humid vapour shed the grownd
With perly deaw, and th' Earthës gloomy shade
Did dim the brightnesse of the welkin rownd,
That every bird and beast, awarned, made
To shrowd themselves, whiles sleepe their sences did invade.

47 Which when Malbecco saw, out of his bush
Upon his hands and feete he crept full light,
And like a gote emongst the gotes did rush;
That, through the helpe of his faire hornes on hight,
And misty dampe of misconceyving night,
And eke through likenesse of his gotish beard,
He did the better counterfeite aright:
So home he marcht emongst the horned heard,
That none of all the Satyres him espyde or heard.

1 *Engore*, pierce. 2 *Lustyhedd*, lustiness. 3 *Brouzes*, twigs.

XLVII. 4. — *His faire hornes.*] His imaginary horns were now become real horns. This is the beginning of his transformation. — UPTON.

48 At night, when all they went to sleepe, he vewd,
Whereas his lovely wife emongst them lay,
Embraced of a Satyre rough and rude,
Who all the night did minde his ioyous play:
Nine times he heard him come aloft ere day,
That all his hart with gealosy did swell:
But yet that nights ensample did bewray
That not for nought his wife them loved so well,
When one so oft a night did ring his matins bell.

49 So closely as he could he to them crept,
When wearie of their sport to sleepe they fell,
And to his wife, that now full soundly slept,
He whispered in her eare, and did her tell,
That it was he which by her side did dwell;
And therefore prayd her wake to heare him plaine.
As one out of a dreame not waked well
She turnd her, and returned backe againe:
Yet her for to awake he did the more constraine.

50 At last with irkesom trouble she abrayd[1];
And then perceiving that it was indeed
Her old Malbecco, which did her upbrayd
With loosenesse of her love and loathly deed,
She was astonisht with exceeding dreed,
And would have wakt the Satyre by her syde;
But he her prayd for mercy or for meed,
To save his life, ne let him be descryde,
But hearken to his lore,[2] and all his counsell hyde.

[1] *Abrayd*, awoke. [2] *Lore*, advice.

51 Tho gan he her perswade to leave that lewd
And loathsom life, of God and man abhord,
And home returne, where all should be renewd
With perfect peace and bandes of fresh accord,
And she receivd againe to bed and bord,
As if no trespas ever had beene donne:
But she it all refused at one word,
And by no meanes would to his will be wonne,
But chose emongst the iolly Satyres still to wonne.[1]

52 He wooed her till day-spring he espyde;
But all in vaine: and then turnd to the heard,
Who butted him with hornes on every syde,
And trode downe in the durt, where his hore beard
Was fowly dight, and he of death afeard.
Early, before the heavens fairest light
Out of the ruddy East was fully reard,
The heardes out of their foldes were loosed quight,
And he emongst the rest crept forth in sory plight.

53 So soone as he the prison dore did pas,
He ran as fast as both his feet could beare,
And never looked who behind him was,
Ne scarsely who before: like as a beare,
That creeping close amongst the hives to reare[2]
An hony-combe, the wakefull dogs espy,
And him assayling sore his carkas teare,
That hardly he with life away does fly,
Ne stayes, till safe himselfe he see from ieopardy.

[1] *Wonne*, dwell. [2] *Reare*, carry off.

54 Ne stayd he, till he came unto the place
Where late his treasure he entombed had;
Where when he found it not, (for Trompart bace
Had it purloyned for his maister bad,)
With extreme fury he became quite mad,
And ran away; ran with himselfe away:
That who so straungely had him seene bestadd,[1]
With upstart haire and staring eyes dismay,
From Limbo lake him late escaped sure would say.

55 High over hilles and over dales he fledd,
As if the wind him on his winges had borne;
Ne banck nor bush could stay him, when he spedd
His nimble feet, as treading still on thorne:
Griefe, and Despight, and Gealosy, and Scorne,
Did all the way him follow hard behynd;
And he himselfe himselfe loath'd so forlorne,[2]
So shamefully forlorne of womankynd:
That, as a snake, still lurked in his wounded mynd.

56 Still fled he forward, looking backward still;
Ne stayd his flight nor fearefull agony
Till that he came unto a rocky hill
Over the sea suspended dreadfully,
That living creature it would terrify
To looke adowne, or upward to the hight:
From thence he threw himselfe dispiteously,
All desperate of his fore-damned spright,
That seemd no help for him was left in living sight.

[1] *Bestadd*, circumstanced. [2] *Forlorne*, forsaken.

57 But, through long anguish and selfe-murdring
thought,
He was so wasted and forpined[1] quight,
That all his substance was consum'd to nought,
And nothing left but like an aery spright;
That on the rockes he fell so flit[2] and light,
That he thereby receiv'd no hurt at all;
But chaunced on a craggy cliff to light,
Whence he with crooked clawes so long did crall,
That at the last he found a cave with entrance small:

58 Into the same he creepes, and thenceforth there
Resolv'd to build his balefull mansion,
n drery darkenes and continuall feare
Of that rocks fall, which ever and anon
Threates with huge ruine him to fall upon,
That he dare never sleepe, but that one eye
Still ope he keepes for that occasion;
Ne ever rests he in tranquillity,
The roring billowes beat his bowre[3] so boystrously.

59 Ne ever is he wont on ought to feed
But todes and frogs, his pasture poysonous,
Which in his cold complexion doe breed
A filthy blood, or humour rancorous,
Matter of doubt and dread suspitious,
That doth with curelesse care consume the hart,
Corrupts the stomacke with gall vitious,
Cros-cuts the liver with internall smart,
And doth transfixe the soule with deathes eternall dart.

1 *Forpined*, pined away.
2 *Flit*, unsubstantial.
3 *Bowre*, abode.

Yet can he never dye, but dying lives,
And doth himselfe with sorrow new sustaine,
That death and life attonce unto him gives,
And painefull pleasure turnes to pleasing paine.
There dwels he ever, miserable swaine,
Hatefull both to himselfe and every wight;
Where he, through privy griefe and horrour vaine,
Is woxen so deform'd that he has quight
Forgot he was a man, and Gelosy is hight.

CANTO XI.

Britomart chaceth Ollyphant;
  Findes Scudamour distrest:
Assayes the House of Busyrane,
  Where Loves spoyles are exprest.

1 O HATEFULL hellish snake! what Furie furst
  Brought thee from balefull house of Proserpine,
  Where in her bosome she thee long had nurst,
  And fostred up with bitter milke of tine[1];
  Fowle Gealosy! that turnest love divine
  To ioylesse dread, and mak'st the loving hart
  With hatefull thoughts to languish and to pine,
  And feed itselfe with selfe-consuming smart,
Of all the passions in the mind thou vilest art!

2 O let him far be banished away,
  And in his stead let Love for ever dwell!
  Sweete Love, that doth his golden wings embay[2]
  In blessed nectar and pure pleasures well,
  Untroubled of vile feare or bitter fell.[3]
  And ye, faire Ladies, that your kingdomes make
  In th' harts of men, them governe wisely well,
  And of faire Britomart ensample take,
That was as trew in love as turtle to her make.[4]

[1] *Tine*, woe.
[2] *Embay*, bathe.
[3] *Fell*, gall.
[4] *Make*, mate.

3 Who with Sir Satyrane, as earst ye red,
Forth ryding from Malbeccoes hostlesse[1] hous,
Far off aspyde a young man, the which fled
From an huge Geaunt, that with hideous
And hatefull outrage long him chaced thus;
It was that Ollyphant, the brother deare
Of that Argantè vile and vitious,
From whom the Squyre of Dames was reft whylere[2];
This all as bad as she, and worse, if worse ought were.

4 For as the sister did in feminine
And filthy lust exceede all woman kinde;
So he surpassed his sex masculine,
In beastly use,[3] all that I ever finde:
Whom when as Britomart beheld behinde
The fearefull boy so greedily poursew,
She was emmoved in her noble minde
T' employ her puissaunce to his reskew,
And pricked fiercely forward where she did him vew.

5 Ne was Sir Satyrane her far behinde,
But with like fiercenesse did ensew[4] the chace;
Whom when the Gyaunt saw, he soone resinde
His former suit, and from them fled apace:
They after both, and boldly bad him bace,

1 *Hostlesse*, inhospitable.
2 *Whylere*, lately.
3 *Use*, habits.
4 *Ensew*, follow.

III. 8. — *Was reft whylere.*] See Canto VII. Stanza 37.

V. 5. — *Bad him bace.*] That is, they pursued the giant, who had been pursuing the young man. The expression is derived

And each did strive the other to outgoe;
But he them both outran a wondrous space,
For he was long, and swift as any roe,
And now made better speed t' escape his feared foe.

6 It was not Satyrane, whom he did feare,
But Britomart the flowre of chastity;
For he the powre of chaste hands might not beare,
But alwayes did their dread encounter fly:
And now so fast his feet he did apply,
That he has gotten to a forrest neare,
Where he is shrowded in security.
The wood they enter, and search everie where;
They searched diversely; so both divided were.

7 Fayre Britomart so long him followed,
That she at last came to a fountaine sheare,[1]
By which there lay a Knight all wallowed
Upon the grassy ground, and by him neare
His haberieon,[2] his helmet, and his speare:
A little of, his shield was rudely throwne,
On which the Winged Boy in colours cleare
Depeincted was, full easie to be knowne,
And he thereby, wherever it in field was showne.

[1] *Sheare*, clear. [2] *Haberieon*, coat of mail.

---

from the rustic game of prison-base, in which the two parties take turns in chasing each other. The meaning here is illustrated by a passage further on:

"So ran they all, as they had bene at bace,
They being chased that did others chace."
Book V. Canto VIII. St. 5. C.

8 His face upon the grownd did groveling ly,
As if he had beene slombring in the shade;
That the brave Mayd would not for courtesy
Out of his quiet slomber him abrade,[1]
Nor seeme too suddeinly him to invade:
Still as she stood, she heard with grievous throb
Him grone, as if his hart were peeces made,
And with most painefull pangs to sigh and sob,
That pitty did the Virgins hart of patience rob.

9 At last forth breaking into bitter plaintes
He sayd: "O soverayne Lord, that sit'st on hye
And raignst in blis emongst thy blessed saintes,
How suffrest thou such shamefull cruelty,
So long unwreaked of thine enimy!
Or hast thou, Lord, of good mens cause no heed?
Or doth thy iustice sleepe and silent ly?
What booteth then the good and righteous deed,
If goodnesse find no grace, nor righteousnes no meed!

10 "If good find grace, and righteousnes reward,
Why then is Amoret in caytive[2] band
Sith that more bounteous[3] creature never far'd[4]
On foot upon the face of living land!
Or if that hevenly iustice may withstand
The wrongfull outrage of unrighteous men,
Why then is Busirane with wicked hand
Suffred, these seven monethes day,[5] in secret den
My Lady and my Love so cruelly to pen?

1 *Abrade*, rouse.
2 *Caytive*, captive.
3 *Bounteous*, virtuous.
4 *Far'd*, walked.
5 *Day*, time.

11 "My Lady and my Love is cruelly pend
In dolefull darkenes from the vew of day,
Whilest deadly torments doe her chast brest rend,
And the sharpe steele doth rive her hart in tway, —
All for she Scudamore will not denay.[1]
Yet thou, vile man, vile Scudamore, art sound,
Ne canst her ayde, ne canst her foe dismay;
Unworthy wretch to tread upon the ground,
For whom so faire a lady feeles so sore a wound."

12 There an huge heape of singulfes[2] did oppresse
His strugling soule, and swelling throbs empeach[3]
His foltring toung with pangs of drerinesse,[4]
Choking the remnant of his plaintife speach,
As if his dayes were come to their last reach.
Which when she heard, and saw the ghastly fit
Threatning into his life to make a breach,
Both with great ruth and terrour she was smit,
Fearing least from her cage the wearie soule would flit.

13 Tho, stouping downe, she him amoved light;
Who, therewith somewhat starting, up gan looke,
And seeing him behind a stranger knight,
Where as no living creature he mistooke,
With great indignaunce he that sight forsooke,[5]
And, downe againe himselfe disdainefully
Abiecting,[6] th' earth with his faire forhead strooke:

1 *Denay*, deny.
2 *Singulfes* (for *singults*), sobs.
3 *Empeach*, hinder.
4 *Drerinesse*, sorrow.
5 *Forsooke*, turned from.
6 *Abiecting*, casting.

XIII. 4. Where he wrongly supposed there was no living creature. C.

Which the bold Virgin seeing, gan apply
Fit medcine to his griefe, and spake thus courtesly:

14 "Ah! gentle Knight, whose deepe-conceived griefe
Well seemes t' exceede the powre of patience,
Yet, if that hevenly grace some good reliefe
You send, submit you to High Providence;
And ever in your noble hart prepense,[1]
That all the sorrow in the world is lesse
Then vertues might and values[2] confidence:
For who nill[3] bide the burden of distresse,
Must not here thinke to live; for life is wretched-
nesse.

15 "Therefore, faire Sir, doe comfort to you take,
And freely read[4] what wicked felon so
Hath outrag'd you, and thrald your gentle make.[5]
Perhaps this hand may helpe to ease your woe,
And wreake your sorrow on your cruell foe;
At least it faire endevour will apply."
Those feeling words so neare the quicke did goe,
That up his head he reared easily;
And, leaning on his elbowe, these few words lett fly:

16 "What boots it plaine[6] that cannot be redrest,
And sow vaine sorrow in a fruitlesse eare;
Sith powre of hand, nor skill of learned brest,
Ne worldly price, cannot redeeme my deare
Out of her thraldome and continuall feare!

1 *Prepense*, consider.
2 *Values*, valor's.
3 *Nill*, will not.
4 *Read*, explain.
5 *Make*, mate.
6 *Plaine*, complain of.

For he, the tyrant, which her hath in ward
By strong enchauntments and blacke magicke leare,[1]
Hath in a dungeon deepe her close embard,
And many dreadfull feends hath pointed to her gard.

17 "There he tormenteth her most terribly,
And day and night afflicts with mortall paine,
Because to yield him love she doth deny,
Once to me yold, not to be yolde againe:
But yet by torture he would her constraine
Love to conceive in her disdainfull brest;
Till so she doe, she must in doole[2] remaine,
Ne may by living meanes be thence relest:
What boots it then to plaine that cannot be redrest!"

18 With this sad hersall[3] of his heavy stresse[4]
The warlike Damzell was empassiond[5] sore,
And sayd: "Sir Knight, your cause is nothing lesse
Then is your sorrow, certes, if not more;
For nothing so much pitty doth implore
As gentle ladyes helplesse misery:
But yet, if please ye listen to my lore,[6]
I will, with proofe of last extremity,
Deliver her fro thence, or with her for you dy."

19 "Ah! gentlest Knight alive," sayd Scudamore,
"What huge heroicke magnanimity
Dwells in thy bounteous brest? what couldst thou more,

[1] *Leare*, lore.
[2] *Doole*, grief.
[3] *Hersall*, rehearsal.
[4] *Stresse*, distress.
[5] *Empassiond*, moved.
[6] *Lore*, teaching, counsel.

If shee were thine, and thou as now am I?
O spare thy happy daies, and them apply
To better boot[1]; but let me die that ought;
More is more losse; one is enough to dy!"
"Life is not lost," said she, "for which is bought
Endlesse renowm, that more then death is to be sought."

20 Thus shee at length persuaded him to rise,
And with her wend to see what new successe
Mote him befall upon new enterprise:
His armes, which he had vowed to disprofesse,
She gathered up and did about him dresse,[2]
And his forwandred[3] steed unto him gott:
So forth they both yfere[4] make their progrésse,
And march, not past the mountenaunce of a shott,[5]
Till they arriv'd whereas their purpose they did plott.

21 There they, dismounting, drew their weapons bold,
And stoutly came unto the Castle gate,
Whereas no gate they found them to withhold,
Nor ward to wait at morne and evening late;
But in the porch, that did them sore amate,[6]
A flaming fire ymixt with smouldry[7] smoke

1 *Boot*, advantage.
2 *Dresse*, dispose.
3 *Forwandred*, strayed away.
4 *Yfere*, together.
5 I. e. a bow-shot's distance.
6 *Amate*, daunt.
7 *Smouldry*, smothering.

XIX. 9. — *That more then death is to be sought.*] The meaning appears to be, that "endlesse renowm" is more to be *sought* than death is to be *avoided*. H.

And stinking sulphure, that with griesly hate
And dreadfull horror did all entraunce choke,
Enforced them their forward footing to revoke.

22 Greatly thereat was Britomart dismayd,
Ne in that stownd[1] wist how herselfe to beare;
For daunger vaine[2] it were to have assayd
That cruell element, which all things feare,
Ne none can suffer to approchen neare:
And, turning backe to Scudamour, thus sayd:
"What monstrous enmity provoke we heare?
Foolhardy as th' Earthes children, the which made
Batteill against the gods, so we a god invade.

23 "Daunger without discretion to attempt,
Inglorious, beast-like, is: therefore, Sir Knight,
Aread[3] what course of you is safest dempt,[4]
And how we with our foe may come to fight."
"This is," quoth he, "the dolorous despight,[5]
Which earst to you I playnd: for neither may
This fire be quencht by any witt or might,
Ne yet by any meanes remov'd away;
So mighty be th' enchauntments which the same do stay.[6]

24 "What is there ells but cease these fruitlesse paines,
And leave me to my former languishing!
Faire Amorett must dwell in wicked chaines,
And Scudamore here die with sorrowing!"

[1] *Stownd*, exigency.
[2] *Vaine*, useless.
[3] *Aread*, declare.
[4] *Dempt*, deemed.
[5] *Dolorous despight*, grievous vexation.
[6] *Stay*, maintain.

"Perdy, not so," saide shee; "for shameful thing
Yt were t' abandon noble chevisaunce,[1]
For shewe of perill, without venturing:
Rather, let try extremities of chaunce
Then enterprised praise for dread to disavaunce.[2]"

25 Therewith, resolv'd to prove her utmost might,
Her ample shield she threw before her face,
And her swords point directing forward right
Assayld the flame; the which eftesoones gave place,
And did itselfe divide with equall space,
That through she passed, as a thonder-bolt
Perceth the yielding ayre, and doth displace
The soring clouds into sad showres ymolt[3];
So to her yold[4] the flames, and did their force revolt.[5]

26 Whome whenas Scudamour saw past the fire
Safe and untoucht, he likewise gan assay
With greedy will and envious desire,
And bad the stubborne flames to yield him way
But cruell Mulciber[6] would not obay
His threatfull pride, but did the more augment
His mighty rage, and with imperious sway
Him forst, maulgre,[7] his fercenes to relent,
And backe retire all scorcht and pitifully brent.[8]

27 With huge impatience he inly swelt,[9]
More for great sorrow that he could not pas

1 *Chevisaunce*, enterprise.
2 *Disavaunce*, retreat from.
3 *Ymolt*, melted.
4 *Yold*, yielded.
5 *Revolt*, roll back.
6 *Mulciber*, Vulcan, the fire.
7 *Maulgre*, in spite of himself.
8 *Brent*, burned.
9 *Swelt*, died. See Vol. III. 124, and IV. 203.

Then for the burning torment which he felt;
That with fell woodnes[1] he effierced[2] was,
And, wilfully him throwing on the gras,
Did beat and bounse his head and brest ful sore:
The whiles the Championesse now entred has
The utmost[3] rowme, and past the formest dore;
The utmost rowme abounding with all precious store:

28 For, round about, the walls yclothed were
With goodly arras of great maiesty,
Woven with gold and silke so close and nere
That the rich metall lurked privily,
As faining to be hidd from envious eye;
Yet here, and there, and every where, unwares
It shewd itselfe and shone unwillingly;
Like to' a discolourd[4] snake, whose hidden snares
Through the greene gras his long bright burnisht back declares.

29 And in those tapets[5] weren fashioned
Many faire pourtraicts, and many a faire feate;
And all of love, and al of lustyhed,[6]
As seemed by their semblaunt,[7] did entreat[8]:

1 *Woodnes*, madness.
2 *Effierced*, enraged.
3 *Utmost*, outermost.
4 *Discolourd*, party-colored.
5 *Tapets*, tapestries.
6 *Lustyhed*, lustfulness.
7 *Semblaunt*, appearance.
8 *Entreat*, treat.

XXIX. 1.—*And in those tapets*, &c.] Spenser here imitates Ovid's description of the tapestry woven by Arachne in her contest with Minerva. (Metam. VI. 103.) As usual with him, the poet departs somewhat from the classical mythology in his version of these stories. UPTON.

And eke all Cupids warres they did repeate,
And cruell battailes, which he whilome fought
Gainst all the gods to make his empire great;
Besides the huge massácres, which he wrought
On mighty kings and kesars[1] into thraldome brought.

30 Therein was writt how often thondring Iove
Had felt the point of his hart-percing dart,
And, leaving heavens kingdome, here did rove
In straunge disguize, to slake his scalding smart;
Now, like a ram, faire Helle to pervart,
Now, like a bull, Europa to withdraw:
Ah, how the fearefull ladies tender hart
Did lively[2] seeme to tremble, when she saw
The huge seas under her t' obay her servaunts law!

31 Soone after that, into a golden showre
Himselfe he chaung'd, faire Danaë to vew;
And through the roofe of her strong brasen towre
Did raine into her lap an hony dew;
The whiles her foolish garde, that litle knew
Of such deceipt, kept th' yron dore fast bard,
And watcht that none should enter nor issew;
Vaine was the watch, and bootlesse all the ward,
Whenas the god to golden hew himselfe transfard.[3]

32 Then was he turnd into a snowy swan,
To win faire Leda to his lovely[4] trade:
O wondrous skill, and sweet wit of the man

1 *Kesars*, emperors.
2 *Lively*, life-like.
3 *Transfard*, transferred.
4 *Lovely*, amorous.

That her in daffadillies sleeping made,
From scorching heat her daintie limbes to shade,
Whiles the proud bird, ruffing[1] his fethers wyde
And brushing his faire brest, did her invade:
Shee slept; yet twixt her eielids closely spyde
How towards her he rusht, and smiled at his pryde.

33 Then shewd it how the Thebane Semelee,
Deceivd of gealous Iuno, did require
To see him in his soverayne maiestee
Armd with his thunderbolts and lightning fire,
Whens dearely she with death bought her desire.
But faire Alcmena better match did make,
Ioying his love in likenes more entire:
Three nights in one they say that for her sake
He then did put, her pleasures lenger to partake.

34 Twise was he seene in soaring eagles shape,
And with wide winges to beat the buxome[2] ayre:
Once, when he with Asterie did scape;
Againe, whenas the Troiane boy so fayre
He snatcht from Ida hill, and with him bare:
Wondrous delight it was, there to behould
How the rude shepheards after him did stare,
Trembling through feare least down he fallen should,
And often to him calling to take surer hould.

[1] *Ruffing*, ruffling. [2] *Buxome*, yielding.

XXXIII. 7.—*In likeness more entire.*] Jupiter appearing to her in a shape more like her own. C.

35 In Satyres shape Antiopa he snatcht;
And like a fire, when he Aegin' assayd:
A shepeheard, when Mnemosyne he catcht;
And like a serpent to the Thracian mayd.
Whyles thus on earth great Iove these pageaunts playd,
The Winged Boy did thrust into his throne,
And, scoffing, thus unto his mother sayd:
"Lo! now the hevens obey to me alone,
And take me for their Iove, whiles Iove to earth is gone."

36 And thou, faire Phœbus, in thy colours bright
Wast there enwoven, and the sad distresse
In which that boy thee plonged, for despight
That thou bewray'dst his mothers wantonnesse,
When she with Mars was meynt[1] in ioyfulnesse:
Forthy he thrild[2] thee with a leaden dart
To love faire Daphne, which thee loved lesse;
Lesse she thee lov'd then was thy iust desart,
Yet was thy love her death, and her death was thy smart.

37 So lovedst thou the lusty Hyacinct;
So lovedst thou the faire Coronis deare:
Yet both are of thy haplesse hand extinct;

1 *Meynt*, mingled   2 *Thrild*, pierced.

XXXV. 4.— *Thracian mayd.*] By the Thracian maid is meant Proserpina. UPTON.

XXXVI. 6.—*Leaden dart.*] The leaden darts of Cupid produced unhappy or unsuccessful passion. H.

Yet both in flowres doe live, and love thee beare,
The one a paunce,[1] the other a sweet-breare:
For griefe whereof, ye mote have lively seene
The god himselfe rending his golden heare,
And breaking quite his garlond ever greene,
With other signes of sorrow and impatient teene.[2]

38 Both for those two, and for his owne deare sonne,
The sonne of Climene, he did repent;
Who, bold to guide the charet of the sunne,
Himselfe in thousand peeces fondly[3] rent,
And all the world with flashing fire brent;
So like, that all the walles did seeme to flame.
Yet cruell Cupid, not herewith content,
Forst him eftsoones to follow other game,
And love a shephards daughter for his dearest dame.

39 He loved Issé for his dearest dame,
And for her sake her cattell fedd awhile,
And for her sake a cowheard vile became:
The servant of Admetus, cowheard vile,
Whiles that from heaven he suffered exile.
Long were to tell each other lovely[4] fitt;
Now, like a lyon hunting after spoile;
Now, like a stag; now, like a faulcon flit:
All which in that faire arras was most lively writ.

1 *Paunce*, pansy.
2 *Teene*, grief.
3 *Fondly*, foolishly.
4 *Lovely*, amorous.

XXXIX. 8. — All the editions have *like a hag*. Jortin suggested *stag*, and this reading is confirmed by a passage cited by Upton from Natalis Comes, according to which Apollo transformed himself into a lion, a *stag*, and a hawk. C.

40 Next unto him was Neptune pictured,
In his divine resemblance wondrous lyke:
His face was rugged, and his hoarie hed
Dropped with brackish deaw; his threeforkt pyke
He stearnly shooke, and therewith fierce did stryke
The raging billowes, that on every syde
They trembling stood, and made a long broad dyke,
That his swift charet might have passage wyde,
Which foure great hippodames[1] did draw in temewise tyde.

41 His seahorses did seeme to snort amayne,
And from their nosethrilles blow the brynie streame,
That made the sparckling waves to smoke agayne
And flame with gold; but the white fomy creame
Did shine with silver, and shoot forth his beame:
The god himselfe did pensive seeme and sad,
And hong adowne his head as he did dreame;
For privy love his brest empierced had,
Ne ought but deare Bisaltis ay could make him glad.

42 He loved eke Iphimedia deare,
And Aeolus faire daughter, Arne hight,
For whom he turnd himselfe into a steare,
And fedd on fodder to beguile her sight.
Also, to win Deucalions daughter bright,
He turnd himselfe into a dolphin fayre;
And, like a winged horse, he tooke his flight
To snaky-locke Medusa to repayre,
On whom he got faire Pegasus that flitteth[2] in the ayre.

[1] *Hippodames*, sea or river horses. [2] *Flitteth*, flieth.

43 Next Saturne was, (but who would ever weene
That sullein Saturne ever weend to love?
Yet love is sullein, and Satúrnlike seene,
As he did for Erigone it prove,)
That to a centaure did himselfe transmove.[1]
So proov'd it eke that gratious god of wine,
When, for to compasse Philliras hard love,
He turnd himselfe into a fruitfull vine,
And into her faire bosome made his grapes decline.

44 Long were to tell the amorous assayes,[2]
And gentle pangues, with which he maked meeke
The mightie Mars, to learne his wanton playes;
How oft for Venus, and how often eek
For many other nymphes, he sore did shreek;
With womanish teares, and with unwarlike smarts,
Privily moystening his horrid[3] cheeke:
There was he painted full of burning dartes,
And many wide woundes launched through his inner partes.

45 Ne did he spare (so cruell was the elfe)
His owne deare mother, (ah, why should he so?)
Ne did he spare sometime to pricke himselfe,
That he might taste the sweet consuming woe,
Which he had wrought to many others moe.
But, to declare the mournfull tragedyes
And spoiles wherewith he all the ground did strow,—
More eath[4] to number with how many eyes
High heven beholdes sad lovers nightly theeveryes.

1 *Transmove*, transform.
2 *Assayes*, attacks.
3 *Horrid*, rough.
4 *Eath*, easy.

46 Kings, queenes, lords, ladies, knights, and damsels gent,
Were heap'd together with the vulgar sort,
And mingled with the raskall rablement,
Without respect of person or of port,[1]
To shew Dan Cupids powre and great effórt:
And round about, a border was entrayld[2]
Of broken bowes and arrowes shivered short;
And a long bloody river through them rayld,[3]
So lively, and so like, that living sence it fayld.[4]

47 And at the upper end of that faire rowme
There was an altar built of pretious stone
Of passing valew and of great renowme,
On which there stood an image all alone
Of massy gold, which with his owne light shone;
And winges it had with sondry colours dight,
More sondry colours then the proud pavone[5]
Beares in his boasted fan, or Iris bright,
When her discolourd bow she spreds through hevens hight.

48 Blyndfold he was; and in his cruell fist
A mortall bow and arrowes keene did hold,
With which he shot at randon when him list,

1 *Port*, carriage.
2 *Entrayld*, entwined.
3 *Rayld*, rolled.
4 *Fayld*, deceived.
5 *Pavone*, peacock.

XLVII. 9.—*Hevens hight.*] All the editions read *heven bright*; but this is so obviously a misprint, that I have made the change suggested by Upton. C.

Some headed with sad[1] lead, some with pure gold;
(Ah man, beware how thou those dartes behold!)
A wounded dragon under him did ly,
Whose hideous tayle his lefte foot did enfold,
And with a shaft was shot through either eye,
That no man forth might draw, ne no man remedye.

49 And underneath his feet was written thus:
Unto the victor of the gods this bee;
And all the people in that ample hous
Did to that image bowe their humble knee,
And oft committed fowle idolatree.
That wondrous sight faire Britomart amazd,
Ne seeing could her wonder satisfie,
But ever more and more upon it gazd,
The whiles the passing brightnes her fraile sences dazd.

50 Tho, as she backward cast her busie eye
To search each secrete of that goodly sted,[2]
Over the dore thus written she did spye:
Bee bold. She oft and oft it over-red,
Yet could not find what sence it figured:
But whatso were therein or writ or ment,
She was no whit thereby discouraged
From prosecuting of her first intent,
But forward with bold steps into the next roome went.

51 Much fayrer then the former was that roome,
And richlier, by many partes,[3] arayd;
For not with arras made in painefull loome,

1 *Sad*, heavy.
2 *Sted*, place.
3 I. e. by many times.

But with pure gold, it all was overlayd,
Wrought with wilde antickes[1] which their follies playd
In the rich metall, as they living were:
A thousand monstrous formes therein were made,
Such as false Love doth oft upon him weare;
For Love in thousand monstrous formes doth oft appeare.

52 And, all about, the glistring walles were hong
With warlike spoiles and with victorious prayes
Of mightie conquerours and captaines strong,
Which were whilóme captíved in their dayes
To cruell love, and wrought their owne decayes[2]:
Their swerds and speres were broke, and hauberques[3] rent,
And their proud girlonds of tryumphant bayes
Troden in dust with fury insolent,
To shew the victors might and mercilesse intent.

53 The warlike Mayd, beholding earnestly
The goodly ordinaunce of this rich place,
Did greatly wonder; ne could satisfy
Her greedy eyes with gazing a long space:
But more she mervaild that no footings trace
Nor wight appear'd, but wastefull emptinesse
And solemne silence over all that place:
Straunge thing it seem'd, that none was to possesse
So rich purveyaunce,[4] ne them keepe with carefulnesse.

1 *Antickes*, fantastic figures.
2 *Decayes*, ruins.
3 *Hauberques*, coats of mail.
4 *Purveyaunce*, furniture.

54 And as she lookt about, she did behold
How over that same dore was likewise writ,
Be bolde, *Be bolde*, and every where, *Be bold ;*
That much she muz'd, yet could not construe it
By any ridling skill or commune wit.
At last she spyde at that rowmes upper end
Another yron dore, on which was writ,
Be not too bold ; whereto though she did bend
Her earnest minde, yet wist not what it might intend.

55 Thus she there wayted untill eventyde,
Yet living creature none she saw appeare.
And now sad shadowes gan the world to hyde
From mortall vew, and wrap in darkenes dreare ;
Yet nould she d'off[1] her weary armes, for feare
Of secret daunger, ne let sleepe oppresse
Her heavy eyes with natures burdein deare,
But drew herselfe aside in sickernesse,[2]
And her welpointed wepons did about her dresse.[3]

1 *Nould she d'off*, would not take off.
2 *Sickernesse*, safety.
3 *Dresse*, dispose.

CANTO XII.

The Maske of Cupid, and th' Enchan
ted Chamber are displayd;
Whence Britomart redeemes faire A-
moret through charmes decayd.[1]

1 THO, whenas chearelesse night ycovered had
Fayre heaven with an universall clowd,
That every wight dismayd with darkenes sad
In silence and in sleepe themselves did shrowd,
She heard a shrilling trompet sound alowd,
Signe of nigh battaill, or got victory:
Nought therewith daunted was her courage prowd,
But rather stird to cruell enmity,
Expecting ever when some foe she might descry.

2 With that, an hideous storme of winde arose,
With dreadfull thunder and lightníng atwixt,
And an earthquake, as if it streight would lose[2]
The worlds foundations from his centre fixt:
A direfull stench of smoke and sulphure mixt
Ensewd, whose noyaunce fild the fearefull sted[3]
From the fourth howre of night untill the sixt;
Yet the bold Britonesse was nought ydred,
Though much emmov'd, but stedfast still persévered.

[1] I. e. wasted by magic arts.
[2] *Lose*, loosen.
[3] *Sted*, place.

3 All suddeinly a stormy whirlwind blew
Throughout the house, that clapped every dore,
With which that yron wicket open flew,
As it with mighty levers had bene tore;
And forth yssėwd, as on the readie flore
Of some theătre, a grave personage,
That in his hand a braunch of laurell bore,
With comely haveour and count'nance sage,
Yclad in costly garments fit for tragicke stage.

4 Proceeding to the midst he stil did stand,
As if in minde he somewhat had to say;
And to the vulgare beckning with his hand,
In signe of silence, as to heare a play,
By lively actions he gan bewray
Some argument of matter passioned[1];
Which doen, he backe retyred soft away,
And, passing by, his name discovered,
Ease, on his robe in golden letters cyphered.

5 The noble Mayd, still standing, all this vewd,
And merveild at his straunge intendiment[2]:
With that a ioyous fellowship issewd
Of minstrales making goodly meriment,

[1] *Passioned*, represented. [2] *Intendiment*, meaning.

III. 6.—*A grave personage*, &c.] The introduction to this procession of maskers was manifestly borrowed from the *dumb show*, which was wont to be exhibited before every act of a tragedy. This consisted of dumb actors, who, by their dress and action, prepared the spectators for the matter and substance of each ensuing act respectively. We have a specimen of this dumb show, introductory to the play in Hamlet. WARTON.

With wanton bardes, and rymers impudent;
All which together song full chearefully
A lay of loves delight with sweet concent[1]:
After whom marcht a iolly company,
In manner of a maske, enranged orderly.

6 The whiles a most delitious harmony
In full straunge notes was sweetly heard to sound,
That the rare sweetnesse of the melody
The feeble sences wholy did confound,
And the frayle soule in deepe delight nigh drownd:
And, when it ceast, shrill trompets lowd did bray,
That their report did far away rebound;
And, when they ceast, it gan againe to play,
The whiles the maskers marched forth in trim aray.

7 The first was Fansy, like a lovely boy
Of rare aspect and beautie without peare,
Matchable ether to that ympe[2] of Troy,
Whom Iove did love and chose his cup to beare;
Or that same daintie lad, which was so deare
To great Alcides, that, when as he dyde,
He wailed womanlike with many a teare,
And every wood and every valley wyde
He fild with Hylas name; the Nymphes eke Hylas cryde.

8 His garment nether was of silke nor say,[3]
But paynted plumes in goodly order dight,

1 *Concent*, harmony.
2 I. e. the youth Ganymede.
3 *Say*, satin.

Like as the sunburnt Indians do aray
Their tawney bodies, in their proudest plight:
As those same plumes, so seemd he vaine and light,
That by his gate might easily appeare;
For still he far'd[1] as dauncing in delight,
And in his hand a windy fan did beare,
That in the ydle ayre he mov'd, still here and theare.

9 And him beside marcht amorous Desyre,
Who seemd of ryper yeares then th' other swayne,
Yet was that other swayne this elders syre,
And gave him being, commune to them twayne:
His garment was disguysed very vayne,
And his embrodered bonet sat awry:
Twixt both his hands few sparks he close did strayne,
Which still he blew and kindled busily,
That soone they life conceiv'd, and forth in flames did fly.

10 Next after him went Doubt, who was yclad
In a discolour'd[2] cote of straunge disguyse,
That at his backe a brode capuccio[3] had,
And sleeves dependaunt Albanesé-wyse[4];
He lookt askew with his mistrustfull eyes,
And nycely[5] trode, as thornes lay in his way,
Or that the flore to shrinke he did avyse[6];

1 *Far'd*, went.
2 *Discolour'd*, many-colored.
3 *Capuccio*, hood.
4 I. e. Albanian fashion.
5 *Nycely*, carefully.
6 *Avyse*, perceive.

And on a broken reed he still did stay
His feeble steps, which shrunck when hard thereon
he lay.

11 With him went Daunger, cloth'd in ragged weed
Made of beares skin, that him more dreadfull made;
Yet his owne face was dreadfull, ne did need
Straunge[1] horrour to deforme his griesly shade:
A net in th' one hand, and a rusty blade
In th' other was; this Mischiefe, that Mishap;
With th' one his foes he threatned to invade,
With th' other he his friends ment to enwrap:
For whom he could not kill he practizd to entrap.

12 Next him was Feare, all arm'd from top to toe,
Yet thought himselfe not safe enough thereby,
But feard each shadow moving too or froe;
And, his owne armes when glittering he did spy
Or clashing heard, he fast away did fly,
As ashes pale of hew, and winged heeld;
And evermore on Daunger fixt his eye,
Gainst whom he alwayes bent a brasen shield,
Which his right hand unarmed fearefully did wield.

13 With him went Hope in rancke, a handsome mayd,
Of chearefull looke and lovely to behold;

1 *Straunge*, foreign, or borrowed.

XII. 9.— *Which his right hand*, &c.] This circumstance is suitable to the nature of Fear, who is here justly represented as being more solicitous to defend himself than to hurt others; he therefore bears his shield on his right arm. CHURCH

In silken samite[1] she was light arayd,
And her fayre lockes were woven up in gold:
She alway smyld, and in her hand did hold
An holy-water-sprinckle, dipt in deowe,
With which she sprinckled favours manifold
On whom she list, and did great liking sheowe,
Great liking unto many, but true love to feowe.

14 And after them Dissemblaunce and Suspect
Marcht in one rancke, yet an unequall paire;
For she was gentle and of milde aspect,
Courteous to all and seeming debonaire,[2]
Goodly adorned and exceeding faire;
Yet was that all but paynted and pourloynd,
And her bright browes were deckt with borrowed haire;
Her deeds were forged, and her words false coynd,
And alwaies in her hand two clewes of silke she twynd:

15 But he was fowle, ill favoured, and grim,
Under his eiebrowes looking still askaunce;
And ever, as Dissemblaunce laught on him,
He lowrd on her with daungerous eye-glaunce,
Shewing his nature in his countenaunce;
His rolling eies did never rest in place,
But walkte[3] each where for feare of hid mischaunce,
Holding a lattis still before his face,
Through which he stil did peep as forward he did pace.

[1] *Samite*, a robe of very fine silk.
[2] *Debonaire*, gracious.
[3] *Walkte*, rolled, roved.

XV. 8. —*Holding a lattis*, &c.] Suspect is drawn with a *lattice*:

16 Next him went Griefe and Fury matcht yfere[1],
Griefe all in sable sorrowfully clad,
Downe hanging his dull head with heavy chere,
Yet inly being more then seeming sad:
A paire of pincers in his hand he had,
With which he pinched people to the hart,
That from thenceforth a wretched life they ladd,
In wilfull languor and consuming smart,
Dying each day with inward wounds of dolours dart.

17 But Fury was full ill appareiled
In rags, that naked nigh she did appeare,
With ghastly looks and dreadfull drerihed[2];
For from her backe her garments she did teare,
And from her head ofte rent her snarled heare:
In her right hand a firebrand shee did tosse
About her head, still roming here and there;
As a dismayed deare in chace embost,[3]
Forgetfull of his safety, hath his right way lost.

18 After them went Displeasure and Pleasaunce,
He looking lompish and full sullein sad,
And hanging downe his heavy countenaunce;
She chearfull, fresh, and full of ioyaunce glad,
As if no sorrow she ne felt ne drad;
That evill matched paire they seemd to bee:
An angry waspe th' one in a viall had,

1 *Yfere*, together.
2 *Drerihed*, sorrow.
3 *Embost*, hard pressed.

---

the allusion is to the Italian name *gelosia;* such blinds or lattices as one may see through, yet not be seen. UPTON.

Th' other in hers an hony-laden bee.
Thus marched these six couples forth in faire degree.[1]

19 After all these there marcht a most faire Dame,
Led of two grysie[2] villeins, th' one Despight,
The other cleped Cruelty by name:
She dolefull lady, like a dreary spright
Cald by strong charmes out of eternall night,
Had deathes owne ymage figurd in her face,
Full of sad signes, fearfull to living sight;
Yet in that horror shewd a seemely grace,
And with her feeble feete did move a comely pace

20 Her brest all naked, as nett[3] yvory
Without adorne of gold or silver bright
Wherewith the craftesman wonts it beautify,
Of her dew honour was despoyled quight;
And a wide wound therein (O ruefull sight!)
Entrenched deep with knyfe accursed keene,
Yet freshly bleeding forth her fainting spright,
(The worke of cruell hand) was to be seene,
That dyde in sanguine red her skin all snowy cleene:

21 At that wide orifice her trembling hart
Was drawne forth, and in silver basin layd,
Quite through transfixed with a deadly dart,
And in her blood yet steeming fresh embayd.[4]

1 *Degree*, step.
2 *Grysie*, squalid. Probably a misprint for *gryslie*.
3 *Nett*, pure.
4 *Embayd*, bathed.

XVIII. 8. — *An hony-laden bee.*] The old editions have *hony-lady bee*. But the quarto of 1590 abounds with misprints in this canto. C.

And those two villeins which her steps upstayd,
When her weake feete could scarcely her sustaine,
And fading vitall powres gan to fade,
Her forward still with torture did constraine,
And evermore encreased her consuming paine.

22 Next after her, the Winged God himselfe
Came riding on a lion ravenous,
Taught to obay the menage of that elfe
That man and beast with powre imperious
Subdeweth to his kingdome tyrannous:
His blindfold eies he bad awhile unbinde,
That his proud spoile of that same dolorous
Faire dame he might behold in perfect kinde[1];
Which seene, he much reioyced in his cruell minde.

23 Of which ful prowd, himselfe uprearing hye,
He looked round about with sterne disdayne,
And did survay his goodly company;
And, marshalling the evill-ordered trayne,
With that the darts which his right hand did straine
Full dreadfully he shooke, that all did quake,
And clapt on hye his coulourd wingës twaine,
That all his many [2] it affraide did make:
Tho, blinding him againe, his way he forth did take.

24 Behinde him was Reproch, Repentaunce, Shame;
Reproch the first, Shame next, Repent behinde:

[1] I. e. with perfect distinctness. [2] *Many*, company.

XXI. 7. — *Fade* should probably be *vade*, or *fading* be *failing*.

Repentaunce feeble, sorowfull, and lame ;
Reproch despightful, carelesse, and unkinde ;
Shame most ill-favourd, bestiall, and blinde :
Shame lowrd, Repentaunce sigh'd, Reproch did scould ;
Reproch sharpe stings, Repentaunce whips entwinde,
Shame burning brond-yrons in her hand did hold :
All three to each unlike, yet all made in one mould.

25 And after them a rude confused rout
Of persons flockt, whose names is hard to read[1].
Emongst them was sterne Strife ; and Anger stout ;
Unquiet Care ; and fond[2] Unthriftyhead ;
Lewd Losse of Time ; and Sorrow seeming dead ;
Inconstant Chaunge ; and false Disloyalty ;
Consuming Riotise ; and guilty Dread
Of heavenly vengeaunce ; faint Infirmity ;
Vile Poverty ; and, lastly, Death with infamy.

26 There were full many moe like maladies,
Whose names and natures I note[3] readen well ;
So many moe, as there be phantasies
In wavering wemens witt, that none can tell,
Or paines in love, or punishments in hell :
All which disguized marcht in masking-wise
About the chamber by the Damozell ;
And then returned, having marched thrise,
Into the inner rowme from whence they first did rise.[4]

1 *Read*, tell.
2 *Fond*, foolish.
3 *Note*, cannot.
4 *Rise*, come forth.

27 So soone as they were in, the dore streightway
Fast locked, driven with that stormy blast
Which first it opened, and bore all away.
Then the brave Maid, which al this while was plast
In secret shade, and saw both first and last,
Issewed forth and went unto the dore
To enter in, but fownd it locked fast:
It vaine she thought with rigorous uprore
For to efforce, when charmes had closed it afore.

28 Where force might not availe, there sleights and art
She cast to use, both fitt for hard emprize:
Forthy[1] from that same rowme not to depart
Till morrow next shee did herselfe avize,[2]
When that same Maske againe should forth arize.
The morrowe next appeard with ioyous cheare,
Calling men to their daily exercize:
Then she, as morrow fresh, herselfe did reare
Out of her secret stand that day for to outweare.[3]

29 All that day she outwore in wandering *
And gazing on that chambers ornament,
Till that againe the second evening
Her covered with her sable vestiment,
Wherewith the worlds faire beautie she hath blent[4]:
Then, when the second watch was almost past,
That brasen dore flew open, and in went

1 *Forthy*, therefore.
2 *Avize*, bethink.
3 *Outweare*, pass.
4 *Blent*, obscured.

* The second folio has *wondering*.

XXIX. 6. — *Second watch.*] The second watch began at nine, and ended at twelve. H.

Bold Britomart, as she had late forecast,[1]
Nether of ydle showes nor of false charmes aghast.

30 So soone as she was entred, rownd about
Shee cast her eies to see what was become
Of all those persons which she saw without.
But lo! they streight were vanisht all and some[2];
Ne living wight she saw in all that roome,
Save that same woefull Lady; both whose hands
Were bounden fast, that did her ill become,[3]
And her small waste girt rownd with yron bands
Unto a brasen pillour, by the which she stands.

31 And, her before, the vile Enchaunter sate,
Figuring straunge charácters of his art;
With living blood he those charácters wrate,
Dreadfully dropping from her dying hart,
Seeming transfixed with a cruell dart;
And all perforce to make her him to love.
Ah! who can love the worker of her smart!
A thousand charmes he formerly did prove[4];
Yet thousand charmes could not her stedfast hart remove.

32 Soone as that Virgin Knight he saw in place,
His wicked bookes in hast he overthrew,
Not caring his long labours to deface;

1 *Forecast*, previously purposed.
2 *All and some*, one and all.
3 I. e. it was unworthy treatment for her.
4 *Prove*, try.

XXXII. 3.—*Not caring*, &c.] Not caring whether he defaced his long labors or not. H.

And, fiercely running to that lady trew,
A murdrous knife out of his pocket drew,
The which he thought, for villeinous despight,
In her tormented bodie to embrew:
But the stout Damzell, to him leaping light,
His cursed hand withheld, and maistered his might.

33 From her, to whom his fury first he ment,
The wicked weapon rashly[1] he did wrest,[2]
And, turning to herselfe his fell intent,
Unwares it strooke into her snowie chest,
That litle drops empurpled her faire brest.
Exceeding wroth therewith the Virgin grew,
Albe the wound were nothing deepe imprest,
And fiercely forth her mortall blade she drew,
To give him the reward for such vile outrage dew.

34 So mightily she smote him, that to ground
He fell halfe dead; next stroke him should have slaine,
Had not the Lady, which by him stood bound,
Dernly[3] unto her called to abstaine
From doing him to dy; for else her paine
Should be remédilesse; sith none but hee
Which wrought it could the same recure againe.
Therewith she stayd her hand, loth stayd to bee;
For life she him envýde, and long'd revenge to see:

35 And to him said: "Thou wicked man, whose meed
For so huge mischiefe and vile villany

1 *Rashly*, quickly.
2 *Wrest*, turn aside.
3 *Dernly*, sadly.

Is death, or if that ought doe death exceed;
Be sure that nought may save thee from to dy
But if that thou this Dame doe presently
Restore unto her health and former state;
This doe, and live; els dye undoubtedly."
He, glad of life, that lookt for death but late,
Did yield himselfe right willing to prolong his date:

36 And, rising up, gan streight to over-looke
Those cursed leaves, his charmes back to reverse.
Full dreadfull thinges out of that balefull booke
He red, and measur'd many a sad verse,
That horrour gan the Virgins hart to perse,
And her faire locks up stared stiffe on end,
Hearing him those same bloody lynes reherse;
And, all the while he red, she did extend
Her sword high over him, if ought he did offend.

37 Anon she gan perceive the house to quake,
And all the dores to rattle round about;
Yet all that did not her dismaied make,
Nor slack her threatfull hand for daungers dout,[1]
But still with stedfast eye and courage stout
Abode, to weet what end would come of all:
At last that mightie chaine, which round about
Her tender waste was wound, adowne gan fall,
And that great brasen pillour broke in peeces small.

38 The cruell steele, which thrild[2] her dying hart,
Fell softly forth, as of his owne accord;
And the wyde wound, which lately did dispart

[1] *Dout*, apprehension. [2] *Thrild*, pierced.

Her bleeding brest and riven bowels gor'd,
Was closed up, as it had not beene bor'd;
And every part to safëty full sownd,
As she were never hurt, was soone restor'd:
Tho, when she felt herselfe to be unbownd
And perfect hole, prostrate she fell unto the grownd;

39 Before faire Britomart she fell prostráte,
Saying: "Ah! noble Knight, what worthy meede
Can wretched lady, quitt from wofull state,
Yield you in lieu of this your gracious deed?
Your vertue selfe her owne reward shall breed,
Even immortall prayse and glory wyde,
Which I, your vassall, by your prowesse freed,
Shall through the world make to be notifyde,[1]
And goodly well advaunce that goodly well was tryde."

40 But Britomart, uprearing her from grownd,
Said: "Gentle Dame, reward enough I weene,
For many labours more then I have found,
This, that in safetie now I have you seene,
And meane of your deliverance have beene:
Henceforth, faire Lady, comfort to you take,
And put away remembraunce of late teene[2];
In sted thereof, know that your loving make[3]
Hath no lesse griefe endured for your gentle sake."

1 *Notifyde*, proclaimed.
2 *Teene*, sorrow.
3 *Make*, mate.

XXXIX. 9.—*And goodly well advaunce*, &c.] And properly extol the qualities that have been so well tried. H.

41 She much was cheard to heare him mentiond,
Whom of all living wightes she loved best.
Then laid the noble Championesse strong hond
Upon th' Enchaunter which had her distrest
So sore, and with foule outrages opprest:
With that great chaine, wherewith not long ygoe
He bound that pitteous lady prisoner now relest,
Himselfe she bound, more worthy to be so,
And captive with her led to wretchednesse and wo.

42 Returning back, those goodly rowmes, which erst
She saw so rich and royally arayd,
Now vanisht utterly and cleane subverst
She found, and all their glory quite decayd,
That sight of such a chaunge her much dismayd.
Thenceforth descending to that perlous porch,
Those dreadfull flames she also found delayd [1]
And quenched quite, like a consumed torch,
That erst all entrers wont so cruelly to scorch.

43 More easie issew now then entrance late
She found; for now that fained-dreadfull flame,
Which chokt the porch of that enchaunted gate
And passage bard to all that thither came,
Was vanisht quite, as it were not the same,
And gave her leave at pleasure forth to passe.
Th' Enchaunter selfe, which all that fraud did frame
To have efforst the love of that faire lasse,
Seeing his worke now wasted, deepe engrieved was.

[1] *Delayd*, abated.

XLI. 7. — Two superfluous syllables have crept in here, probably through the carelessness of the printer.

44 But when the Victoresse arrived there
Where late she left the pensife Scudamore
With her own trusty squire, both full of feare,
Neither of them she found where she them lore[1]:
Thereat her noble hart was stonisht sore;
But most faire Amoret, whose gentle spright
Now gan to feede on hope, which she before
Conceived had, to see her own deare knight,
Being thereof beguyld, was fild with new affright.

45 But he, sad man, when he had long in drede
Awayted there for Britomarts returne,
Yet saw her not, nor signe of her good speed,
His expectation to despaire did turne,
Misdeeming[2] sure that her those flames did burne;
And therefore gan advize with her old squire,
Who her deare nourslings losse no lesse did mourne,
Thence to depart for further aide t' enquire:
Where let them wend at will, whilest here I doe re-
spire.*

1 *Lore*, left. 2 *Misdeeming*, judging wrongly.

---

* In the first edition of the Faerie Queene the five last stanzas of this canto bring the story of Sir Scudamore to a happy conclusion. In the place of them, the three concluding stanzas as given above are substituted in the second edition. By these alterations this third book not only connects better with the fourth, but the reader is kept in that suspense which is necessary in a well-told story. The stanzas which are omitted in the second edition, and printed in the first, are the following: —

43 At last she came unto the place, where late
She left Sir Scudamour in great distresse,

Twixt dolour and despight halfe desperate,
Of his loves succour, of his owne redresse,
And of the hardie Britomarts successe:
There on the cold earth him now thrown she found,
In wilfull anguish, and dead heavinesse,
And to him cald; whose voices knowen sound
Soone as he heard, himself he reared light from ground.

44 There did he see, that most on earth him ioyd,
His dearest love, the comfort of his dayes,
Whose too long absence him had sore annoyd,
And wearied his life with dull delayes:
Straight he upstarted from the loathed layes,[1]
And to her ran with hasty egernesse,
Like as a deare, that greedily embayes [2]
In the coole soile,[3] after long thirstinesse,
Which he in chace endured hath, now nigh breathlesse.

45 Lightly he clipt [4] her twixt his armës twaine,
And streightly [5] did embrace her body bright,
Her body, late the prison of sad paine,
Now the sweet lodge of love and deare delight:
But the faire Lady, overcommen quight
Of huge affection, did in pleasure melt,
And in sweete ravishment pourd out her spright.
No word they spake, nor earthly thing they felt,
But like two senceles stocks in long embracement dwelt.

46 Had ye them seene, ye would have surely thought
That they had beene that faire Hermaphrodite,
Which that rich Romane of white marble wrought,
And in his costly bath causd to bee site [6];
So seemd those two, as growne together quite,
That Britomart, halfe envying their blesse,
Was much empassiond in her gentle sprite,

1 *Layes*, lease, lea.
2 *Embayes*, bathes.
3 *Soile*, water in which a deer takes refuge.
4 *Clipt*, embraced.
5 *Streightly*, closely.
6 *Site*, placed.

XLVI. 4. —*Costly bath.*] This statue was found in the baths of Diocletian.

And to her selfe oft wisht like happinesse:
In vaine she wisht, that fate n'ould[1] let her yet possesse.

47 Thus doe those lovers with sweet countervayle,[2]
Each other of loves bitter fruit despoile.
But now my teme begins to faint and fayle,
All woxen weary of their iournall[3] toyle;
Therefore I will their sweatie yokes assoyle[4]
At this same furrowes end, till a new day:
And ye, faire Swayns, after your long turmoyle,
Now cease your worke, and at your pleasure play;
Now cease your worke; to-morrow is an holy-day.

1 *N'ould*, would not.
2 *Countervayle*, exchange.
3 *Iournall*, daily.
4 *Assoyle*, loosen, release.

APPENDIX.

VARIATIONS FROM THE FIRST EDITION.

Page 5, st. 5, v. 9, straunge (ed. 1609), Q. straung.
" 8, st. 12, v. 9, as (2d ed.), Q. in.
" 11, st. 21, v. 5, infernall (2d ed.), Q. internall.
" 12, st. 24, v. 7, ought (2d ed.), Q. nought.
" 16, st. 36, v. 4, yron (ed. 1609), Q. dying.
" 18, st. 40, v. 7, but (2d ed.), Q. and.
" 18, st. 40, v. 7, golden (2d ed.), Q. yron.
" 25, st. 60, v. 4, intemperate (2d ed.), Q. more temperate.
" 30, st. 3, v. 8, come hether, hether (ed. 1609), Q. come hether, come hether.
" 45, st. 44, v. 8, no more (2d ed.), Q. not thore.
" 47, st. 48, v. 8, Prince Arthur (ed. 1609), Q. Sir Guyon.
" 53, st. 6, v. 9, Arthegall, Q. Arthogall.
" 54, st. 9, v. 1, weete, Q. wote.
" 57, st. 15, v. 3, capitaine (ed. 1609), Q. captaine.
" 59, st. 21, v. 1, them (2d ed.), Q. him.
" 66, st. 37, v. 8, you love, Q. your love.
" 70, st. 48, v. 3, these (2d ed.), Q. this.
" 75, st. 60, v. 2, antiquitee, Q. antiquitiee.
" 81, st. 15, v. 1, straunge (ed. 1609), Q. straung.
" 85, st. 24, v. 8, it (2d ed.), Q. he.
" 92, st. 43, v. 1, Sisillus, Q. and all the editions, Sifillus.
" 109, st. 9, v. 9, they that bulwarke sorely rent (2d ed.), Q. they against that bulwarke lent.
" 114, st. 21, c. 8, there — there, Q. their — their.
" 118. st. 32, v. 5, unrest (2d ed.), Q. infest.
" 125, Arg., v. 1, by (2d ed.), Q. through.
" 125, Arg., v. 2, passing through (2d ed.), Q. through passing.
" 132, st. 21, v. 1, heedfull (2d ed.), Q. earnest.
" 134, st. 23, v. 9, monoceroses, Q. monoceros.

Page 143, st. 47, v. 6, foresee, Q. forsee.
" 144, st. 51, v. 1, thereto (2d ed.), Q. therewith.
" 146, st. 54, v. 7, hyacine (2d fol.), Q. hyacint.
" 159, st. 1, v. 2, that (2d ed.), Q. the.
" 164, st. 7, v. 6, thee, Q. the.
" 177, st. 41, v. 8, lightly (ed. 1609), Q. highly.
" 180, st. 47, v. 7, which (2d ed.), Q. that.
" 185, st. 60, v. 8, wary (ed. 1609), Q. weary.
" 198, st. 25, v. 6, Arthegall, Q. Arthogall.
" 225, st. 44, v. 6, ere they to former (ed. 1609), Q. ere they unto their former.
" 228, st. 50, v. 9, as earst (supplied from ed. 1609), Q. omitted.
" 235, st. 5, v. 8, she (2d ed.), Q. he.
" 236, st. 8, v. 9, these (2d ed.), Q. thy.
" 238, st. 15, v. 6, speare (ed. 1609), Q. speares.
" 243, st. 27, v. 6, fleshly (2d ed.), Q. fleshy.
" 244, st. 30, v. 6, swowne, Q. swownd.
" 247, st. 39, v. 9, sith we no more shall meet (2d ed.), Q. till we againe may meet.
" 255, st. 59, v. 5, dayes dearest children (2d ed.), Q. the children of day.
" 263, st. 19, v. 5, no, Q. now.
" 270, st. 39, v. 9, his (2d ed.), Q. their.
" 270, st. 40, v. 4, loves sweet teene (2d ed.), Q. sweet loves teene.
" 270, st. 40, v. 9, living (2d ed.), Q. liking.
" 275, st. 53, v. 9, weare (ed. 1609), Q. were.
" 279, st. 5, v. 3, bare, Q. bore.
" 281, st. 12, v. 2, aspect, Q. aspects.
" 286, st. 25, v. 5, which as a fountaine (ed. 1609), Q. from which a fountaine.
" 286, st. 26, v. 4, both farre and nere (supplied from 2d ed.), Q. omitted.
" 292, st. 42, v. 5, heavy (2d ed.), Q. heavenly.
" 293, st. 45, v. 4, supplied from ed. 1609, Q. wanting.
" 296, st. 52, v. 9, launched, Q. launch.
" 297, st. 1, v. 8, she did heare, Q. he did heare.
" 300, st. 9, v. 3, to, Q. and all editions, two.
" 303, st. 18, v. 5, might be by the witch, Q. might by the witch.
" 314, st. 48, v. 4, and many hath to foule confusion brought (2d ed.), Q. till him Chylde Thopas to confusion brought.

Page 321, st. 5, v. 1, advice (2d ed.), Q. device.
" 323, st. 9, v. 9, whom (ed. 1609), Q. who.
" 326, st. 17, v. 3, brought through, Q. broght throgh.
" 333, st. 37, v. 9, hight (2d ed.), Q. high.
" 339, st. 2, v. 4, attone, Q. attonce.
" 341, st. 7, v. 3, misdonne, Q. disdonne.
" 348, st. 27, v. 5, that (ed. 1609), Q. with.
" 355, st. 45, v. 3, neck (ed. 1609), Q. necks.
" 362, st. 8, v. 9, to (2d ed.), Q. with.
" 365, st. 18, v. 4, then (2d ed.), Q. so.
" 370, st. 31, v. 3, with thy (2d ed.), Q. that with.
" 370, st. 31, v. 7, vertues pay (ed. 1609), Q. vertuous pray.
" 373, st. 40, v. 1, addresse, Q. addrest.
" 373, st. 40, v. 3, wastefull, (2d ed.), Q. faithfull.
" 381, st. 2, v. 3, golden (ed. 1609), Q. golding.
" 389, st. 22, v. 8, as th' Earthes children, the which made (2d ed.), Q. as the Earthes children which made.
" 389, st. 23, v. 2, inglorious, beast-like (2d fol.), Q. inglorious and beastlike.
" 391, st. 27, v. 7, entred (2d ed.), Q. decked.
" 394, st. 36, v. 7, thee, Q. the.
" 395, st. 39, v. 6, each (2d ed.), Q. his.
" 395, st. 39, v. 8. stag, Q. and all editions, hag.
" 398, st. 47, v. 9, hevens hight, Q. and all editions, heven bright.
" 404, st. 7. v. 8, wood, Q. word.
" 405, st. 9, v. 3, other, Q. others.
" 408, st. 18, v. 5, drad, Q. dread.
" 409, st. 18, v. 8, hony-laden, Q. and all editions, hony-lady.
" 410, st. 21, v. 8, still (2d ed.), Q. skill.
" 412, st. 27, v. 3, and bore all away (2d ed.), Q. nothing did remayne.
" 412, st. 28, v. 1, there (ed. 1609), Q. their.
" 414, st. 33, v. 3, to herselfe (2d ed.), Q. to the next.
" 414, st. 34, v. 4, her (ed. 1609), Q. him.
" 416, st. 38, v. 5, bor'd (2d ed.), Q. sor'd.

END OF VOL. II.

www.ingramcontent.com/pod-product-compliance
Lightning Source LLC
LaVergne TN
LVHW021149110826
845150LV00005B/1172